Intermediate Spanish

Edited by
Enrique Montes

 **LIVING LANGUAGE**®

Content in this program has been modified and enhanced from *Starting Out in Spanish* and *Complete Course Spanish: The Basics*, both published in 2008.

Published in the United States by Living Language, an imprint of Random House, Inc.

www.livinglanguage.com

Editor: Suzanne McQuade
Production Editor: Carolyn Roth
Production Manager: Tom Marshall
Interior Design: Sophie Chin
Illustrations: Sophie Chin

First Edition

Library of Congress Cataloging-in-Publication Data

Montes, Enrique.
Intermediate Spanish / edited by Enrique Montes.—1st ed.
p.   cm.
ISBN 978-0-307-97163-0
1. Spanish language—Textbooks for foreign speakers—English.   2. Spanish language—Grammar.
3. Spanish language—Spoken Spanish.   I. Montes, Enrique.   II. Title.
PC4129.E5I58 2011
468.2'421—dc23   2011021881

This book is available at special discounts for bulk purchases for sales promotions or premiums. Special editions, including personalized covers, excerpts of existing books, and corporate imprints, can be created in large quantities for special needs. For more information, write to Special Markets/ Premium Sales, 1745 Broadway, MD 3-1, New York, New York 10019 or e-mail specialmarkets@ randomhouse.com.

PRINTED IN THE UNITED STATES OF AMERICA

16 15 14 13 12

Acknowledgments

Thanks to the Living Language team: Amanda D'Acierno, Christopher Warnasch, Suzanne McQuade, Laura Riggio, Erin Quirk, Amanda Munoz, Fabrizio LaRocca, Siobhan O'Hare, Sophie Chin, Sue Daulton, Alison Skrabek, Carolyn Roth, Ciara Robinson, and Tom Marshall.

How to Use This Course 9

UNIT 1: Talking about Yourself and Your Family 14

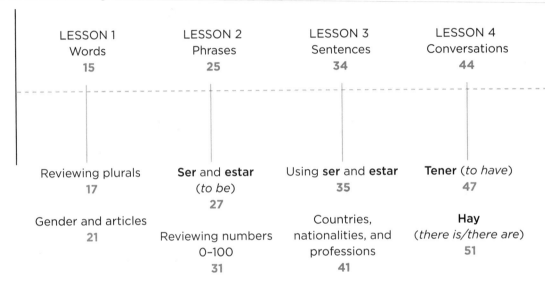

LESSON 1	LESSON 2	LESSON 3	LESSON 4
Words	Phrases	Sentences	Conversations
15	25	34	44

Reviewing plurals
17

Gender and articles
21

Ser and **estar**
(*to be*)
27

Reviewing numbers
0–100
31

Using **ser** and **estar**
35

Countries,
nationalities, and
professions
41

Tener (*to have*)
47

Hay
(*there is/there are*)
51

UNIT 2: Everyday Life 62

LESSON 5	LESSON 6	LESSON 7	LESSON 8
Words	Phrases	Sentences	Conversations
63	74	84	96

Numbers above 100
64

Telling time
68

Adjective
agreement
76

More on adjective
agreement
80

Question words
86

More question
words
91

Yes/no questions
99

Saying what you
like to do
104

UNIT 3: Health and the Human Body **119**

LESSON 9	LESSON 10	LESSON 11	LESSON 12
Words	Phrases	Sentences	Conversations
120	128	136	148

Possessive adjectives (singular) 121

Possession with **de** + pronoun 130

Possessive pronouns 138

Conjugation of -er verbs and **ver** (*to see*) 150

Conjugation of -ar verbs 143

Possessive adjectives (plural) 125

More possession with **de** 132

Conjugation of -ir verbs 156

COURSE

UNIT 4: Using the Telephone and Making Appointments 172

LESSON 13 Words 173	LESSON 14 Phrases 181	LESSON 15 Sentences 192	LESSON 16 Conversations 200
Demonstrative adjectives 174	Negation 183	Irregular verbs **hacer** (*to make, to do*), **poner** (*to put*), **traer** (*to bring*), and **caer** (*to fall*) 193	**Ir** (*to go*) 204
Demonstrative pronouns 177	Indefinite pronouns 187	Irregular verbs **salir** (*to go out*) and **decir** (*to say*) 197	**Querer** (*to want, to love*) 207

UNIT 5: Getting Around Town **221**

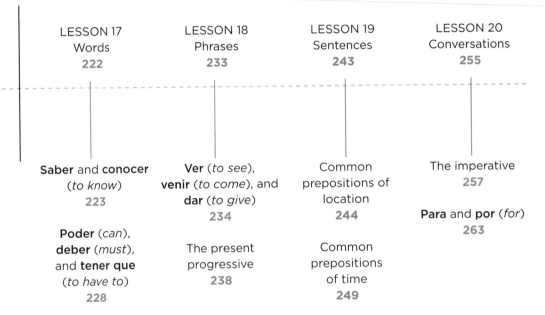

LESSON 17 Words 222	LESSON 18 Phrases 233	LESSON 19 Sentences 243	LESSON 20 Conversations 255
Saber and **conocer** (*to know*) 223	**Ver** (*to see*), **venir** (*to come*), and **dar** (*to give*) 234	Common prepositions of location 244	The imperative 257
Poder (*can*), **deber** (*must*), and **tener que** (*to have to*) 228	The present progressive 238	Common prepositions of time 249	**Para** and **por** (*for*) 263

Pronunciation Guide **281**
Grammar Summary **287**
Glossary **315**

How to Use This Course

¡Bienvenidos! Welcome to *Living Language Intermediate Spanish*!

Before we begin, let's take a quick look at what you'll see in this course.

CONTENT

Intermediate Spanish is a continuation of *Essential Spanish*. It will review, expand on, and add to the foundation that you received in *Essential Spanish*. In other words, this course contains:

- an in-depth review of important vocabulary and grammar from *Essential Spanish*;

- an expanded and more advanced look at some key vocabulary and grammar from *Essential Spanish*;

- an introduction to idiomatic language and more challenging Spanish grammar.

UNITS

There are five units in this course. Each unit has four lessons arranged in a "building block" structure: the first lesson will present essential *words*, the second will introduce longer *phrases*, the third will teach *sentences*, and the fourth will show how everything works together in everyday *conversations*.

At the beginning of each unit is an introduction highlighting what you'll learn in that unit. At the end of each unit you'll find the Unit Essentials, which reviews the key information from that unit, and a self-graded Unit Quiz, which tests what you've learned.

LESSONS

There are four lessons per unit for a total of 20 lessons in the course. Each lesson has the following components:

- **Introduction** outlining what you will cover in the lesson.

- **Word Builder 1** (first lesson of the unit) presenting key words and phrases.

- **Phrase Builder 1** (second lesson of the unit) introducing longer phrases and expressions.

- **Sentence Builder 1** (third lesson of the unit) teaching sentences.

- **Conversation 1** (fourth lesson of the unit) for a natural dialogue that brings together important vocabulary and grammar from the unit.

- **Take It Further** providing extra information about the new vocabulary you just saw, expanding on certain grammar points, or introducing additional words and phrases.

- **Word/Phrase/Sentence/Conversation Practice 1** practicing what you learned in Word Builder 1, Phrase Builder 1, Sentence Builder 1, or Conversation 1.

- **Grammar Builder 1** guiding you through important Spanish grammar that you need to know.

- **Work Out 1** for a comprehensive practice of what you saw in Grammar Builder 1.

- **Word Builder 2/Phrase Builder 2/Sentence Builder 2/Conversation 2** for more key words, phrases, or sentences, or a second dialogue.

- **Take It Further** for expansion on what you've seen so far and additional vocabulary.

- **Word/Phrase/Sentence/Conversation Practice 2** practicing what you learned in Word Builder 2, Phrase Builder 2, Sentence Builder 2, or Conversation 2.

Intermediate Spanish

- **Grammar Builder 2** for more information on Spanish grammar.

- **Work Out 2** for a comprehensive practice of what you saw in Grammar Builder 2.

- **Tip or Culture Note** for a helpful language tip or useful cultural information related to the lesson or unit.

- **Word Recall** reviewing important grammar and vocabulary from the lesson.

- **How Did You Do?** outlining what you learned in the lesson.

UNIT ESSENTIALS

You will see the **Unit Essentials** at the end of every unit. This section summarizes and reviews the key information from the unit, but with missing vocabulary information for you to fill in. In other words, each Unit Essentials works as both a study guide and a blank "cheat sheet." Once you complete it, you'll have your very own reference for the most essential vocabulary and grammar from the unit.

UNIT QUIZ

After each Unit Essentials, you'll see a **Unit Quiz**. The quizzes are self-graded so it's easy for you to test your progress and see if you should go back and review.

PROGRESS BAR

You will see a **Progress Bar** on each page that has course material. It indicates your current position within the unit and lets you know how much progress you're making. Each line in the bar represents a Grammar Builder section.

AUDIO

Look for the symbol ⊙ to help guide you through the audio as you're reading the book. It will tell you which track to listen to for each section that has audio. When you see the symbol, select the indicated track and start listening! If you don't see the symbol, then there isn't any audio for that section. You'll also see ⏸, which will tell you where that track ends.

The audio can be used on its own—in other words, without the book—when you're on the go. Whether in your car or at the gym, you can listen to the audio on its own to brush up on your pronunciation or review what you've learned in the book.

PRONUNCIATION GUIDE, GRAMMAR SUMMARY, GLOSSARY

At the back of this book you will find a **Pronunciation Guide**, **Grammar Summary**, and **Glossary**. The Pronunciation Guide provides information on Spanish pronunciation and the phonetics system used in this course. The Grammar Summary contains a helpful, brief overview of key points in the Spanish grammar system. The Glossary (Spanish–English and English–Spanish) includes all of the essential words from the five units of *Intermediate Spanish*, as well as some additional vocabulary.

FREE ONLINE TOOLS

Go to **www.livinglanguage.com/languagelab** to access your free online tools. The tools are organized around the units in this course, with audiovisual flashcards, as well as interactive games and quizzes for each unit. These tools will help you review and practice the vocabulary and grammar that you've seen in the units, as well as provide some bonus words and phrases related to the unit's topic.

Unit 1:

Talking About Yourself and Your Family

In this unit, you'll learn how to talk about yourself and your family as well as how to describe where you live. You'll also expand your knowledge of Spanish grammar by reviewing gender, plurals, the forms of *to be*, the verb *to have*, and more. By the end of this unit, you should be able to:

☐ Understand how articles work

☐ Identify the gender of words

☐ Name some family members

☐ Name some rooms of the house and items found around the house

☐ Confidently conjugate ser and estar

☐ Count to 100 without difficulty, and combine some numbers and words

☐ Clearly understand the difference in usage between ser and estar

☐ Identify nationalities and professions

☐ Confidently conjugate the verb tener and use it in several idiomatic expressions

☐ Use the expression Hay ... to express *there is, there are*

    ▶ Look for this symbol to help guide you through the audio as you're reading the book. It will tell you which track to listen to for each section that has audio. However, keep in mind that the audio can also be used on its own when you're on the go!

Lesson 1: Words

By the end of this lesson, you will be able to:

☐ Understand how articles work

☐ Identify the gender of words

☐ Name some family members

☐ Name some rooms of the house and items found around the house

Word Builder 1

Let's start by looking at a list of words that refer to family members.

▶ 1A Word Builder 1 (CD 4, Track 1)

la madre	mother
el padre	father
el/la niño/a	boy/girl
el/la hijo/a	son/daughter
el/la hermano/a	brother/sister
el/la abuelo/a	grandfather/grandmother
el/la tío/a	aunt/uncle
el/la primo/a	cousin
el/la sobrino/a	nephew/niece
el/la esposo/a	husband/wife
el/la nieto/a	grandson/granddaughter
el/la suegro/a	father-in-law/mother-in-law
la nuera	daughter-in-law

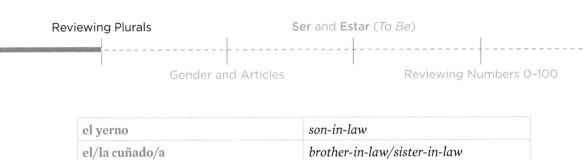

| el yerno | son-in-law |
| el/la cuñado/a | brother-in-law/sister-in-law |

Take It Further

Here are a few extra words that will appear in this lesson, either in the examples or in the exercises. Study them at your leisure, or return to this section when you come across them and want a review.

la tarjeta	card
el libro	book
el bolígrafo	pen
la carta	letter
el lápiz	pencil
la luz	light
la cafetera	coffeemaker
el premio	prize
el código	code
el nombre	name
el cheque	check
la nacionalidad	nationality
la profesión	profession

✎ Word Practice 1

Match the Spanish word on the right with its English translation on the left.

1. *nephew*	a. la nieta
2. *granddaughter*	b. el cuñado
3. *brother-in-law*	c. la sobrina
4. *daughter-in-law*	d. el sobrino
5. *niece*	e. la nuera
6. *sister-in-law*	f. la cuñada

ANSWER KEY

1. d; 2. a; 3. b; 4. e; 5. c; 6. f

Grammar Builder 1
REVIEWING PLURALS

▷ 1B Grammar Builder 1 (CD 4, Track 2)

Let's review how the plural is formed in Spanish.

VOWEL ENDING	-S
un hombre (*a man*)	unos hombres (*some men*)
una abuela (*a grandmother*)	unas abuelas (*some grandmothers*)

CONSONANT ENDING (OTHER THAN -Z)	-ES
un señor (*a gentleman*)	unos señores (*some gentlemen*)
una mujer (*a woman*)	unas mujeres (*some women*)

-Z ENDING	DROP -Z, ADD -CES
un lápiz (*a pencil*)	unos lápices (*some pencils*)
una luz (*a light*)	unas luces (*some lights*)

Note that the plural of **padre** (*father*) means *parents*. Similarly, other masculine plural nouns referring to family members can take on a more general sense and do not necessarily refer to males only. This depends on context, of course.

hijos	children (sons and daughters)
abuelos	grandparents
hermanos	brothers and sisters, siblings
primos	cousins
nietos	grandchildren

✎ Work Out 1

We'll give you one object; you give us back more than one by making the following nouns plural and translating your answers.

1. tarjeta _____

2. hermano _____

3. señor _____

4. abogado _____

5. hija _____

6. premio _____

7. nombre _____

8. cafetera _____

9. madre _____

10. padre _____

ANSWER KEY

1. tarjetas (*cards*); 2. hermanos (*brothers*); 3. señores (*gentlemen*); 4. abogados (*lawyers*); 5. hijas (*daughters*); 6. premios (*prizes*); 7. nombres (*names*); 8. cafeteras (*coffeemakers*); 9. madres (*mothers*); 10. padres (*fathers/parents*)

Word Builder 2

Here are some words that can be used when talking about where we live.

▶ 1C Word Builder 2 (CD 4, Track 3)

la casa	house
el edificio	building
el apartamento	apartment
la sala	living room
el comedor	dining room
la cocina	kitchen
el baño	bathroom
la habitación	bedroom
el jardín	garden
el balcón	balcony
el escritorio	desk/study
la puerta	door
la ventana	window
la silla	seat
la mesa	table

✎ Word Practice 2

Fill in the floorplan below with as many room names as you can come up with based on the vocabulary you just learned.

1. _____
2. _____
3. _____
4. _____

Grammar Builder 2
GENDER AND ARTICLES

▶ 1D Grammar Builder 2 (CD 4, Track 4)

You probably remember from *Essential Spanish* that all nouns and adjectives indicate gender, either masculine or feminine. You'll remember that for nouns with natural gender, this is easy: hombre *(man)*, muchacho *(boy)*, and abogado *(male lawyer)* are all masculine, while mujer *(woman)*, muchacha *(girl)*, and abogada *(female lawyer)* are all feminine. In cases where there is no natural gender, masculine nouns usually end in -o, and feminine nouns end in -a.

MASCULINE	FEMININE
libro *(book)*	tarjeta *(card)*
bolígrafo *(pen)*	carta *(letter)*

Take It Further

As a general rule, nouns and adjectives ending in -dad or -ción are feminine, and most nouns and adjectives that end in -e are masculine. For now, the best thing to do is simply memorize the gender of each new noun you learn. Let's look at the genders of some of the nouns you've learned so far.

MASCULINE	FEMININE
premio *(prize)*	tarjeta *(card)*
código *(code)*	cafetera *(coffeemaker)*
nombre *(name)*	nacionalidad *(nationality)*
cheque *(check)*	profesión *(profession)*

As in English, Spanish has articles that translate as *a, an, some,* and *the*. But remember that in Spanish, they have to match the gender and number of the noun they precede. Singular indefinite articles are translated as *a/an,* while plurals are translated as *some*.

	MASCULINE	FEMININE
singular	un	una
plural	unos	unas

un hombre (*a man*)	unos niños (*some boys/children*)
una mujer (*a woman*)	unas niñas (*some girls*)

Notice that the plural masculine form unos is used as long as at least one of the members of the group is male. The feminine plural form unas is used exclusively for groups with only female members.

The definite article in Spanish corresponds to *the* in English. And again, there are four forms that agree in gender and number with the nouns they modify.

	MASCULINE	FEMININE
singular	el	la
plural	los	las

el estudiante (*the male student*)	la estudiante (*the female student*)
el bebé (*the baby boy*)	la bebé (*the baby girl*)

Note that the plurals of the above words with their articles would be as follows:

los estudiantes (*the male students*)	las estudiantes (*the female students*)
los bebés (*the baby boys*)	las bebés (*the baby girls*)

✎ Work Out 2

Replace the indefinite article with the definite article, and then translate your answers.

1. unas habitaciones _____

2. un abuelo _____

3. unos padres _____

4. una cocina _____

5. una prima _____

6. unas hermanas _____

7. un niño _____

8. un jardín _____

ANSWER KEY
1. las habitaciones (*the bedrooms*); 2. el abuelo (*the grandfather*); 3. los padres (*the fathers/parents*);
4. la cocina (*the kitchen*); 5. la prima (*the female cousin*); 6. las hermanas (*the sisters*); 7. el niño (*the boy*); 8. el jardín (*the garden*)

⊕ Culture Note

Spanish speakers around the world use slightly different words for the same things. Here are a few differences.

In Spain, for example, you will hear people talking about their piso when referring to un apartamento (*apartment*). They'll also refer to their parents as madre (*mother*) and padre (*father*). Spaniards usually talk about their young children as el crío (*kid, m.*) or la cría (*kid, f.*).

In Latin America, people will use the words cuarto and dormitorio to refer to una habitación (*bedroom*). There is also the word estudio, which is used instead of escritorio, in the sense of *study* or *office*. And you will hear Latin Americans use the words mamá (*mom*) and papá (*dad*), or even mami and papi, when talking about their parents. In some parts of Latin America, you'll hear the word párvulo in reference to young children.

The words habitación and cuarto are literally translated as *room*. However, in many countries they are used to mean specifically a *bedroom*. Spanish has two other words that literally mean *bedroom*: alcoba and dormitorio. But habitación is also commonly used to refer to rooms in a hotel.

How Did You Do?

Let's see how you did! By now, you should be able to:

☐ Understand how articles work
(Still unsure? Jump back to page 21.)

☐ Identify the gender of words
(Still unsure? Jump back to page 21.)

☐ Name some family members
(Still unsure? Jump back to page 15.)

☐ Name some rooms of the house and items found around the house
(Still unsure? Jump back to page 19.)

✎ Word Recall

Place the appropriate indefinite article in front of each of the following nouns.

1. _____ hermano

2. _____ amigo

3. _____ abuelo

4. _____ hermana

5. _____ amiga

6. _____ abuela

7. _____ hermanos

8. _____ amigos

9. _____ abuelos

10. _____ hermanas

11. _____ amigas

12. _____ abuelas

ANSWER KEY
1–3: un; 4–6: una; 7–9: unos; 10–12: unas

Lesson 2: Phrases

By the end of this lesson, you should be able to:

☐ Confidently conjugate ser and estar

☐ Count to 100 without difficulty, and combine some numbers and words

Phrase Builder 1

Here are some phrases that can be used to talk about family and friends. You'll see them again in the dialogues in this unit.

▶ 2A Phrase Builder 1 (CD 4, Track 5)

| como ya sabes | *as you already know* |

el mayor	the oldest (male)
la menor	the youngest (female)
diferencia de edades	difference in ages
el centro de atracción	center of attraction
es natural	it's natural
y encima …	and on top of that …
situación familiar	family situation
tienes que …	you have to …
en un mismo apartamento	in the same apartment

(II)

Take It Further

In this lesson, you will also encounter several other words related to professions. Let's take a look at them briefly.

el/la abogado/a	lawyer
el/la artista	artist
el/la secretaria	secretary
el/la profesor/a	professor
la universidad	university

✎ Phrase Practice 1

Translate the phrases you just learned from English into Spanish. Don't be ashamed to go back to the list of phrases for some help!

1. *as you already know* _____

2. *the oldest (male)* _____

3. *the youngest (female)* _____

4. *difference in ages* _____

5. *center of attraction* _____

6. *it's natural* _____

7. *and on top of that …* _____

8. *family situation* _____

9. *you have to …* _____

10. *in the same apartment* _____

ANSWER KEY

1. como ya sabes; 2. el mayor; 3. la menor; 4. diferencia de edades; 5. el centro de atracción;
6. es natural; 7. y encima …; 8. situación familiar; 9. tienes que …; 10. en un mismo apartamento

Grammar Builder 1
SER AND ESTAR (*TO BE*)

▶ 2B Grammar Builder 1 (CD 4, Track 6)

Before we go further into the differences between ser and estar in the next
lesson, let's review their conjugations.

SER (*TO BE*)			
yo soy	*I am*	**nosotros/as somos**	*we are*
tú eres	*you are (infml.)*	**vosotros/as sois**	*(all of) you are (pl. infml.)*
él/ella/usted es	*he/she is, you are (fml.)*	**ellos/ellas/ ustedes son**	*they are, (all of) you are (pl. fml.)*

ESTAR *(TO BE)*			
yo estoy	*I am*	nosotros/as estamos	*we are*
tú estás	*you are (infml.)*	vosotros/as estáis	*(all of) you are (pl. infml.)*
él/ella/usted está	*he/she is, you are (fml.)*	ellos/ellas/ ustedes están	*they are, (all of) you are (pl. fml.)*

✎ Work Out 1

A. Fill in the blanks with the correct form of ser.

1. Mi nombre _____ Marliz Camargo.

2. Yo _____ Ana Benavides. _____ la secretaria de la universidad.

3. ¿Cuál _____ su número de teléfono, por favor?

4. Nosotros _____ abogados, ¿y ustedes?

5. Vosotros _____ de Bolivia y ellas _____ de España.

6. Tú _____ profesora de inglés.

7. Él _____ soltero y ella _____ casada.

8. Ellos _____ venezolanos.

9. ¿_____ usted casado o soltero?

10. Ustedes _____ muy inteligentes.

B. Now fill in the blanks with the correct form of the verb estar.

1. Yo _____ en el apartamento.

2. Vosotros _____ felices.

3. Ellos _____ en la casa.

4. ¿Cómo _____ usted?

5. ¿Cómo _____ vosotros?

6. Yo _____ bien, ¿y tú?

ANSWER KEY
A. 1. es; 2. soy/Soy; 3. es; 4. somos; 5. sois/son; 6. eres; 7. es/es; 8. son; 9. Es; 10. son
B. 1. estoy; 2. estáis; 3. están; 4. está; 5. estáis; 6. estoy

Phrase Builder 2

Let's look at some common expressions using ser and estar.

▶ 2C Phrase Builder 2 (CD 4, Track 7)

¿Es usted también español?	*Are you also from Spain?*
¿Cuál es su profesión?	*What's your profession?*
Soy abogada.	*I'm a lawyer.*
¿Sois de Argentina?	*Are you from Argentina?*
No, somos colombianos.	*No, we're Colombian.*
Ustedes son artistas.	*You're artists.*
¿Cuál es su número de fax?	*What's your fax number?*
¿Cuál es su dirección de correo electrónico?	*What's your email address?*
Nosotros no somos de Brasil.	*We're not from Brazil.*
¿Cómo estás?	*How are you?*
Estoy bien, gracias.	*I'm fine, thanks.*
Estoy cansado.	*I'm tired. (male)*
Estoy cansada.	*I'm tired. (female)*

Estoy triste.	I'm sad.
Estás feliz.	You're happy.
Está mal.	He/She is not doing well.
¿Donde está la universidad?	Where's the university?
Está en la Avenida Palacios.	It's on Avenida Palacios.
El horno está caliente.	The oven is hot.
El agua está fría.	The water is cold.

Take It Further

Notice that you say el agua instead of la agua. That's because agua begins with a stressed vowel. If a feminine word begins with a stressed a- or ha-, use el instead of la. In the plural, though, use the regular las.

| el agua/las aguas | the water/the waters |
| el hacha/las hachas | the axe/the axes |

✎ Phrase Practice 2

Match the Spanish sentence on the right with its English translation on the left.

1. *I'm tired. (male)*
2. *He/She is not doing well.*
3. *I'm tired. (female)*
4. *The water is cold.*
5. *You're happy.*
6. *I'm sad.*

a. Estás feliz.
b. Estoy triste.
c. Estoy cansado.
d. Está mal.
e. El agua está fría.
f. Estoy cansada.

ANSWER KEY

1. c; 2. d; 3. f; 4. e; 5. a; 6. b

Grammar Builder 2
REVIEWING NUMBERS 0–100

▶ 2D Grammar Builder 2 (CD 4, Track 8)

Before we move on to the next lesson, let's take a moment to review the numbers from 0 to 100 in Spanish. (Just remember: the more you practice, the better you'll be at recalling these when you need them!)

0	cero	20	veinte
1	uno	21	veintiuno
2	dos	22	veintidós
3	tres	23	veintitrés
4	cuatro	24	veinticuatro
5	cinco	25	veinticinco
6	seis	26	veintiséis
7	siete	27	veintisiete
8	ocho	28	veintiocho
9	nueve	29	veintinueve
10	diez	30	treinta
11	once	31	treinta y uno
12	doce	32	treinta y dos
13	trece	40	cuarenta
14	catorce	50	cincuenta
15	quince	60	sesenta
16	dieciséis (*or* diez y seis)	70	setenta
17	diecisiete (*or* diez y siete)	80	ochenta
18	dieciocho (*or* diez y ocho)	90	noventa
19	diecinueve (*or* diez y nueve)	100	cien

Notice that once you go above thirty, the numbers are formed with the tens followed by **y** (*and*) and then the number.

45	cuarenta y cinco	(*lit., forty and five*)
77	setenta y siete	(*lit., seventy and seven*)
82	ochenta y dos	(*lit., eighty and two*)

✎ Work Out 2

Match the sequence of numbers on the left with the Spanish translations on the right. Be sure to say each number out loud as you answer.

1. 77, 11, 31
2. 45, 35, 25
3. 90, 100, 15
4. 67, 10, 21
5. 100, 81, 20
6. 45, 65, 19

a. sesenta y siete, diez, veintiuno
b. cien, ochenta y uno, veinte
c. setenta y siete, once, treinta y uno
d. cuarenta y cinco, treinta y cinco, veinticinco
e. cuarenta y cinco, sesenta y cinco, diecinueve
f. noventa, cien, quince

ANSWER KEY
1. c; 2. d; 3. f; 4. a; 5. b; 6. e

⊕ Culture Note

You'll hear the word **hombre** (*man*) used conversationally when two men are addressing each other. This is very similar to the conversational English use of *man*. Today, women are also beginning to use the word **mujer** (*woman*) in the same way. Also, many times, a Spanish speaker will refer to his wife as **mi mujer**, which literally means *my woman*. It is, however, not meant in a disrespectful way; that's just the word that's used. Women usually refer to their husbands as **mi marido**. The most commonly used expression for one's spouse in Latin America, however, is **mi esposa/esposo** (*my wife/husband*).

How Did You Do?

By now, you should be able to:

☐ Confidently conjugate ser and estar
(Still unsure? Jump back to page 27.)

☐ Count to 100 without difficulty, and combine some numbers and words
(Still unsure? Jump back to page 31.)

✎ Word Recall

Fill in the blanks with the correct form of the verb ser.

1. Yo _____ inteligente.

2. Tú _____ inteligente.

3. Él/Ella/Ud. _____ inteligente.

4. Nosotros _____ inteligentes.

5. Vosotros _____ inteligentes.

6. Ellos/Ellas/Uds. _____ inteligentes.

ANSWER KEY

1. soy; 2. eres; 3. es; 4. somos; 5. sois; 6. son

Lesson 3: Sentences

By the end of this lesson, you will be able to:

☐ Clearly understand the difference in usage between ser and estar

☐ Identify nationalities and professions

Sentence Builder 1

▶ 3A Sentence Builder 1 (CD 4, Track 9)

¿Cuántos años tienen?	*How old are they?*
¿Cómo se llaman?	*What are their names?*
No me siento muy bien.	*I don't feel very well.*
Ella está un poco celosa.	*She's a bit jealous.*
Eso no es todo.	*That's not all.*
Hay cuatro alcobas.	*There are four rooms.*
Hay una cocina.	*There's a kitchen.*
Tengo dos hijos.	*I have two sons.*
No hay otra solución.	*There's no other solution.*
No me digas.	*Really? (lit., Don't tell me.)*

⏸

Take It Further

Notice that a few new words were introduced in the above sentences.

la solución	*solution*
decir	*to say*

Tener (*To Have*)

Countries, Nationalities,
and Professions

Hay (*There Is/There Are*)

todo/a	all
celoso/a	jealous

Don't forget the distinction in gender!

✎ Sentence Practice 1

Fill in the blanks with the word that completes the sentence based on the English translations provided.

1. _____ muy bien. *I don't feel very well.*

2. Ella está un poco _____. *She's a bit jealous.*

3. Eso no es _____. *That's not all.*

4. Hay cuatro _____. *There are four rooms.*

5. Tengo _____. *I have two sons.*

6. No hay _____. *There's no other solution.*

7. _____. *Really? (lit., Don't tell me.)*

ANSWER KEY

1. No me siento; 2. celosa; 3. todo; 4. alcobas; 5. dos hijos; 6. otra solución; 7. No me digas.

Grammar Builder 1
USING SER AND ESTAR

▶ 3B Grammar Builder 1 (CD 4, Track 10)

So, how are **ser** and **estar** used? The major difference, in a nutshell, is that **ser** expresses permanent, or at least long-lasting, qualities, while **estar** expresses qualities that are likely to change. **Estar** is also used to describe location, even of something that's not likely to move.

Let's start with **ser**, which is generally used in the following ways.

1. To express origin or nationality

Soy de Argentina.
I'm from Argentina.

Eres francesa.
You're French.

2. To identify people and things

¿Cuál es su nombre?
What's your name?

Mi nombre es Marta.
My name is Marta.

¿Cuál es su número de teléfono?
What's your phone number?

Es el tres dos cero tres cuatro cinco seis.
It's 320-3456.

3. To express occupation

Ella es profesora de matemáticas.
She's a professor of mathematics.

Ellos son ingenieros.
They're engineers.

4. To express permanent or inherent characteristics

El hielo es frío.
Ice is cold.

Las rosas son hermosas.
Roses are beautiful.

The verb estar, on the other hand, is used in the following circumstances.

1. To show location or place things in space and time

Mi hermana está en el apartamento.
My sister is in the apartment.

Londres está en Inglaterra.
London is in England.

2. To express what is temporal or accidental

El café está frío.
The coffee is cold (right now).

3. To express feelings and emotions

¡Estoy feliz!
I am happy (right now)!

As you can see, one of the main differences between ser and estar is the fact that ser expresses a permanent characteristic and estar a temporal condition or location. So, depending on the speaker's intention, in some cases either ser or estar can be used. Notice the differences.

Ella es bonita.
She's pretty (by nature).

Ella está bonita.
She looks pretty right now.

Es (un) borracho.
He's a drunk (as a characteristic).

Está borracho.
He's drunk right now.

Es triste.
He's gloomy (by nature).

Está triste.
He's feeling down.

¿Cómo eres?
What are you like? (Describe yourself.)

¿Cómo estás?
How are you? (How's your current state?)

Countries, Nationalities,   Hay (*There Is/There Are*)
and Professions

✎ Work Out 1

Choose the verb that best completes the sentence.

1. **Buenos Aires (es, está) en Argentina.** _____

2. **Juan, Pedro, y Miguel (están, son) profesores.** _____

3. **¡Hola! ¿Cómo (estás, eres)?** _____

4. **Tú y María (sois, estáis) portuguesas.** _____

5. **Yo (estoy, soy) en mi casa.** _____

6. **Mi tía y mi hermana (están, son) en el apartamento.** _____

7. **Yo (estoy, soy) un estudiante.** _____

8. **¡Hola! ¿Cómo (estáis, sois)?** _____

ANSWER KEY
1. está; 2. son; 3. estás; 4. sois; 5. estoy; 6. están; 7. soy; 8. estáis

Sentence Builder 2

You learned the most common greetings in *Essential Spanish*. Here are a few more informal ways to greet someone and a few sentences that can be used to make small talk.

▶ 3C Sentence Builder 2 (CD 4, Track 11)

¿Qué tal?	What's up?
¿Qué pasa?	How's it going?
¿Qué hay?	What's up? What's going on?
¿Cómo va todo?	How's everything?
Así, así.	So-so.
Pues, nada.	Not much.

Pues, aquí estamos.	*Here we are.*
Y la familia, ¿cómo está?	*How's your family doing?*
Y su esposa/o, ¿cómo va?	*How's your wife/husband?*
¿Y sus hijos?	*What about your children?*
¿Qué tal andan todos?	*How's everyone?*
Pues, bien.	*Fine.*
¿Cómo te trata la vida?	*How's life treating you?*

⑪

✎ Sentence Practice 2

Translate the following English phrases into Spanish.

1. *How's everything?* _____

2. *So-so.* _____

3. *Not much.* _____

4. *Here we are.* _____

5. *How's your family doing?* _____

6. *How's your wife/husband?* _____

7. *What about your children?* _____

8. *How's everyone?* _____

9. *Fine.* _____

10. *How's life treating you?* _____

ANSWER KEY

1. ¿Cómo va todo? 2. Así, así. 3. Pues, nada. 4. Pues, aquí estamos. 5. Y la familia, ¿cómo está? 6. Y su esposa/o, ¿cómo va? 7. ¿Y sus hijos? 8. ¿Qué tal andan todos? 9. Pues, bien. 10. ¿Cómo te trata la vida?

Grammar Builder 2
COUNTRIES, NATIONALITIES, AND PROFESSIONS

▷ 3D Grammar Builder 2 (CD 4, Track 12)

Let's look at a list of a few nationalities and countries.

País (country)	Nacionalidad (nationality)
Argentina	argentino/a
Bolivia	boliviano/a
Brasil	brasilero/a
Canadá	canadiense
Chile	chileno/a
Colombia	colombiano/a
Ecuador	ecuatoriano/a
España	español/a
Estados Unidos	estadounidense
Inglaterra	inglés/inglesa
México	mexicano/a
Perú	peruano/a
Uruguay	uruguayo/a
Venezuela	venezolano/a

Ⅱ

Take It Further
Let's also look at some common professions.

el periodista/la periodista	journalist
el abogado/la abogada	lawyer
el arquitecto/la arquitecta	architect

el médico/la médica	doctor
el policía/la policía	police officer
el profesor/la profesora	teacher, professor
el pintor/la pintora	painter

✎ Work Out 2

We'll give you a country, an industry, and a gender; you tell us their nationality and profession.

1. *Spain, engineering, female* _____

2. *Uruguay, academia, male* _____

3. *Mexico, the arts, male* _____

4. *USA, law, female* _____

5. *Chile, law enforcement, female* _____

ANSWER KEY

1. la arquitecta española; 2. el profesor uruguayo; 3. el pintor mexicano; 4. la abogada estadounidense; 5. la policía chilena

☀ Tip!

In trying to learn how to use ser and estar, don't get too hung up on the rules. Try to remember the basic differences and then experiment, and pay attention to how Spanish speakers use them. One way of exploring this difference is to type fragments like "el presidente/la doctora/María es" and "el presidente/la doctora/María está" into a search engine. See if you can decipher the results and identify the different nuances. You'll see that, with time, it will all start making more sense. Remember, be patient with yourself, and most of all, have fun learning the language.

How Did You Do?

By now, you should be able to:

☐ Clearly understand the difference in usage between ser and estar
(Still unsure? Jump back to page 35.)

☐ Identify nationalities and professions
(Still unsure? Jump back to page 41.)

✎ Word Recall

Read each of the sentences below. Decide which form of *to be* you need to use,
then write the appropriate form of ser or estar in the blank.

1. Mi madre _____ simpática y responsable.

2. Mi madre _____ colombiana.

3. ¿ _____ mi madre estudiante de la universidad regional?

4. Mi madre _____ buena estudiante.

5. Mi madre _____ en España.

6. Mi madre _____ muy contenta y feliz.

7. ¿ _____ mi madre enferma?

8. Mi madre _____ en el restaurante nuevo.

ANSWER KEY

1–4: es; 5–8: está

Lesson 4: Conversations

By the end of this lesson, you will be able to:

☐ Confidently conjugate the verb tener and use it in several idiomatic expressions

☐ Use the expression Hay … to express *there is, there are*

Conversation 1

Farina is on her third date with Fabio. She's telling him a little bit more about her personal life and her family.

▶ 4A Conversation 1 (CD 4, Track 13 - Spanish Only; Track 14 - Spanish and English)

Farina:	Como ya sabes, estoy divorciada de mi segundo esposo y tengo dos hijos.
Fabio:	¿Cuántos años tienen?
Farina:	Bueno, el mayor tiene venticinco años y la menor tiene ocho años.
Fabio:	Es una diferencia de edades muy grande, ¿no? ¿Cómo se llaman?
Farina:	Carlos es de mi primer matrimonio y Carolina del segundo. Carlos está casado y tiene una bebita de dieciséis meses.
Fabio:	¡Así que eres abuela!
Farina:	Sí, soy abuela y me siento muy bien. ¡Estoy feliz!
Fabio:	¡Y tu hija ya es tía!
Farina:	Sí, pero ella está un poco celosa de mi nieta.
Fabio:	Es natural. La bebé es en este momento el centro de atracción de la familia.

Farina:	*As you already know, I'm divorced from my second husband and I have two children.*
Fabio:	*How old are they?*

Farina:	Well, the older one is twenty-five and the younger one is eight.
Fabio:	That's a big age difference, don't you think? What are their names?
Farina:	Carlos is from my first marriage and Carolina from the second. Carlos is married and has a sixteen-month-old baby.
Fabio:	So, you're a grandmother!
Farina:	Yes, I'm a grandmother and I feel good. I'm happy!
Fabio:	And your daughter is already an aunt!
Farina:	Yes, but she's a bit jealous of my granddaughter.
Fabio:	It's natural. Right now the baby is the center of attention of the whole family.

Take It Further

In *Essential Spanish*, you learned how to ask for someone's name like this: ¿Cuál es su nombre? That's one possibility, but Spanish speakers generally use the verb llamarse *(to be called)* instead.

¿Cómo se llaman?
What are their names?

¿Cómo se llama?
What is your name?

Me llamo María.
My name is María.

In the next unit, we'll learn how to conjugate regular verbs like this one.

Also remember from *Essential Spanish* that mi is the possessive adjective meaning *my*. We'll review the other possessive adjectives again in a later unit.

✎ Conversation Practice 1

Fill in the blanks below with the appropriate word based on the English translations and the dialogue above.

1. **Estoy divorciada de mi segundo esposo y** _____.

   I'm divorced from my second husband and I have two children.

2. **¿Cuántos años** _____**?** *How old are they?*

3. **El mayor tiene** _____ **y la menor tiene**

   _____**.** *The older one is twenty-five and the younger one is eight.*

4. **¡Así que eres** _____**!** *So, you're a grandmother!*

5. **¡Y tu** _____ **ya es** _____**!** *And your daughter is already an aunt!*

6. **Ella está un poco** _____ **de mi nieta.** *She's a bit jealous of my*

   granddaughter.

   ANSWER KEY
   1. tengo dos hijos; 2. tienen; 3. venticinco años /ocho años; 4. abuela; 5. hija /tía; 6. celosa

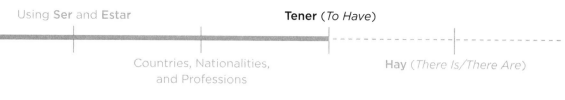
Grammar Builder 1
TENER (*TO HAVE*)

▶ 4B Grammar Builder 1 (CD 4, Track 15)

Let's learn more about the verb tener (*to have*). You'll remember from *Essential Spanish* that tener is an irregular verb, so let's review its forms.

TENER (*TO HAVE*)			
yo tengo	*I have*	nosotros/as tenemos	*we have*
tú tienes	*you have (infml.)*	vosotros/as tenéis	*(all of) you have (pl. fml.)*
él/ella/usted tiene	*he/she has, you have (fml.)*	ellos/ellas/ ustedes tienen	*they have, (all of) you have (pl. fml.)*

Remember that you use tener to tell a person's age.

¿Cuántos años tiene Pedro?
How old is Pedro? (lit., How many years does Pedro have?)

Pedro tiene veintitrés años.
Pedro is twenty-three years old.

It's also used to show possession, just as in English.

Tengo un apartamento en México y una casa en Paraguay.
I have an apartment in Mexico and a house in Paraguay.

The verb tener is also used to describe certain physical, mental, and emotional states. In most of the cases where Spanish uses tener, English uses *to be*.

tener frío	*to be cold*
tener calor	*to be warm*
tener sed	*to be thirsty*
tener hambre	*to be hungry*
tener sueño	*to be sleepy*
tener cansancio	*to be tired*
tener prisa	*to be in a hurry*
tener miedo	*to be scared*
tener razón	*to be right*

¿Tienes hambre?
Are you hungry?

Tengo sueño ahora.
I'm sleepy now.

Tenemos frío en enero.
We're cold in January.

⑪

✎ Work Out 1

Fill in the blanks with the correct form of tener.

1. Nosotros _____ hambre y sed.

2. Ella _____ veintisiete años y él _____ cuarenta.

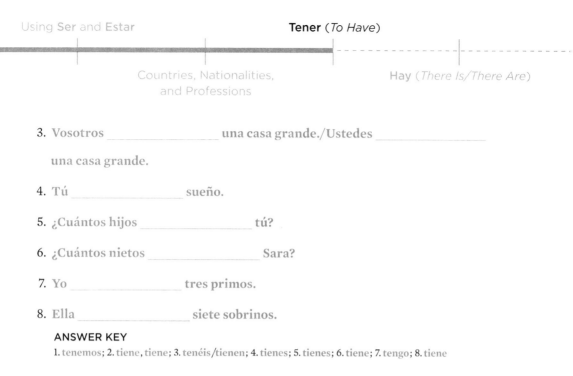

3. Vosotros _____ una casa grande./Ustedes _____ una casa grande.

4. Tú _____ sueño.

5. ¿Cuántos hijos _____ tú?

6. ¿Cuántos nietos _____ Sara?

7. Yo _____ tres primos.

8. Ella _____ siete sobrinos.

ANSWER KEY

1. tenemos; 2. tiene, tiene; 3. tenéis/tienen; 4. tienes; 5. tienes; 6. tiene; 7. tengo; 8. tiene

Conversation 2

A day after his date, Fabio meets up with his friend Jorge and tells him about the woman he's been dating.

▶ 4C Conversation 2 (CD 4, Track 16 - Spanish Only; Track 17 - Spanish and English)

Fabio:	¡Está divorciada!
Jorge:	¿Tiene hijos?
Fabio:	Sí, dos. ¡Y encima es abuela!
Jorge:	¡No me digas!
Fabio:	Pero eso no es todo. Ella vive con sus hijos, su nuera y su nieta en un mismo apartamento.
Jorge:	¿Es un apartamento grande o pequeño?
Fabio:	Hay cuatro alcobas y una sala-comedor. Hay también una cocina y un balcón.
Jorge:	No está mal.
Fabio:	¿No está mal? ¡Los dos ex esposos viven en el edificio también!
Jorge:	Bueno, tienes razón. El problema es gordo.

Fabio:	Farina es una mujer muy atractiva y divertida pero su situación familiar es difícil.

Fabio:	She's divorced!
Jorge:	Does she have children?
Fabio:	Yes, two. And, on top of that, she's a grandmother!
Jorge:	No kidding!
Fabio:	But that's not all. She lives with her children, her daughter-in-law, and her granddaughter in the same apartment.
Jorge:	Is it a big or a small apartment?
Fabio:	There are four bedrooms and a living room–dining room. There's also a kitchen and a balcony.
Jorge:	Not bad.
Fabio:	Not bad? Her two ex-husbands are living in the building too!
Jorge:	Well, you're right. That's a major problem.
Fabio:	Farina is a very attractive and fun woman, but her family situation is very difficult.

Take It Further

Notice that at the beginning of the dialogue, Fabio refers to the woman he's been on a date with as la tía (*the aunt*). In colloquial Spanish, the words tío and tía are used very frequently to refer to a man or a woman, just like we use the words *guy* and, less commonly, *gal* in English.

✎ Conversation Practice 2

Fill in the blanks below with the appropriate word based on the English translations and the dialogue above.

1. ¡Y encima es _____! *And, on top of that, she's a grandmother!*

2. _____ cuatro alcobas y una sala-comedor. *There are four bedrooms and a living room–dining room.*

3. ¡Los dos ex- _____ viven en el edificio también! *Her two ex-husbands are living in the building too!*

4. Bueno, tienes _____. *Well, you're right.*

5. Farina es una mujer muy _____ y _____ pero su situación familiar es difícil. *Farina is a very attractive and fun woman, but her family situation is very difficult.*

ANSWER KEY
1. abuela; 2. Hay; 3. esposos; 4. razón; 5. atractiva, divertida

Grammar Builder 2
HAY (*THERE IS/THERE ARE*)

▶ 4D Grammar Builder 2 (CD 4, Track 18)

Let's review some sentences using the word hay, which means both *there is* and *there are*.

Hay una persona en la clase.
There's one person in the classroom.

En la casa hay tres habitaciones y un estudio.
There are three bedrooms and a study in the house.

¿Cuántas personas hay en su familia?
How many people are there in your family?

(II)

✎ Work Out 2

Translate the following sentences, writing out the numbers in Spanish.

1. *There are seventy men and twenty women in the room.* _____

   _____

2. *The house has fifteen bathrooms.* _____

   _____

3. *I'm hungry.* _____

4. *The coffee is hot.* _____

5. *She's sleepy.* _____

6. *You (fml. sg.) are right.* _____

7. *We're hot.* _____

8. *They're scared.* _____

ANSWER KEY

1. **Hay setenta hombres y veinte mujeres en la habitación.** 2. **La casa tiene quince baños.** 3. **Tengo hambre.** 4. **El café está caliente.** 5. **Ella tiene sueño.** 6. **Usted tiene razón.** 7. **Tenemos calor.** 8. **Tienen miedo.**

✎ Word Recall

Which tener expression would you use for each of the following? Answer using Tengo . . . .

1. *You are tired and need to sleep.* _____

2. *It's very hot.* _____

3. *It's cold.* _____

4. *You are thirsty.* _____

5. *You're hungry.* _____

ANSWER KEY
1. Tengo sueño. 2. Tengo calor. 3. Tengo frío. 4. Tengo sed. 5. Tengo hambre.

How Did You Do?

By now, you should be able to:

☐ Confidently conjugate the verb **tener** and use it in several idiomatic expressions
(Still unsure? Jump back to page 47.)

☐ Use the expression **Hay** ... to express *there is*, *there are*
(Still unsure? Jump back to page 51.)

Don't forget to practice and reinforce what you've learned by visiting **www.livinglanguage.com/languagelab** for flashcards, games, and quizzes for Unit 1!

Unit 1 Essentials

You're almost at the end of the first unit of *Intermediate Spanish*!

You will see Unit Essentials at the end of every unit. They are divided into two sections: Vocabulary Essentials and Grammar Essentials. The Vocabulary Essentials section is a blank "cheat sheet" for you to fill in and test yourself on the vocabulary you learned in the past four lessons. Once you've completed it, you will be able to use it along with the Grammar Essentials as your very own reference guide for all of the key material from each unit.

Vocabulary Essentials

FAMILY

	mother
	father
	boy/girl
	son/daughter
	brother/sister
	grandfather/grandmother
	aunt/uncle
	husband/wife

[Pg. 15] (If you're stuck, visit this page to review!)

OBJECTS

	book
	pen
	letter
	pencil

[Pg. 16]

HOME

	house
	building
	apartment
	living room
	dining room
	kitchen
	bathroom
	bedroom
	door
	window
	table

[Pg. 19]

PROFESSIONS

	lawyer
	artist
	secretary
	professor
	university

[Pg. 26]

EXPRESSIONS

	There is/There are …
	How are you?
	I'm fine, thanks.
	I'm tired. (male/female)
	to be cold
	to be warm
	to be thirsty
	to be hungry

[Pg. 48]

NUMBERS

	0		20
	1		21
	2		22
	3		23
	4		24
	5		25

	6		26
	7		27
	8		28
	9		29
	10		30
	11		31
	12		32
	13		40
	14		50
	15		60
	16		70
	17		80
	18		90
	19		100

[Pg. 31]

Grammar Essentials

ARTICLES

INDEFINITE ARTICLES	MASCULINE	FEMININE
singular	un	una
plural	unos	unas

DEFINITE ARTICLES	MASCULINE	FEMININE
singular	el	la
plural	los	las

VERBS

SER - *(TO BE)* (ORIGIN OR NATIONALITY; IDENTIFYING PEOPLE AND THINGS; OCCUPATION; PERMANENT OR INHERENT CHARACTERISTICS)			
soy	*I am*	somos	*we are*
eres	*you are (infml.)*	sois	*you are (pl. infml.)*
es	*he/she is, you are (fml.)*	son	*they are, you are (pl. fml.)*

ESTAR - *(TO BE)* (LOCATION IN SPACE AND TIME; TEMPORAL OR ACCIDENTAL; FEELINGS AND EMOTIONS)			
estoy	*I am*	estamos	*we are*
estás	*you are (infml.)*	estáis	*you are (pl. fml.)*
está	*he/she is, you are (fml.)*	están	*they are, you are (pl. fml.)*

TENER - *(TO HAVE)*			
tengo	*I have*	tenemos	*we have*
tienes	*you have (infml.)*	tenéis	*you have (pl. fml.)*
tiene	*he/she has, you have (fml.)*	tienen	*they have, you have (pl. fml.)*

Unit 1 Quiz

Let's put the most essential Spanish words and grammar points you've learned and reviewed so far to practice in a few exercises. It's essential that you have this mastered before you move on; score yourself at the end of the review and see if you need to go back for further review, or if you're ready to move on to more Spanish learning.

A. Finish the English sentence with the most appropriate word in Spanish using the proper definite article:

1. *My father's brother is my:* _____

2. *My mother's mother is my:* _____

3. *The room where we eat dinner is:* _____

4. *The room where we cook dinner is:* _____

5. *A woman who represents a defendant in court is:* _____

B. Fill in the blank in each sentence with the most appropriate word from the following list: dirección, francesa, número, años, eres

1. ¿Cuál es su _____ de teléfono?

2. Tú _____ profesora en la universidad.

3. ¿Cuál es su _____ de correo electrónico?

4. La muchacha _____ es de París.

5. Carlos tiene treinta _____.

C. Choose the best conjugation of the word in parentheses for each
sentence below.

1. Ella _____ (ser) bonita.

2. Usted _____ (tener) calor.

3. Yo _____ (estar) en Nueva York.

4. Nosotros _____ (ser) americanos.

5. ¿_____ (tener, tú) hambre?

D. Blank Family Tree

Give the Spanish word for each of the family members below. Don't forget to
include the definite article.

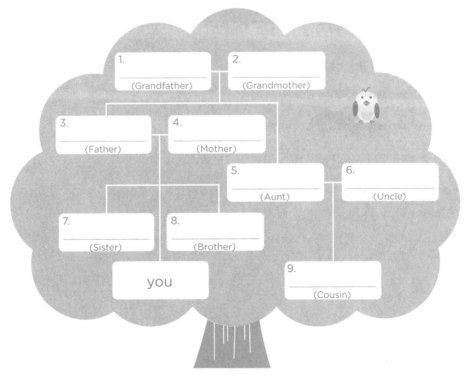

How Did You Do?

Give yourself a point for every correct answer, then use the following key to determine whether or not you're ready to move on:

0–7 points: It's probably best to go back and study the lessons again to make sure you understood everything completely. Take your time; it's not a race! Make sure you spend time reviewing vocabulary with the flashcards and reading through each grammar note carefully.

8–16 points: If the questions you missed were in sections A or B, you may want to review the vocabulary again; if you missed answers mostly in sections C or D, check the unit essentials to make sure you have your conjugations and other grammar basics down.

17–20 points: Feel free to move on to the next unit! You're doing a great job.

 points

Unit 2:
Everyday Life

In this unit you'll learn how to talk about your everyday life, what you do and when you do it, what you like to do, and what you don't like to do. You'll also learn how to ask someone about their everyday life.

By the end of this unit, you should be able to:

☐ Say the names of the days of the week

☐ Say the names of the months of the year

☐ Use numbers above 100

☐ Express the time

☐ Say good-bye in a variety of ways

☐ Talk about different times of the day

☐ Use adjectives to describe people and things

☐ Make plans with someone

☐ Ask questions using question words

☐ Tell someone what you do on certain days

☐ Ask yes/no questions and use tag questions

☐ Say what you like to do and what you don't like to do

Lesson 5: Words

By the end of this lesson, you should be able to:

☐ Say the names of the days of the week

☐ Say the names of the months of the year

☐ Use numbers above 100

☐ Express the time

Word Builder 1

▶ 5A Word Builder 1 (CD 4, Track 19)

Let's review the days of the week in Spanish and add some other useful vocabulary to your list.

la semana	week
el día	day
lunes	Monday
martes	Tuesday
miércoles	Wednesday
jueves	Thursday
viernes	Friday
sábado	Saturday
domingo	Sunday
el fin de semana	weekend
semanal	weekly
diario	daily
la mañana	morning

la tarde	*afternoon*
la noche	*evening, night*

Remember that in Spanish, the days of the week are not written with a capital letter.

✎ Word Practice 1

Match the days of the week in Spanish to their English translations.

1. miércoles
2. viernes
3. domingo
4. sábado
5. martes
6. jueves
7. lunes

a. *Sunday*
b. *Tuesday*
c. *Wednesday*
d. *Friday*
e. *Monday*
f. *Thursday*
g. *Saturday*

ANSWER KEY
1. c; 2. d; 3. a; 4. g; 5. b; 6. f; 7. e

Grammar Builder 1
NUMBERS ABOVE 100

▷ 5B Grammar Builder 1 (CD 4, Track 20)

You already know the numbers 0 to 100. So, let's keep on counting and add some important information about using numbers above 100.

cien	*100*
ciento uno/una	*101*
ciento dos	*102*

doscientos/as	200
trescientos/as	300
cuatrocientos/as	400
quinientos/as	500
seiscientos/as	600
setecientos/as	700
ochocientos/as	800
novecientos/as	900
mil	1,000
mil novecientos noventa y ocho	1,998
diez mil	10,000
veinte mil	20,000
un millón	1,000,000

The hundreds not only have a masculine and a feminine form, but they are also plural.

doscientos hombres	200 men
cuatrocientas mujeres	400 women
quinientos treinta y tres niños	533 boys (children)
seiscientas quince niñas	615 girls

Usually the word cien is used before a noun, and the word ciento before any number except mil (thousand).

cien días	100 days
cien personas	100 people
ciento tres dólares	103 dollars
ciento setenta y siete años	177 years
cien mil pesos	100,000 pesos

Finally, the word millón (*million*) and others formed by using it are followed by the preposition de (*of*).

un millón de casas	1,000,000 houses
cuatro millones de personas	4,000,000 people

✎ Work Out 1

Translate the following phrases. Write out the numbers in Spanish.

1. *365 days* _____

2. *52 weeks* _____

3. *10,000 people* _____

4. *1,565,000 houses* _____

5. *100 children* _____

6. *555 women* _____

7. *145 prizes* _____

8. *278 rooms* _____

ANSWER KEY

1. trescientos sesenta y cinco días 2. cincuenta y dos semanas 3. diez mil personas 4. un millón quinientos sesenta y cinco mil casas. 5. cien niños 6. quinientas cincuenta y cinco mujeres 7. ciento cuarenta y cinco premios 8. doscientas setenta y ocho habitaciones

Word Builder 2

▶ 5C Word Builder 2 (CD 4, Track 21)

Let's review the months of the year and add some other useful vocabulary.

el año	year
el mes	month
enero	January
febrero	February
marzo	March
abril	April
mayo	May
junio	June
julio	July
agosto	August
septiembre	September
octubre	October
noviembre	November
diciembre	December
la década	decade
el siglo	century
la estación	season
la primavera	spring
el verano	summer
el otoño	fall
el invierno	winter

Like the days of the week, the months and seasons are not capitalized in Spanish.

⏸

✎ Word Practice 2

The months below are scrambled. Can you put them in their proper order?

septiembre	junio
diciembre	octubre
enero	mayo
noviembre	abril
marzo	febrero
agosto	julio

ANSWER KEY
enero; febrero; marzo; abril; mayo; junio; julio; agosto; septiembre; octubre; noviembre; diciembre

Grammar Builder 2
TELLING TIME

▶ 5D Grammar Builder 2 (CD 4, Track 22)

The verb **ser** comes in very handy when telling time. You can ask for the time using any of the following expressions.

¿Qué hora es?
What time is it?

¿Qué horas son?
What time is it?

¿Qué hora tiene?
What time do you have?

Usually, you answer by using the verb ser + la(s), because the noun hora is feminine. Notice that with most hours you use son las ..., but with one o'clock you use es la ...

Son las doce (en punto).
12:00/It's twelve o'clock (sharp).

Es la una.
1:00/It's one o'clock.

Son las dos.
2:00/It's two o'clock.

Son las seis en punto.
6:00/It's six o'clock sharp.

Use y (*and*) to add minutes past the hour. Notice that you can use cuarto (*quarter*) or quince (*fifteen*) for a quarter of an hour and media (*half*) or treinta (*thirty*) for a half an hour.

Es la una y diez.
1:10/It's ten after one.

Son las cuatro y veinte.
4:20/It's twenty after four.

Es la una y quince.
1:15/It's one fifteen.

Son las tres y cuarto.
3:15/It's a quarter after three.

Son las nueve y treinta.
9:30/It's nine thirty.

Son las once y media.
11:30/It's eleven thirty.

Son las siete y cuarenta y cinco.
7:45/It's seven forty-five.

When telling time past the half hour, you subtract the minutes from the hour and use menos (*less*), like this.

Es la una menos cinco.
12:55/It's five to one.

Es la una menos cuarto.
12:45/It's a quarter to one.

Son las cuatro menos veinte.
3:40/It's twenty to four.

Son las ocho menos cuarto.
7:45/It's a quarter to eight.

You learned a few words for divisions of the day in your word list. Here they are again, with a few more expressions that will come in handy in telling the time.

la mañana	*morning*
el mediodía	*noon*
la tarde	*afternoon*
la noche	*evening, night*

| la media noche | *midnight* |
| la madrugada | *late night, early morning (from midnight till daybreak)* |

Because we normally don't use military time, you can specify the time of day when telling time with phrases like the following.

Es la una y diez de la madrugada.
1:10/It's ten after one in the morning.

Son las cuatro menos veinte de la mañana.
3:40/It's twenty to four in the morning.

Son las nueve y treinta de la noche.
9:30/It's nine thirty at night.

Es la una y diez de la tarde.
1:10/It's ten after one in the afternoon.

Notice that when the preposition de is followed by the masculine article el, it forms the contraction del.

Son las doce del mediodía.
It's twelve noon.

Ⅱ

✎ Work Out 2

What time is it? Write out your answers in complete words in Spanish.

1. *7:15 p.m.* _____

_____

2. *3:20 p.m.*

3. *1:45 a.m.*

4. *8:00 a.m.*

5. *2:30 p.m.*

6. *12:55 p.m.*

7. *6:45 a.m.*

8. *1:35 p.m.*

9. *9:10 a.m.*

ANSWER KEY

1. Son las siete y cuarto (y quince) de la noche. 2. Son las tres y veinte de la tarde. 3. Es la una y cuarenta y cinco de la madrugada./Son las dos menos cuarto de la madrugada. 4. Son las ocho de la mañana. 5. Son las dos y treinta (y media) de la tarde. 6. Son las doce y cincuenta y cinco del medio día./Es la una menos cinco. 7. Son las seis y cuarenta y cinco de la mañana./Son las siete menos cuarto de la mañana. 8. Es la una y treinta y cinco de la tarde./Son las dos menos veinticinco de la tarde. 9. Son las nueve y diez de la mañana.

Take It Further

Take a closer look at how numbers are written in Spanish and in English. Those little commas and periods we all love (especially when dealing with large amounts of money) signal something completely different.

5.000 (cinco mil)
5,000 (five thousand)

19,95 (diecinueve coma noventa y cinco)
19.95 (nineteen point ninety-five)

10.540,80 (diez mil quinientos cuarenta coma ochenta)
10,540.80 (ten thousand, five hundred forty point eighty)

✎ Word Recall

What time is it? Below you will find different times; express what time it is in Spanish.

1. *1:00 p.m.* _____

_____

2. *1:15 p.m.* _____

_____

3. *1:30 p.m.* _____

_____

4. *1:45 p.m.* _____

_____

5. *2:00 p.m.* _____

_____

ANSWER KEY
1. Es la una de la tarde. 2. Es la una y cuarto/quince de la tarde. 3. Es la una y media de la tarde. 4. Es la una y cuarenta y cinco de la tarde./Son las dos menos cuarto de la tarde. 5. Son las dos de la tarde.

How Did You Do?

By now you should be able to:

☐ Say the names of the days of the week
(Still unsure? Jump back to page 63.)

☐ Say the names of the months of the year
(Still unsure? Jump back to page 67.)

☐ Use numbers above 100
(Still unsure? Jump back to page 64.)

☐ Express the time
(Still unsure? Jump back to page 68.)

Lesson 6: Phrases

By the end of this lesson, you should be able to:

☐ Say good-bye in a variety of ways

☐ Talk about different times of the day

☐ Use adjectives to describe people and things

Phrase Builder 1

▶ 6A Phrase Builder 1 (CD 4, Track 23)

You've already seen a number of different ways to greet someone. How about saying good-bye? Here are a few phrases to help you out.

Adiós.	Good-bye.
Hasta luego.	Until later.
Hasta pronto.	See you soon. (lit., Until soon).
Hasta mañana.	Until tomorrow.
Hasta más tarde.	Until later.
Hasta entonces.	Till then.
Chao.	Bye.
Nos vemos.	See you. (lit., We see each other.)
Que estés bien. (infml.)	Take care. (lit., May you be well.)
Que esté bien. (fml.)	Take care. (lit., May you be well.)

Ⅱ

✎ Phrase Practice 1

Translate the phrases you just learned into Spanish.

1. *Good-bye.* _____

2. *Until later.* _____

3. *See you soon. (lit., Until soon).* _____

4. *Until tomorrow.* _____

5. *Till then.* _____

6. *See you. (lit., We see each other.)* _____

7. *Take care.(lit., May you be well.) (infml.)* _____

ANSWER KEY
1. Adiós. 2. Hasta luego./Hasta más tarde. 3. Hasta pronto. 4. Hasta mañana. 5. Hasta entonces.
6. Nos vemos. 7. Que estés bien. *(infml.)*

Grammar Builder 1
ADJECTIVE AGREEMENT

▷ 6B Grammar Builder 1 (CD 4, Track 24)

Remember that adjectives are words that you use to describe nouns. So *big,*
intelligent, interesting, and *horrible* are adjectives in English. Don't forget that
nouns in Spanish have gender (masculine or feminine) and number (singular or
plural), and adjectives must agree with the nouns that they describe or modify.

un hombre panameño	a Panamanian man
una mujer panameña	a Panamanian woman
unos hombres panameños	a few Panamanian men
unas mujeres panameñas	a few Panamanian women

As you can see from the above examples, adjectives usually come after the nouns
they modify. The typical adjective endings are -o for masculine singular, -a for
feminine singular, -os for masculine plural, and -as for feminine plural. If an
adjective ends in -e, (grande, *big*), then it has the same form in the singular for
both genders (grande) and adds -s for both genders in the plural (grandes). There
are a few irregularities that we'll get to, but that's the basic picture.

Here are some adjectives you can use to describe people and things. Notice that
just the singular forms are given. You can make the plurals just by adding -s to the
appropriate singular form.

| alto(a)/bajo(a) | tall/short |
| gordo(a)/delgado(a) | fat/thin |

largo(a)/corto(a)	long/short
ancho(a)/angosto(a)	wide/narrow
grande/pequeño(a)	big/small
rico(a)/pobre	rich/poor
costoso(a)/barato(a)	expensive/cheap
limpio(a)/sucio(a)	clean/dirty
libre/ocupado(a)	free/busy
bueno(a)/malo(a)	good/bad
agradable/desagradable	pleasant/unpleasant
temprano/tarde	early/late
divertido(a)/aburrido(a)	fun/boring
bonito(a)/feo(a)	pretty/ugly

Here are some examples using ser. Remember that the adjectives all agree with the person or thing they modify.

Soy alto.
I'm tall.

Eres delgada.
You're thin.

El apartamento es pequeño.
The apartment is small.

Ella es rica.
She's rich.

Somos pobres.
We are poor.

Vosotros sois divertidos.
You are fun.

Ellos son agradables.
They are pleasant.

Son bajos.
They are short.

Let's look at some more examples, this time with tener.

Tengo una casa grande.
I have a big house.

Tiene una abuela rica.
He/She has a rich grandmother.

Tenemos un día libre.
We have a free day.

Tienen un tío divertido.
They have a fun uncle.

Ⅱ

✎ Work Out 1

Connect each noun on the left with its appropriate matching adjective on the right and answer in a complete sentence using a form of ser.

1. el día
2. el libro

a. larga
b. costosas

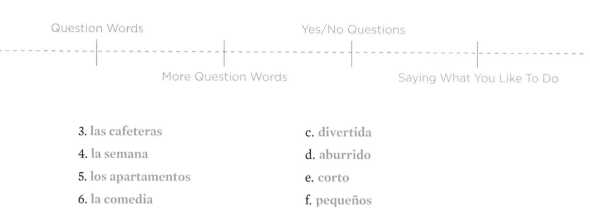

3. las cafeteras
4. la semana
5. los apartamentos
6. la comedia

c. divertida
d. aburrido
e. corto
f. pequeños

ANSWER KEY
1. El día es corto. 2. El libro es aburrido. 3. Las cafeteras son costosas. 4. La semana es larga. 5. Los apartamentos son pequeños. 6. La comedia es divertida.

Phrase Builder 2

6C Phrase Builder 2 (CD 4, Track 25)

por la mañana	in the morning
por la tarde	in the afternoon
por la noche	in the evening, at night
al mediodía	at noon
a la medianoche	at midnight
a la madrugada	in the early morning, at dawn
al* amanecer	at dawn
al atardecer	at dusk
Se me hace tarde.	I'm late.
Es muy temprano.	It's very early.

*Remember how de + el = del? Well, the same thing happens with a (to, at) plus el: a + el = al (to the, at the) in the expressions al amanecer and al atardecer.

Phrase Practice 2

Translate the phrases below.

1. *in the morning* _____

2. *in the afternoon* _____

3. *in the evening, at night* _____

4. *at noon* _____

5. *at midnight* _____

6. *I'm late.* _____

7. *It's very early.* _____

ANSWER KEY

1. **por la mañana**; 2. **por la tarde**; 3. **por la noche**; 4. **al mediodía**; 5. **a la medianoche**; 6. **Se me hace tarde.** 7. **Es muy temprano.**

Grammar Builder 2
MORE ON ADJECTIVE AGREEMENT

▶ 6D Grammar Builder 2 (CD 4, Track 26)

Let's get back to adjectives and adjective agreement, so you know how to describe things in Spanish. Again, as with nouns, adjectives ending in -o are masculine, and the feminine is formed by changing the -o to -a. To form the plural, just add -s to the singular form.

	MASCULINE SINGULAR	FEMININE SINGULAR	MASCULINE PLURAL	FEMININE PLURAL
pretty	bonito	bonita	bonitos	bonitas
ugly	feo	fea	feos	feas

Es un jardín muy bonito.
It's a very pretty garden.

Es una foto muy fea.
It's a very ugly photo.

Tienen unos jardines bonitos.
They have some pretty gardens.

Tienen unas fotos feas.
They have some ugly pictures.

As you know, there are some adjectives that end in **-e**, like **grande** (*big*), **pobre** (*poor*), **libre** (*free*), and so on. These adjectives only have one singular form for both masculine and feminine. There are other adjectives that end in a consonant, like **difícil** (*difficult*) and **fácil** (*easy*). These adjectives also only have one singular form. Both of these types of adjectives end in **-es** in the plural.

Ella es una niña inteligente.
She's an intelligent girl.

Él es un chico inteligente.
He's an intelligent kid.

Son inteligentes.
They're intelligent.

Notice that **trabajador** (*hardworking*) ends in a consonant but has two singular forms.

Tienen un hermano trabajador.
They have a hardworking brother.

Ella es trabajadora.
She's hardworking.

Tienen unos padres trabajadores.
They have hardworking parents.

The exceptions to the above rule are those adjectives used to denote nationalities. Most of them end in a consonant, and the feminine is formed by adding **-a** to the end.

Yo soy española y él es alemán.
I'm Spanish and he's German.

Ella es alemana y ellos son franceses.
She's German and they're French.

Tú eres francesa y él es español.
You're French and he's Spanish.

Ⓘ

✎ Work Out 2

Form sentences using the words given. Make sure you use the correct form of the verb. Adjectives are given in the singular, masculine form, so you may have to change them.

1. yo / tener / treinta / películas / divertido _____

   _____

2. casas / ser / feo _____

   _____

3. tú / tener / dos apartamentos / grande _____

   _____

4. ella / ser / inglés _____

   _____

5. las niñas / ser / alto y bonito _____

   _____

6. yo / tener / un día / libre _____

_____

7. vosotros / tener / unos tíos / rico _____

_____

8. ustedes / tener / unos tíos / rico _____

_____

ANSWER KEY

1. Yo tengo treinta películas divertidas. 2. Las casas son feas. 3. Tú tienes dos apartamentos grandes. 4. Ella es inglesa. 5. Las niñas son altas y bonitas. 6. Yo tengo un día libre. 7. Vosotros tenéis unos tíos ricos. 8. Ustedes tienen unos tíos ricos.

Culture Note

You've probably heard the term realismo mágico (*magical realism*), which refers to a Latin American literary movement. The origin of the term has been attributed to the Cuban writer Alejo Carpentier, who first applied it to Latin American fiction in 1949. The main characteristic of magical realism is the matter-of-fact incorporation of fantastic or dreamlike elements into otherwise realistic fiction. The Colombian writer Gabriel García Márquez is probably the movement's best known proponent. His most famous novel is Cien años de soledad (*One Hundred Years of Solitude*). Other magic realist writers include Guatemala's Miguel Ángel Asturias, Argentina's Julio Córtazar, Mexico's Carlos Fuentes, and Chile's Isabel Allende.

Reading short stories by these writers might be a good way for you to get an introduction to Latin American literature and, in doing so, learn some adjectives!

Word Recall

Write the correct form of the adjective bonito.

1. El apartamento es _____.

2. **El niño es** _____.

3. **La casa es** _____.

4. **La niña es** _____.

5. **Los apartamentos son** _____.

6. **Los niños son** _____.

7. **Las casas son** _____.

8. **Las niñas son** _____.

ANSWER KEY
1-2: bonito; 3-4: bonita; 5-6: bonitos; 7-8: bonitas

How Did You Do?

By now you should be able to:

☐ Say goodbye in a variety of ways
  (Still unsure? Jump back to page 75.)

☐ Talk about different times of the day
  (Still unsure? Jump back to page 79.)

☐ Use adjectives to describe people and things
  (Still unsure? Jump back to pages 76 and 80.)

Lesson 7: Sentences

By the end of this lesson, you should be able to:

☐ Make plans with someone

☐ Ask questions using question words

Sentence Builder 1

▶ 7A Sentence Builder 1 (CD 4, Track 27)

¿Cómo estás de tiempo?	Do you have time?/How are you doing for time?
¿Qué tal si nos encontramos para almorzar?	How about if we meet for lunch?
¿Qué te parece si nos reunimos al mediodía?	How about if we meet at noon?
¿Conoces el lugar?	Do you know the place?
¿Qué tal si vamos al cine?	How about if we go to the movies?
¿Tienes la cartelera de cine a la mano?	Do you have the movie listings handy?
Quedamos a las ocho, ¿no?	We meet at eight, don't we?
¿Por qué no escogemos una comedia?	Why don't we choose a comedy?

Ⅱ

✎ Sentence Practice 1

Translate the following questions into Spanish.

1. *Do you have time?/How are you doing for time?* _____

_____

2. *How about if we meet for lunch?* _____

_____

3. *How about if we meet at noon?* _____

_____

4. *Do you know the place?* _____

_____

5. *How about if we go to the movies?* _____

_____

6. *Do you have the movie listings handy?* _____

_____

7. *We meet at eight, don't we?* _____

_____

8. *Why don't we choose a comedy?* _____

_____

ANSWER KEY

1. ¿Cómo estás de tiempo? 2. ¿Qué tal si nos encontramos para almorzar? 3. ¿Qué te parece si nos reunimos al mediodía? 4. ¿Conoces el lugar? 5. ¿Qué tal si vamos al cine? 6. ¿Tienes la cartelera de cine a la mano? 7. Quedamos a las ocho, ¿no? 8. ¿Por qué no escogemos una comedia?

Grammar Builder 1
QUESTION WORDS

▷ 7B Grammar Builder 1 (CD 4, Track 28)

You have seen examples of yes/no questions previously in this course, for instance: ¿**Es Marta de Madrid o de Barcelona?** (*Is Marta from Madrid or Barcelona?*). We'll come back to yes/no questions in a moment. For now let's look

at questions with question words like *who, what, where, when,* and so on. Here are a few question words in Spanish.

cómo	how
qué	what
quién	who
cuándo	when

You already know how to use **cómo** to greet people and to ask for a description of something or someone. It's also used when you don't understand what has been said. Notice that **cómo** comes at the beginning of the question and that the subject (if it's not dropped) and verb are reversed.

¿Cómo estás?
How are you?

¿Cómo es la película?
How's the movie?

¿Cómo se llama?
What is your name? (lit., How are you called?)

¿Cómo se llama la profesora?
What's the teacher's name?

¿Cómo?
What?/Pardon me?

The word **qué** is used to ask for an explanation or an identification. It's also used to ask when something is happening.

¿Qué es eso?
What is that?

¿Qué es la filosofía?
What is philosophy?

¿Qué hora es?
What time is it?

¿A qué hora es la película?
At what time is the movie?

Quién is used to request the identification of a person. In Spanish it has a plural form (quiénes).

¿Quién es ella?
Who is she?

¿Quiénes son ustedes?
Who are you?

¿Quién es su padre?
Who's your father?

¿Quiénes son sus padres?
Who are your parents?

Finally, cuándo is used to ask when something is taking place.

¿Cuándo es la película?
When is the movie?

¿Cuándo tienes el día libre?

When do you have a free day?

¿Cuándo está ocupada?

When is she busy?

✎ Work Out 1

Translate the following sentences.

1. *When do you have time? (infml. sg.)* _____

_____

2. *How are you doing? (infml. pl.)* _____

_____

3. *At what time is the movie?* _____

_____

4. *Who are the children?* _____

_____

5. *How's the coffee?* _____

_____

6. *What time is it?* _____

_____

ANSWER KEY

1. ¿Cuándo tienes tiempo? 2. ¿Cómo estáis? 3. ¿A qué hora es la película? 4. ¿Quiénes son los niños?
5. ¿Cómo está el café? 6. ¿Qué hora es?

Sentence Builder 2

▶ 7C Sentence Builder 2 (CD 4, Track 29)

El lunes trabajo horas extras.	On Monday I work extra hours.
Los martes tengo clases en la universidad.	On Tuesday I have classes at the university.
Esa es una mejor idea.	That's a better idea.
No, al mediodía no me va bien.	No, noontime is not good for me.
Hablamos luego.	We'll talk later.
A mí tampoco me gustan.	I don't like them either.
Estoy muy ocupada.	I'm very busy.
¿Tienes la cartelera de cine a la mano?	Do you have the movie listings handy?

⏸

✎ Sentence Practice 2

Translate the following sentences into Spanish.

1. *On Monday I work extra hours.* _____

   _____

2. *On Tuesday I have classes at the university.* _____

   _____

3. *That's a better idea.* _____

   _____

4. *No, noontime is not good for me.* _____

   _____

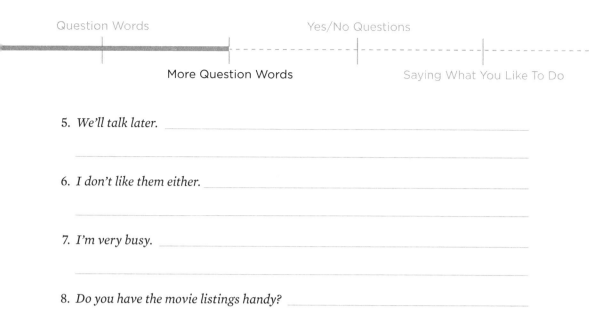

5. *We'll talk later.*

6. *I don't like them either.*

7. *I'm very busy.*

8. *Do you have the movie listings handy?*

ANSWER KEY

1. El lunes trabajo horas extras. 2. Los martes tengo clases en la universidad. 3. Esa es una mejor idea. 4. No, al mediodía no me va bien. 5. Hablamos luego. 6. A mí tampoco me gustan. 7. Estoy muy ocupada. 8. ¿Tienes la cartelera de cine a la mano?

Grammar Builder 2
MORE QUESTION WORDS

▶ 7D Grammar Builder 2 (CD 5, Track 1)

Here are some more useful question words.

dónde	where
cuánto	how much, how many
cuál	which
por qué	why

Dónde is used with **estar** to ask for the location of something. In order to ask for the origin of something/someone, the phrase **de dónde** (*from where*) is used along with the verb **ser**.

¿Dónde está el restaurante?
Where is the restaurant?

¿Dónde están las niñas?
Where are the girls?

¿De dónde eres?
Where are you from?

Cuánto has a feminine form, **cuánta**, and the plural forms **cuántos/as**.

¿Cuánto es el apartamento?
How much is the apartment?

¿Cuánto dinero tienes?
How much money do you have?

¿Cuánta leche quieres?
How much milk do you want?

¿Cuántos días hay en una semana?
How many days are there in a week?

¿Cuántas horas tiene un día?
How many hours does a day have?

Cuál also has a plural form (**cuáles**) and is used when asking about something
that belongs to a group.

¿Cuál es su casa?
Which is your house?

¿Cuáles son sus libros?
Which are your books?

Finally, there is por qué, which means *why*.

¿Por qué es delgado?
Why is he thin?

¿Por qué está María en Costa Rica?
Why is María in Costa Rica?

¿Por qué tienes sueño?
Why are you sleepy?

Ⓘ

✎ Work Out 2

Write a question for each of the following answers.

1. **El hotel tiene cuatrocientas cincuenta habitaciones.** _____

_____

2. **La película es a las tres y media de la tarde.** _____

_____

3. **Colombia está en Sudamérica.** _____

_____

4. **Estoy cansado.** _____

_____

5. Tengo cinco hermanos. _____

_____

ANSWER KEY

1. ¿Cuántas habitaciones tiene el hotel? 2. ¿A qué hora es la película? 3. ¿Dónde está Colombia?
4. ¿Cómo estás/está? 5. ¿Cuántos hermanos tienes/tiene?

Take It Further

In Spanish, the context of a sentence is very important, because speakers tend to drop the subject pronouns and only use them when they want to show emphasis or when they're absolutely necessary for clarity. In all cases, the verb ending helps you determine who the subject of the sentence is. But this is not the case with the third person singular and plural, because these verb endings are used with a few different subjects. Let's take a look at the following question.

¿Cuándo está libre?

This could be referring to usted, él, or ella.

And how about this one:

¿Cuándo están libres?

It could be referring to ustedes, ellos, or ellas.

When you need to use the pronoun for clarification, simply insert it after the verb.

¿Cuándo está usted libre?
When are you free?

¿Cuándo está ella libre?
When is she free?

¿Cuándo están ustedes libres?
When are you free?

¿Cuándo están ellos libres?
When are they free?

✎ Word Recall

Fill in the blank according to the hint in parentheses.

1. ¿_____ es la película? (*when?*)

2. ¿_____ es el almuerzo? (*when?*)

3. ¿_____ trabajas? (*where?*)

4. ¿_____ comes? (*where?*)

5. ¿_____ es el muchacho? (*who?*)

6. ¿_____ es la muchacha? (*who?*)

7. ¿_____ son los muchachos? (*who?*)

8. ¿_____ son las muchachas? (*who?*)

ANSWER KEY
1-2: Cuándo; 3-4: Dónde; 5-6: Quién; 7-8: Quiénes

How Did You Do?

By now, you should be able to:

☐ Make plans with someone
(Still unsure? Jump back to page 85.)

☐ Ask questions using question words
(Still unsure? Jump back to pages 86 and 91.)

Lesson 8: Conversations

By the end of this lesson, you should be able to:

☐ Tell someone what you do on certain days

☐ Ask yes/no questions and use tag questions

☐ Say what you like to do and what you don't like to do

⁏ Conversation 1
▶ 8A Conversation 1 (CD 5, Track 2 - Spanish Only; Track 3 - Spanish and English)

Clara and Margarita have been friends since high school. They haven't seen each other since graduation, and they're trying to set up a time to meet.

Clara:	¿Cómo estás de tiempo? Cualquier día después del trabajo me viene bien.
Margarita:	Estoy muy ocupada. El lunes trabajo horas extras en la oficina. Los martes y jueves tengo clases en la universidad. Y los miércoles practico deporte. El único día que tengo libre es el viernes y generalmente se lo dedico a mi novio.
Clara:	Sí, entiendo … Bueno, y ¿qué tal si nos encontramos para almorzar?
Margarita:	Esa es una mejor idea. ¿Qué te parece si nos reunimos este martes al mediodía?
Clara:	No, el martes al mediodía no me va bien. Mejor por la tarde y tomamos un café. ¿Conoces un sitio que se llama "Chocolate y churros"?

Margarita: Sí, es un lugar muy agradable. Me gustan mucho las tortas que tienen, pero son un poco costosas.

Clara: Ay, lo siento Margarita, ya son las dos y media y se me hace tarde. Hablamos luego.

Margarita: Bueno, que estés bien. Adiós.

Clara: Chao.

Clara: *Do you have time? Any day after work is fine with me.*

Margarita: *I'm very busy. On Monday I work extra hours in the office. On Tuesdays and Thursdays I have classes at school. And Wednesdays I play sports. The only day I have free is Friday, and I usually set that aside for my boyfriend (lit., dedicate it to him, to my boyfriend).*

Clara: *Yes, I understand … Well, and how about if we meet for lunch?*

Margarita: *That's a better idea. How about if we meet this Tuesday at noon?*

Clara: *No, Tuesday at noon is not good for me. It'd be better in the afternoon for a coffee. Do you know a place called "Chocolate y churros"?*

Margarita: *Yes, it's a very nice place. I like the cakes they have very much, but they're a bit expensive.*

Clara: *Oh, sorry, Margarita, it's already two thirty and I'm running late. We'll talk later.*

Margarita: *Okay … take care. Good-bye.*

Clara: *Bye.*

Take It Further

Notice that the days of the week are masculine, so the masculine article is always used except after the verb ser.

Trabajo horas extras el lunes.
I work extra hours on Monday.

Hoy es martes.
Today is Tuesday.

Also notice that when talking about an activity that happens with a certain frequency on a certain day of the week, the plural is used.

Los miércoles hago deporte.
I play sports on Wednesdays.

Estudio los sábados.
I study on Saturdays.

There are plenty of examples of new verbs in this dialogue: trabajo (*I work*), practico (*I play, I practice*), dedico (*I dedicate*), and so on. You'll learn all about verb conjugation in the next unit.

Conversation Practice 1

Unscramble the sentences from the dialogue above. The English sentence is unscrambled.

1. ¿/estás/de/cómo/tiempo/? *Do you have time?* _____

_____

2. una/idea/es/mejor/esa/. *That's a better idea.* _____

_____

3. ¿/un/llama/sitio/se/"Chocolate y churros"/que/conoces/? *Do you know a place called "Chocolate y Churros"?* _____

_____

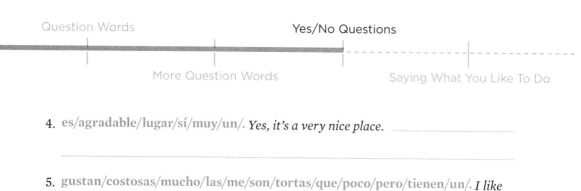
4. es/agradable/lugar/sí/muy/un/. *Yes, it's a very nice place.* _____

_____

5. gustan/costosas/mucho/las/me/son/tortas/que/poco/pero/tienen/un/. *I like*

the cakes they have very much, but they're a bit expensive. _____

_____

ANSWER KEY

1. ¿Cómo estás de tiempo? 2. Es una idea mejor. 3. Conoces un sitio que se llama "Chocolate y churros"?
4. Sí, es un lugar muy agradable. 5. Me gustan mucho las tortas que tienen, pero son un poco costosas.

Grammar Builder 1
YES/NO QUESTIONS

▶ 8B Grammar Builder 1 (CD 5, Track 4)

Question words like the ones we saw in Lesson 7 are one way of making questions.
Yes/no questions are another type of question, and they're very simple to form.
All you need to do is put the verb at the beginning of the sentence.

¿Eres boliviana?
Are you Bolivian?

¿Tienes hermanos?
Do you have brothers and sisters?

Notice that subject pronouns are often left out; they are only used for emphasis or
to clarify. If they are used, or if a subject noun is used, they come after the verb.

¿Es (usted) profesora?
Are you a teacher?

¿Tiene (ella) el libro?
Does she have the book?

¿Es Marta de Costa Rica?
Is Marta from Costa Rica?

¿Tienen los niños tiempo?
Do the children have time?

Or-questions are formed in a similar way.

¿Eres soltero o casado?
Are you single or married?

¿Está Jorge en la casa o en la oficina?
Is Jorge at home or in the office?

In English, you can ask what's called a *tag question,* as in *He's a blast, isn't he?* or *They aren't much fun, are they?* In Spanish, the equivalents of tag questions can be formed with either ¿no? (*no?*) or ¿verdad? (*right?*) at the end of the question. Notice the difference in punctuation.

Eres soltera, ¿no?
You're single, aren't you?

Tienes dos hermanos, ¿verdad?
You have two brothers, don't you?

Él está en Londres y ella en Bogotá, ¿no?
He's in London and she's in Bogotá, right?

Ⅱ

✎ Work Out 1

Fill in the blank with the correct form of the verb in parentheses.

1. Ellos _____ una casa en Madrid, ¿verdad? (tener)

2. ¿ _____ usted colombiana? (ser)

3. Tú _____ en la oficina, ¿verdad? (estar)

4. ¿Cuántas habitaciones _____ el apartamento? (tener)

5. Nosotros _____ solteros. (ser)

6. Vosotros _____ en Quito, ¿verdad? (estar)

7. ¿Por qué _____ usted sed? (tener)

8. ¡Nosotros _____ hambre! (tener)

ANSWER KEY
1. tienen; 2. Es; 3. estás; 4. tiene; 5. somos; 6. estáis; 7. tiene; 8. tenemos

▣ Conversation 2

▶ 8C Conversation 2 (CD 5, Track 5 - Spanish Only; Track 6 - Spanish and English)

Clara and Margarita had so much fun having coffee together and remembering
the good old days that they have decided to get together over the weekend and go
to the movies with their boyfriends. They're setting it all up over the phone.

Clara:	Bueno, y ¿qué tal si vamos los cuatro al cine este fin de semana?
Margarita:	Sí, sería divertido.
Clara:	¿Qué películas les gustan?
Margarita:	A mí me gustan mucho las películas de suspenso, pero Rafael las detesta.
Clara:	A mí tampoco me gustan. Prefiero las películas románticas o las comedias.

Margarita:	Bueno, ¿por qué no escogemos una comedia? ¿Tienes la cartelera de cine a la mano?
Clara:	Sí, aquí la tengo. A ver ... Bueno, solamente hay dos películas: Dos bobos en apuros y Chanchitos en el espacio.
Margarita:	No sé ... pero Chanchitos en el espacio suena divertida. La otra película parece aburrida, ¿no crees?
Clara:	Sí, tienes razón.
Margarita:	¿A qué hora la dan?
Clara:	A las diez menos cuarto de la noche.
Margarita:	Ya está ... Quedamos a las ocho en el bar que está al otro lado del teatro, ¿no?
Clara:	A las ocho es muy temprano. Mejor a las nueve. Hasta entonces.
Margarita:	Hasta luego.

Clara:	Well, how about if the four of us go to the movies this weekend?
Margarita:	Yes, that would be fun.
Clara:	What movies do you like?
Margarita:	I like suspense movies very much, but Rafael hates them.
Clara:	I don't like them either. I prefer romantic or funny movies.
Margarita:	Well, how about if we choose a comedy? Do you have the movie listings handy?
Clara:	Yes, here they are. Let's see ... There are only two movies: Two Dummies in a Jam and Piglets in Space.
Margarita:	I don't know ... but Piglets in Space sounds like fun. The other movie seems boring, don't you think?
Clara:	Yes, you're right.
Margarita:	What time is it playing?
Clara:	At a quarter to ten.
Margarita:	That's it. We're meeting at eight at the bar that's across from the theater, right?
Clara:	Eight is too early. Nine is better. See you then.
Margarita:	See you then.

Take It Further

In Spanish, a simple sí or no is enough to answer short yes/no questions. However, because this way of answering is a bit brief, it is better to try to give a bit more information by using other short phrases or repeating the verb used in the question.

¿Tienes la cartelera de cine a la mano?
Do you have the movie listings handy?

Sí, aquí la tengo.
Yes, here they are (lit., Yes, I have it here.)

¿Están tus padres en casa?
Are your parents home?

Sí, sí están.
Yes, they are.

✎ Conversation Practice 2

Fill in the blanks below with the appropriate word based on the English translations and the dialogue above.

1. ¿Qué películas les _____? *What movies do you like?*

2. A mí me gustan mucho las películas de suspenso, pero Rafael las _____.

   I like suspense movies very much, but Rafael hates them.

3. _____ las películas románticas o las comedias. *I prefer romantic or funny movies.*

4. **La otra película parece** _____, **¿no crees?** *The other movie seems boring, don't you think?*

5. **A las** _____ **de la noche.** *At a quarter to ten.*

6. _____ **a las ocho en el bar que está al otro lado del teatro, ¿no?** *We're meeting at eight at the bar that's across from the theater, right?*

ANSWER KEY
1. gustan; 2. detesta; 3. Prefiero; 4. aburrida; 5. diez menos cuarto; 6. Quedamos

Grammar Builder 2
SAYING WHAT YOU LIKE TO DO

▷ 8D Grammar Builder 2 (CD 5, Track 7)

Here are some verbs that may come in handy when talking about things you usually do.

trabajar	*to work*
bailar	*to dance*
cantar	*to sing*
comer	*to eat*
beber	*to drink*
nadar	*to swim*
trotar	*to jog*
escribir	*to write*
dormir	*to sleep*

All of these verbs are in the infinitive, or basic, form, which corresponds to the *to* form in English. In the next unit, you'll learn how verbs are conjugated

in Spanish—for example, how to say *I swim* or *she swims* instead of *to swim*. But before that, you can start using these infinitive forms with the very useful expression me gusta (*I like*).

Me gusta bailar.
I like to dance.

Me gusta nadar.
I like to swim.

Me gusta hablar español.
I like to speak Spanish.

Gusta is a form of the verb gustar, which literally means *to be pleasing.* In Spanish, when you say *I like X,* you say *X is pleasing to me.* If the thing you like is a verb, the form gusta is always used, as in the above examples. You also use gusta if you like a singular person or thing.

Me gusta el libro.
I like the book.

Me gusta el nuevo profesor.
I like the new teacher.

If you like more than one person or thing, you use gustan.

Me gustan los fines de semana.
I like weekends.

Me gustan los libros interesantes.
I like interesting books.

Me gustan los actores mexicanos.
I like Mexican actors.

To say that you don't like something, use no me gusta or no me gustan (*I don't like*).

No me gusta cantar.
I don't like to sing.

No me gusta trotar.
I don't like to jog.

No me gustan los lunes.
I don't like Mondays.

No me gustan las películas de horror.
I don't like horror movies.

Ⅱ

🖊 Work Out 2

Fill in the blanks with the correct form of gustar.

1. Me _____ **los apartamentos grandes.**

2. No me _____ **los hombres altos.**

3. Me _____ **los niños.**

4. No me _____ **trabajar.**

5. Me _____ **los viernes.**

6. No me _____ **los libros largos.**

7. Me _____ las comedias.

ANSWER KEY
1. gustan; 2. gustan; 3. gustan; 4. gusta; 5. gustan; 6. gustan; 7. gustan

Take It Further

You may be wondering by now about accent marks on some words, like cómo. Accent marks are used for two purposes: to show where the stress or emphasis falls on a word when it's pronounced, and to help differentiate between identically spelled words. We won't get into all the rules here, but here are some general rules for when and why accents are used.

If a word ends in a vowel, -n, or -s, stress normally falls on the second-to-last syllable.

libro, hombre, España, computadora, gustan, tienen, cartas, tienes, estas

If a word ends in a consonant other than -n or -s, it is normally stressed on the last syllable.

mujer, español, celebrar, ciudad, escuchar

An accent mark overrides this rule:

fotografía, cárcel, tomó, sótano, estás

An accent mark is also used to distinguish between two words that are pronounced the same way but mean different things.

solo (*adjective: sole, only, alone*)	sólo (*adverb: merely, solely, only*)
que (*conjunction: that, that which*)	qué (*interrogative: what*)
si (*if*)	sí (*yes*)
el (*the, masc.*)	él (*he*)

✎ Word Recall

Form sentences expressing your likes and dislikes based on the clues in parentheses.

1. el actor americano *(I like)* _____

_____

2. la casa pequeña *(I like)* _____

_____

3. los actores americanos *(I like)* _____

_____

4. los sábados y los domingos *(I like)* _____

_____

5. el actor americano *(I don't like)* _____

_____

6. la casa pequeña *(I don't like)* _____

_____

7. los actores americanos *(I don't like)* _____

_____

8. los sábados ni los domingos *(I don't like)* _____

_____

ANSWER KEY
1. Me gusta el actor americano. 2. Me gusta la casa pequeña. 3. Me gustan los actores americanos.
4. Me gustan los sábados y los domingos. 5. No me gusta el actor americano. 6. No me gusta la casa
pequeña. 7. No me gustan los actores americanos. 8. No me gustan los sábados ni los domingos.

How Did You Do?

By now, you should be able to:

☐ Tell someone what you do on certain days
(Still unsure? Jump back to page 97.)

☐ Ask yes/no questions and use tag questions
(Still unsure? Jump back to page 99.)

☐ Say what you like to do and what you don't like to do
(Still unsure? Jump back to page 104.)

Don't forget to practice and reinforce what you've learned by visiting **www.livinglanguage.com/ languagelab** for flashcards, games, and quizzes for Unit 2!

Unit 2 Essentials

Vocabulary Essentials

DAYS OF THE WEEK

	Monday
	Tuesday
	Wednesday
	Thursday
	Friday
	Saturday
	Sunday

[Pg. 63]

MONTHS OF THE YEAR

	January
	February
	March
	April
	May
	June
	July
	August
	September
	October
	November

	December

[Pg. 67]

OTHER TIME AND SEASONAL EXPRESSIONS

	week
	day
	weekend
	weekly
	daily
	morning
	afternoon
	evening, night
	year
	month
	decade
	century
	season
	spring
	summer
	fall
	winter

[Pg. 63, Pg. 67]

PARTING EXPRESSIONS

	Good-bye.
	Until later.
	See you soon. (lit., Until soon).
	Until tomorrow.
	Until later.
	Till then.
	Bye.
	See you. (lit., We see each other.)
	Take care.(lit., May you be well.)
	May you be well.

[Pg. 75]

NUMBERS 100–1,000,000

	100
	101
	102
	200
	300
	400
	500
	600
	700
	800
	900
	1,000

	1,998
	10,000
	20,000
	1,000,000

[Pg. 64]

ADJECTIVES

	tall/short
	fat/thin
	long/short
	wide/narrow
	big/small
	rich/poor
	expensive/cheap
	clean/dirty
	free/busy
	good/bad
	pleasant/unpleasant
	early/late
	fun/boring
	pretty/ugly

[Pg. 76]

VERBS

	to work
	to dance

	to sing
	to eat
	to drink
	to swim
	to jog
	to write
	to sleep

[Pg. 104]

Grammar Essentials

ADJECTIVE AGREEMENT

	MASCULINE SINGULAR	FEMININE SINGULAR	MASCULINE PLURAL	FEMININE PLURAL
pretty	bonito	bonita	bonitos	bonitas
ugly	feo	fea	feos	feas

QUESTION WORDS

cómo	*how*
qué	*what*
quién/quiénes	*who*
cuándo	*when*
dónde	*where*
cuánto/cuánta/cuántos/cuántas	*how much, how many*
cuál/cuáles	*which*
por qué	*why*

YES/NO QUESTIONS

To form a yes/no question, put the verb at the beginning of the sentence. Subject pronouns are often omitted; they are only used for emphasis or to clarify. If they are used, or if a subject noun is used, they come after the verb.

TAG QUESTIONS

Tag questions are formed in Spanish by adding either ¿no? (*no?*) or ¿verdad? (*right?*) at the end of the question.

TO LIKE/TO NOT LIKE

	SINGULAR	PLURAL
I like	me gusta	me gustan
I don't like	no me gusta	no me gustan

Unit 2 Quiz

A. Give the day or month that follows the one listed below.

1. abril: _____

2. martes: _____

3. julio: _____

4. sábado: _____

5. diciembre: _____

6. jueves: _____

7. septiembre: _____

8. viernes: _____

9. mayo: _____

10. lunes _____

B. Fill in the blank in each sentence with the most appropriate word from the following list: mañana, hora, es, son, quién, quiénes

1. ¿Qué _____ es?

2. _____ las siete y media de la mañana.

3. Adiós, hasta _____.

4. ¿ _____ es ella?

5. ¿ _____ son ellas?

6. _____ la una y veinte de la tarde.

C. Give the number that goes before and after the number given below.

1. _____ veintiocho _____

2. _____ noventa y nueve _____

3. _____ quinientos

cuarenta y seis _____

4. _____

mil doscientos cincuenta y cuatro _____

_____

5. _____

tres mil setecientos noventa y nueve _____

_____

D. Find the opposite of the word given.

1. temprano	a. pequeño
2. gordo	b. malo
3. rico	c. sucio
4. grande	d. tarde
5. limpio	e. delgado
6. bueno	f. bajo
7. libre	g. ocupado
8. alto	h. pobre

How Did You Do?

Give yourself a point for every correct answer, then use the following key to determine whether or not you're ready to move on:

0–7 points: It's probably best to go back and study the lessons again to make sure you understood everything completely. Take your time; it's not a race! Make sure you spend time reviewing vocabulary with the flashcards and reading through each grammar note carefully.

8–16 points: If the questions you missed were in sections A or B, you may want to review the vocabulary again; if you missed answers mostly in sections C or D, check the unit essentials to make sure you have your conjugations and other grammar basics down.

17–20 points: Feel free to move on to the next unit! You're doing a great job.

 points

Unit 3:
Health and the Human Body

In this unit you'll learn a lot of new and useful vocabulary related to the human body and health. By the end of the unit, you should know how to:

☐ Talk about parts of the body

☐ Express possession with possessive adjectives like *my* and *your*

☐ Talk about your physical state with a doctor

☐ Feel familiar with some idiomatic expressions using body parts

☐ Express possession using de + pronoun

☐ Express possession using de in other expressions

☐ Talk to a doctor about specific problems

☐ Use possessive pronouns to express *mine* and *yours*

☐ Use verbs like *to walk, to taste, to speak*

☐ Use verbs like *to run, to eat, to see*

☐ Use verbs like *to write, to live, to leave*

☐ Talk about the present tense using time expressions

Lesson 9: Words

By the end of this lesson, you should know how to:

☐ Talk about parts of the body

☐ Express possession with possessive adjectives like *my* and *your*

Word Builder 1

▶ 9A Word Builder 1 (CD 5, Track 8)

Let's learn a few words pertaining to the head and face.

la cabeza	*head*
la cara	*face*
el pelo	*hair*
la frente	*forehead*
la oreja	*ear*
el ojo	*eye*
la nariz	*nose*
la mejilla	*cheek*
la boca	*mouth*
el labio	*lip*
la lengua	*tongue*
el diente	*tooth*
la muela	*molar*
la garganta	*throat*
la barbilla	*chin*
el cuello	*neck*

✎ Word Practice 1

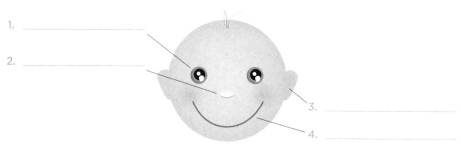

1. _____

2. _____

3. _____

4. _____

Fill in the appropriate Spanish words in the illustration above.

ANSWER KEY
1. el ojo; 2. la nariz; 3. la oreja; 4. la boca

Grammar Builder 1
POSSESSIVE ADJECTIVES (SINGULAR)

▶ 9B Grammar Builder 1 (CD 5, Track 9)

Let's look at some useful little words called possessive adjectives, which correspond to the English *my, your, his, her, our,* and *their.* Because these are adjectives in Spanish, they must agree in gender and number with the nouns they modify. Let's start with the possessive adjectives that correspond to the singular personal pronouns (yo, tú, él, ella, usted).

mi(s)	*my*
tu(s)	*your (infml.)*
su(s)	*his, her, your (fml.)*

The possessive adjectives mi, tu, and su are used with singular possessions (mi libro, tu casa), and mis, tus, and sus are used with plural possessions (mis libros, tus casas). The gender of the possession doesn't make any difference in these cases. Let's see some more examples.

Mi pelo es rojo.
My hair is red.

Mis ojos son grandes.
My eyes are big.

Tu cara es bonita.
Your face is pretty.

Tus dientes son blancos.
Your teeth are white.

Su nariz es larga.
His/Her/Your nose is long.

Sus piernas son gordas.
His/Her/Your legs are fat.

Notice that there is only one form for *his, her,* and *your (fml.)*—su. The context
will tell you what, exactly, su means.

(II)

✎ Work Out 1

Translate the following sentences:

1. *I like your eyes.* _____

_____

2. *His nose is long.* _____

_____

3. *My family is in Caracas.* _____

_____

4. *Your (infml.) granddaughter is hungry.* _____

_____

5. *Her hair is short.* _____

_____

6. *My apartment is small.* _____

_____

7. *Your grandparents are tired.* _____

_____

8. *My house is your (fml.) house.* _____

_____

ANSWER KEY

1. **Me gustan tus ojos.** 2. **Su nariz es larga.** 3. **Mi familia está en Caracas.** 4. **Tu nieta tiene hambre.** 5. **Su pelo es corto.** 6. **Mi apartamento es pequeño.** 7. **Tus abuelos están cansados.** 8. **Mi casa es su casa.**

Word Builder 2

▶ 9C Word Builder 2 (CD 5, Track 10)

Here are some more words related to the rest of the human body.

el cuerpo	the body
el brazo	arm
la espalda	back
la columna vertebral	backbone, spinal column
el hombro	shoulder
el codo	elbow

la muñeca	wrist
la mano	hand
el dedo	finger, toe
el estómago	stomach
el pecho	chest
la pierna	leg
la rodilla	knee
el pie	foot
el corazón	heart
la cadera	hip

✎ Word Practice 2

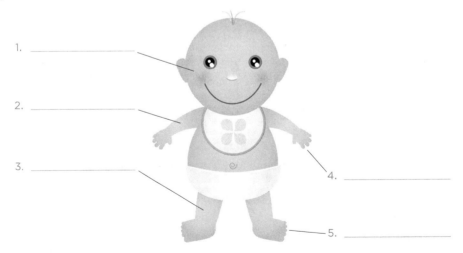

1. _____
2. _____
3. _____
4. _____
5. _____

Fill in the appropriate body parts in the illustration.

ANSWER KEY
1. la cabeza; 2. el brazo; 3. la pierna; 4. la mano; 5. el pie

Grammar Builder 2
POSSESSIVE ADJECTIVES (PLURAL)

▶ 9D Grammar Builder 2 (CD 5, Track 11)

Let's take a look at the possessive adjectives that correspond to the plural subject pronouns (nosotros, vosotros, ellos, ellas, ustedes).

nuestro/a(s)	*our*
vuestro/a(s)	*your (infml.)*
su(s)	*their, your (fml.)*

Notice that the first two plural forms change depending on both the gender and the number of the possession—for example, nuestro libro (*our book*), nuestra casa (*our house*), nuestros libros (*our books*), and nuestras casas (*our houses*). Here are some more examples. Again, don't forget that the vuestro forms are not very common in Latin America, where su(s) is used instead.

Nuestra casa es grande.
Our house is big.

Nuestro apartamento está en Quito.
Our apartment is in Quito.

Vuestros/Sus hijos son altos.
Your children are tall.

Sus hijos son altos.
Their/Your children are tall.

Vuestras/Sus manos son pequeñas.
Your hands are small.

Sus manos son pequeñas.
Their/Your hands are small.

Su familia es boliviana.
Their/Your family is Bolivian.

Sus abuelos son italianos.
Their/Your grandparents are Italian.

✎ Work Out 2

Fill in the blank with the correct form of the possessive adjective. The English possessive is given in parentheses.

1. _____ primos son venezolanos. (*their*)

2. En _____ casa hay catorce habitaciones. (*our*)

3. _____ padres están divorciados. (*your, fml.*)

4. _____ familias son grandes. (*our*)

5. En _____ familia hay muchos niños. (*your, infml.*)

6. _____ apartamento está en Nueva York. (*our*)

7. _____ libros están en la oficina. (*your, fml.*)

8. _____ coche no es muy grande. (*our*)

ANSWER KEY
1. Sus; 2. nuestra; 3. Sus; 4. Nuestras; 5. vuestra; 6. Nuestro; 7. Sus; 8. Nuestro

Take It Further

Although names of body parts are used in much the same manner in Spanish as in English, there is one significant difference—in Spanish, they are frequently preceded by a definite article (el, la, los, or las). In most cases, the possessive adjective is only used when it's not clear from the context to whose body something belongs. Here are a few examples.

Tengo la cara larga y los ojos azules.
I have a long face and blue eyes.

Tiene los dedos largos.
He/She has long fingers./You have long fingers.

Me gustan tus manos.
I like your hands.

✎ Word Recall

Let's practice possession in Spanish. Tell whose item it is by writing the correct possessive adjective in the blank.

1. **Yo tengo un libro. Es** _____ libro.

2. **Yo tengo unos libros. Son** _____ libros.

3. **Tú tienes un libro. Es** _____ libro.

4. **Tú tienes unos libros. Son** _____ libros.

5. **Ella tiene un libro. Es** _____ libro.

6. **Ella tiene unos libros. Son** _____ libros.

ANSWER KEY
1. mi; 2. mis; 3. tu; 4. tus; 5. su; 6. sus

How Did You Do?

By now, you should know how to:

☐ Talk about parts of the body
(Still unsure? Jump back to page 120.)

☐ Express possession with possessive adjectives like *my* and *your*
(Still unsure? Jump back to pages 121 and 125.)

Lesson 10: Phrases

By the end of this lesson, you should be able to:

☐ Talk about your physical state with a doctor

☐ Feel familiar with some idiomatic expressions using body parts

☐ Express possession using **de** + pronoun

☐ Express possession using **de** in other expressions

Phrase Builder 1

▷ 10A Phrase Builder 1 (CD 5, Track 12)

Here are some phrases you can use when visiting the doctor or talking about your physical state. Notice the use of **tener**.

tener dolor de cabeza	*to have a headache*
tener dolor de garganta	*to have a sore throat*
tener fiebre	*to have a fever*

tener tos	to have a cough
tener mal de estómago	to have an upset stomach
tener mareo	to be dizzy
tener la tensión alta (tener la presión alta)	to have high blood pressure
tener la tensión baja (tener la presión baja)	to have low blood pressure
tener náusea	to be nauseated, to have nausea
hacer un examen de sangre	to take a blood test
tomar la tensión (tomar la presión)	to take the blood pressure
tomar un medicamento	to take medication

✎ Phrase Practice 1

Match the Spanish phrase to its appropriate English translation.

1. tener fiebre

2. tener mareo

3. tener náusea

4. tener tos

5. tener mal de estómago

6. tener dolor de garganta

7. tener dolor de cabeza

a. to have a cough

b. to have a headache

c. to have an upset stomach

d. to be nauseated, to have nausea

e. to have a sore throat

f. to be dizzy

g. to have a fever

ANSWER KEY
1. g; 2. f; 3. d; 4. a; 5. c; 6. e; 7. b

Grammar Builder 1
POSSESSION WITH DE + PRONOUN

▶ 10B Grammar Builder 1 (CD 5, Track 13)

A definite article and the preposition de (*of*) can be used with a subject pronoun in place of the more ambiguous su(s).

su pierna	his/her/their/your leg
la pierna de él	his leg
la pierna de ella	her leg
la pierna de ellos	their leg
la pierna de ellas	their leg
la pierna de usted	your leg
la pierna de ustedes	your leg

su cuerpo	his/her/their/your body
el cuerpo de él	his body
el cuerpo de ella	her body
el cuerpo de ellos	their body
el cuerpo de ellas	their body
el cuerpo de usted	your body
el cuerpo de ustedes	your body

In the plural form, simply use the plural feminine or masculine article, depending on the gender of the noun.

las piernas de él	his legs
los cuerpos de ustedes	your bodies

⏸

✎ Work Out 1

Can you say each of the sentences below in another way? Follow the example:

Ex. Son los padres de mis padres.
Son mis abuelos.

1. Es el hijo de mi hermano. _____

2. Son los hermanos de mi esposo. _____

3. Es la esposa de tu padre. _____

4. Son las hijas de nuestra hija. _____

5. Son los padres de Juan. _____

6. Son los hijos de nuestra tía. _____

ANSWER KEY
1. Es mi sobrino. 2. Son mis cuñados. 3. Es tu madre. 4. Son nuestras nietas. 5. Son sus padres. 6. Son nuestros primos.

Phrase Builder 2

▶ 10C Phrase Builder 2 (CD 5, Track 14)

Just as in English, Spanish has a few idioms using words for parts of the body.

estar en buenas manos	to be in good hands
pararse de cabeza	to go crazy, to go out of one's mind
dar la cara	to face the circumstances
tener cara dura	to be shameless
tener los pies en la tierra	to have both feet on the ground
perder la cabeza	to lose one's head
tener la cabeza fría	to keep a cool head
ojo por ojo	an eye for an eye

Ⓜ

✎ Phrase Practice 2

Fill in the missing verb in each phrase.

1. _____ en buenas manos *to be in good hands*

2. _____ de cabeza *to go crazy, to go out of one's mind*

3. _____ la cara *to face the circumstances*

4. _____ la cabeza *to lose one's head*

5. _____ la cabeza fría *to keep a cool head*

ANSWER KEY
1. estar 2. pararse 3. dar 4. perder 5. tener

Grammar Builder 2
MORE POSSESSION WITH DE

▶ 10D Grammar Builder 2 (CD 5, Track 15)

The preposition **de** comes in very handy when talking about possession. While English uses apostrophe *-s*, Spanish uses a phrase with **de**. This is similar to another way of showing possession in English with *of*. Let's take a look at some examples.

el corazón de la señora Suárez
Mrs. Suárez's heart

los primos de María
María's cousins

el restaurante de Jorge
Jorge's restaurant

las ventanas de la casa
the windows of the house

la puerta de la oficina
the door of the office

Remember that when de is followed by the masculine article (el), it becomes del.

la casa del padre de Juan.
Juan's father's house

la cola del caballo
the horse's tail

Please be careful! When using de + the masculine pronoun él, there is no contraction.

La casa de él es grande.
His house is big.

Here's how you can ask questions about possession. Notice that ¿de quién? means *whose*.

¿De quién es la casa?
Whose house is it?

¿De quién es el restaurante?
Whose restaurant is it?

¿De quién son los primos?
Whose cousins are they?

(II)

✎ Work Out 2

Translate the following sentences:

1. *His parents are divorced.* _____

2. *Whose heart is it?* _____

3. *Roberto's mother has high blood pressure.* _____

4. *It's María's sister's uncle.* _____

5. *Their sister's husband has a headache.* _____

ANSWER KEY

1. Sus padres están divorciados. 2. ¿De quién es el corazón? 3. La madre de Roberto tiene la presión alta. 4. Es el tío de la hermana de María. 5. El esposo de su hermana tiene dolor de cabeza.

Take It Further

Here are some useful phrases you can use to describe yourself and others.

tener la cara larga	*to have a long face*
tener la cara redonda	*to have a round face*
ser rubio/a	*to be blond*
ser moreno/a	*to be dark skinned*
ser blanco/a	*to be white*

tener los ojos negros/azules/ marrones/verdes	to have black/blue/brown/green eyes
tener el cabello largo/corto	to have long/short hair
ser calvo/a	to be bald
ser alto/a	to be tall
ser bajo/a	to be short

Let's take a look at some examples.

Soy bajo y rubio. Tengo los ojos verdes.
I'm short and blond. I have green eyes.

Soy morena de ojos azules.
I'm dark skinned with blue eyes.

Ella tiene el cabello largo y es alta.
She has long hair and is tall.

✎ Word Recall

Let's practice possession using the preposition de.

1. *my mother's book* _____

2. *my sister's book* _____

3. *the boy's book* _____

4. *Juan's book* _____

5. *his book* _____

6. *the man's book* _____

7. *Lina's book* _____

8. *their book* _____

ANSWER KEY
1. el libro de mi madre; 2. el libro de mi hermana; 3. el libro del niño/chico; 4. el libro de Juan; 5. el libro de él; 6. el libro del hombre; 7. el libro de Lina; 8. el libro de ellos/ellas

How Did You Do?

By now, you should be able to:

☐ Talk about your physical state with a doctor
(Still unsure? Jump back to page 128.)

☐ Feel familiar with some idiomatic expressions using body parts
(Still unsure? Jump back to page 131.)

☐ Express possession using de + pronoun
(Still unsure? Jump back to page 130.)

☐ Express possession using de in other expressions
(Still unsure? Jump back to page 132.)

Lesson 11: Sentences

By the end of this lesson, you should be able to:

☐ Talk to a doctor about specific problems

☐ Use possessive pronouns to express *mine* and *yours*

☐ Use verbs like *to walk, to taste, to speak*

Sentence Builder 1

▶ 11A Sentence Builder 1 (CD 5, Track 16)

Here are sentences that may come in handy at a doctor's office.

¿Cuál es el problema?	What's the problem?
Tengo dolor de garganta y tos.	I have a sore throat and a cough.
Me siento mareado.	I feel dizzy.
Tengo náusea y diarrea.	I have nausea and diarrhea.
¿Toma algún medicamento en este momento?	Are you taking any medication right now?
¿Sufre de alguna enfermedad?	Do you suffer from any illnesses?
¿Fuma usted?	Do you smoke?
¿Tiene la presión alta?	Do you have high blood pressure?
¿Lo han operado de algo?	Have you had any operations?
¿En dónde tiene dolor?	Where do you have pain?
¿Tiene problemas del corazón?	Do you have heart problems?
¿Tiene alergias?	Do you have any allergies?
Soy alérgico a la penicilina.	I'm allergic to penicillin.
¿Tiene hijos?	Do you have children?
¿Hace deporte con frecuencia?	Do you play sports regularly?

⏸

✎ Sentence Practice 1

Fill in the missing word in the following sentences.

1. ¿Sufre de _____? Do you suffer from any illnesses?

2. ¿_____ usted? Do you smoke?

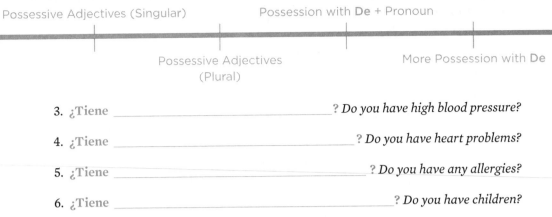

3. ¿Tiene _____? *Do you have high blood pressure?*

4. ¿Tiene _____? *Do you have heart problems?*

5. ¿Tiene _____? *Do you have any allergies?*

6. ¿Tiene _____? *Do you have children?*

ANSWER KEY
1. alguna enfermedad; 2. Fuma; 3. la presión alta; 4. problemas del corazón; 5. alergias; 6. hijos

Grammar Builder 1
POSSESSIVE PRONOUNS

▶ 11B Grammar Builder 1 (CD 5, Track 17)

Another way to talk about the things we own is by using possessive pronouns, which are equivalent to the English *mine, yours, his, hers, ours,* and *theirs.* They usually take the place of a noun and are normally used with a definite article.

el mío/la mía, los míos/las mías	*mine*
el tuyo/la tuya, los tuyos/las tuyas	*yours (infml.)*
el suyo/la suya, los suyos/las suyas	*his, hers, yours (fml.)*
el nuestro/la nuestra, los nuestros/las nuestras	*ours*
el vuestro/la vuestra, los vuestro/las vuestras	*yours (infml.)*
el suyo/la suya, los suyos/las suyas	*theirs, yours (fml.)*

Notice that all of the possessive pronouns agree in both gender and number with the nouns they stand in for. Let's look at some examples to see how this works.

Mi cara es redonda y la tuya es larga.
My face is round and yours is long.

Tu cabello es rubio y el nuestro es negro.
Your hair is blond and ours is black.

Vuestros hijos están en Brasil y los suyos en Costa Rica.
Your children are in Brazil and hers/his/theirs/yours (are) in Costa Rica.

In the first example, la tuya is standing in for la cara. In the second, el nuestro is standing in for el cabello. In the third, los suyos is standing in for los hijos.

As we saw in Lesson 10, the use of the possessive adjective su can be clarified by using the preposition de and the corresponding pronoun. The same thing can be done with possessive pronouns, but in this case, only a definite article is used before the de phrase. Let's first take a look at the feminine.

Mi casa es grande y la suya es pequeña.
My house is big and his/hers/theirs/yours is small.

Mi casa es grande y la de él es pequeña.
My house is big and his is small.

Mi casa es grande y la de ella es pequeña.
My house is big and hers is small.

Mi casa es grande y la de ellos es pequeña.
My house is big and theirs is small.

Mi casa es grande y la de ellas es pequeña.
My house is big and theirs is small.

Mi casa es grande y la de usted es pequeña.
My house is big and yours is small.

Mi casa es grande y la de ustedes es pequeña.
My house is big and yours is small.

Now, let's take a look at the masculine.

Mi cabello es largo y el suyo es corto.
My hair is long and his/hers/theirs/yours is short.

Mi cabello es largo y el de él es corto.
My hair is long and his is short.

Mi cabello es largo y el de ella es corto.
My hair is long and hers is short.

Mi cabello es largo y el de ellos es corto.
My hair is long and theirs is short.

Mi cabello es largo y el de ellas es corto.
My hair is long and theirs is short.

Mi cabello es largo y el de usted es corto.
My hair is long and yours is short.

Mi cabello es largo y el de ustedes es corto.
My hair is long and yours is short.

Let's take a few examples with the plural feminine and masculine.

Nuestras manos son pequeñas y las de él son grandes.
Our hands are small and his are big.

Tus padres están en Londres y los de ellos en Guadalajara.
Your parents are in London and theirs are in Guadalajara.

When the possessive pronoun comes after the verb ser, the article is left out.

La casa grande es mía.
The big house is mine.

La habitación treinta y dos es tuya/suya.
Room 32 is yours.

Ⓘ

✎ Work Out 1

Join the two sentences by using a possessive pronoun. Follow the example:

Ex. El padre de Juan está en La Paz. El padre de Margarita está en Francia.
El padre de Juan está en La Paz y el suyo está en Francia.

1. Nuestra profesora es alta. La profesora tuya y la de Luis es baja. _____

   _____

2. Las manos de Ángela son bonitas. Mis manos son feas. _____

   _____

3. La madre de Pedro tiene sesenta y siete años. La madre de Enrique y Sara

   tiene ochenta y ocho. _____

   _____

4. Mi hermano es abogado. Tu hermano es astronauta. _____

   _____

5. La habitación de María es grande. La habitación de Claudia es pequeña. _____

   _____

ANSWER KEY

1. Nuestra profesora es alta y la vuestra es baja. 2. Las manos de Ángela son bonitas y las mías son feas. 3. La madre de Pedro tiene sesenta y siete años y la suya tiene ochenta y ocho. 4. Mi hermano es abogado y el tuyo es astronauta. 5. La habitación de María es grande y la suya es pequeña.

Sentence Builder 2

▶ 11C Sentence Builder 2 (CD 5, Track 18)

Tengo un cosquilleo muy desagradable.	*I have a very unpleasant tingling feeling.*
¿Se le hinchan los pies y las manos?	*Do your feet and hands swell?*
Sí, con mucha frecuencia.	*Yes, very frequently.*
¿Y, qué quiere decir eso?	*So, what does that mean?*
¿Es grave?	*Is it serious?*
¿Cuál es el tratamiento a seguir?	*What is the treatment to be followed?*
Tiene un brote en todo el cuerpo.	*She has a rash all over her body.*
¿Es él su pediatra de cabecera?	*Is he your regular pediatrician?*
Él tiene paciencia con los niños.	*He is patient with children.*
Le gusta mucho la homeopatía.	*He likes homeopathy very much.*

⏸

✎ Sentence Practice 2

Translate the following sentences.

1. *I have a very unpleasant tingling feeling.* _____

_____

2. *Do your feet and hands swell?* _____

_____

3. *So, what does that mean?* _____

_____

4. *Is it serious?* _____

_____

5. *She has a rash all over her body.* _____

_____

ANSWER KEY

1. Tengo un cosquilleo muy desagradable. 2. ¿Se le hinchan los pies y las manos? 3. ¿Y, qué quiere decir eso? 4. ¿Es grave? 5. Tiene un brote en todo el cuerpo.

Grammar Builder 2
CONJUGATION OF -AR VERBS

▶ 11D Grammar Builder 2 (CD 5, Track 19)

Now let's look at how to conjugate verbs in Spanish. A conjugation is the pattern of endings (or other changes) that a verb undergoes to agree with a subject, as in the English *I sing, you sing, she sings,* etc. In Spanish, there are slightly different conjugations for different types of verbs. Verbs are grouped according to three different infinitive endings: -ar verbs, -er verbs, and -ir verbs. Examples from each group are hablar (*to speak*), comer (*to eat*), and vivir (*to live*). There are both regular and irregular verbs—that is, those that follow a regular pattern of conjugation and those that don't. But don't panic. Most verbs are regular!

Let's start with a list of some common -ar verbs.

caminar	to walk
hablar	to talk, to speak
tocar	to touch, to play an instrument
escuchar	to listen to

| saborear | to taste |
| estudiar | to study |

To conjugate any verb, take off the infinitive ending, which, in this case, is -ar. Then you're left with the verb stem, and you add certain endings to that stem depending on the subject. For regular -ar verbs, you will add the following endings:

yo	-o	nosotros	-amos
tú	-as	vosotros	-áis
él/ella/usted	-a	ellos/ellas/ustedes	-an

Let's look at the conjugation of a regular -ar verb, caminar:

CAMINAR *(TO WALK)*			
yo camino	*I walk*	nosotros caminamos	*we walk*
tú caminas	*you walk (infml.)*	vosotros camináis	*you walk (pl. fml.)*
él/ella/usted camina	*he/she walks, you walk (fml.)*	ellos/ellas/ustedes caminan	*they walk, you walk (pl. fml.)*

All of the -ar verbs from the list above are conjugated in exactly this way. Here are some examples.

Los fines de semana nosotros caminamos en el parque.
We walk in the park on weekends.

Yolanda toca la guitarra muy bien.
Yolanda plays the guitar very well.

Ellos hablan cuatro idiomas.
They speak four languages.

Yo escucho música todas las noches.
I listen to music every night.

Notice that in English, you *listen to* something, but in Spanish, you don't need a preposition; escuchar is perfectly fine on its own. You'll see this sort of difference a lot when you compare two languages. Sometimes one language will use a preposition where the other won't, and sometimes the situation is reversed. As a general tip, be wary of translating prepositions literally; in fact, it's better not even to assume that you need one in another language just because your native language uses one. Prepositions are often used in very different ways from one language to another!

Ⅱ

✎ Work Out 2

Fill in the blank with the appropriate form of the verb in parentheses.

1. Nosotros _____ por la mañana. (caminar)

2. Ustedes _____ el piano. (tocar)

3. Yo _____ música clásica los fines de semana. (escuchar)

4. Tú _____ el vino. (saborear)

5. Ellos _____ español. (hablar)

6. Él _____ por la mañana. (caminar)

7. Vosotras _____ por teléfono. (hablar)

8. Yo _____ la radio. (escuchar)

ANSWER KEY
1. caminamos; 2. tocan; 3. escucho; 4. saboreas; 5. hablan; 6. camina; 7. habláis; 8. escucho

Take It Further

Don't forget that Spanish speakers tend to drop the subject pronouns because the verb endings indicate who the subject is. This is true for yo, tú, nosotros/as, and vosotros/as. In the case of él, ella, usted, ellos, ellas, and ustedes, it is not always clear who the subject is. Therefore, the pronoun may be used.

Hablas por teléfono.
You talk on the phone. (infml.)

Habla por teléfono.
He/She talks on the phone./You talk on the phone.

Él habla por teléfono.
He talks on the phone.

✎ Word Recall

Rewrite the sentence in each line using the subject in parentheses. Make sure that you write the correct form of the -ar verb.

1. **Yo camino mucho. (Tú)** _____

_____

2. **Yo camino mucho. (Nosotros)** _____

_____

3. **Yo camino mucho. (Usted)** _____

_____

4. Yo camino mucho. (Él) _____

_____

5. Roberto y Luisa hablan por teléfono. (Yo) _____

_____

6. Roberto y Luisa hablan por teléfono. (Roberto) _____

_____

7. Roberto y Luisa hablan por teléfono. (Tú) _____

_____

8. Roberto y Luisa hablan por teléfono. (Ustedes) _____

_____

ANSWER KEY
1. Tú caminas mucho. 2. Nosotros caminamos mucho. 3. Usted camina mucho. 4. Él camina mucho.
5. Yo hablo por teléfono. 6. Roberto habla por teléfono. 7. Tú hablas por teléfono. 8. Ustedes hablan
por teléfono.

How Did You Do?

By now, you should be able to:

☐ Talk to a doctor about specific problems
(Still unsure? Jump back to page 137.)

☐ Use possessive pronouns to express *mine* and *yours*
(Still unsure? Jump back to page 138.)

☐ Use verbs like *to walk*, *to taste*, *to speak*
(Still unsure? Jump back to page 143.)

Lesson 12: Conversations

By the end of this lesson, you should know how to:

☐ Use verbs like *to run, to eat, to see*

☐ Use verbs like *to write, to live, to leave*

☐ Talk about the present tense using time expressions

Conversation 1

▶ 12A Conversation 1 (CD 5, Track 20 - Spanish Only; Track 21 - Spanish and English)

Listen in while Gloria visits the doctor.

Médico:	Buenos días, Doña Solís, ¿cuál es el problema?
Gloria:	Tengo mucho dolor en las muñecas, sobre todo la derecha.
Médico:	¿Tiene dolor en el cuello o la espalda?
Gloria:	No, para nada. Pero por las noches tengo un cosquilleo muy desagradable en los dedos de mi mano derecha.
Médico:	¿Toma algún medicamento en este momento?
Gloria:	Sí, estoy tomando una pastilla para bajar la tensión.
Médico:	¿Se le hinchan los pies o las manos, sobre todo por las tardes?
Gloria:	Sí, con mucha frecuencia.
Médico:	Bueno, son los clásicos síntomas del síndrome del túnel del carpio.
Gloria:	¿Y, qué quiere decir eso? ¿Es grave?
Médico:	No, simplemente tiene bloqueados los nervios del carpio, que son los que conectan la muñeca con el resto de la mano.
Gloria:	¿Y cuál es el tratamiento a seguir?
Médico:	La acupuntura ayuda mucho. Así que vamos a comenzar con una sesión dos veces por semana por un mes.

Doctor:	Good morning, Mrs. Solís. What seems to be the problem?
Gloria:	I have a lot of pain in my wrists, especially the right one.
Doctor:	Do you have pain in your neck or your back?
Gloria:	No, not at all. But at nighttime I have a very unpleasant tingling sensation in the fingers of my right hand.
Doctor:	Are you taking any medication right now?
Gloria:	Yes, I'm taking a pill to lower my blood pressure.
Doctor:	Do your feet and hands swell, especially in the afternoons?
Gloria:	Yes, very frequently.
Doctor:	Well, those are the typical symptoms of carpal tunnel syndrome.
Gloria:	What does that mean? Is it serious?
Doctor:	No, it only means that the carpal nerves, which connect your wrist to the hand, are blocked.
Gloria:	What treatment is there?
Doctor:	Acupuncture helps a lot. So we're going to begin with one session twice a week for a month.

Take It Further

Two polite titles that you may hear are don and doña, although they're dying out. They are usually used before the first name of a person who deserves respect on the basis of his or her age or status in society. They are usually accompanied by the given name of the person being addressed. You will very often see them used to address the Spanish king and queen: Don Juan Carlos y Doña Sofía. In Latin America, they are commonly used by workers to address their employers, especially in rural areas.

Notice that the doctor asked: ¿Toma algún medicamento en este momento? The English translation is: *Are you taking any medication right now?* In Spanish, the present tense (toma, for example) can be translated into English as the simple present (*you take*), the present continuous or progressive (*you are taking*), or even the present emphatic (*you do take*). It all depends on the context.

✎ Conversation Practice 1

Fill in the blanks below with the appropriate word based on the English
translations and the dialogue above.

1. ¿Tiene dolor en el _____ o la _____? *Do you have pain in your neck or your back?*

2. Pero por las noches tengo un cosquilleo muy _____

   en los dedos de mi mano derecha. *But at nighttime I have a very unpleasant*

   tingling sensation in the fingers of my right hand.

3. ¿Y, qué _____ decir eso? ¿Es grave? *What does that mean? Is it serious?*

4. Sí, estoy tomando _____ para bajar la tensión. *Yes, I'm*

   taking a pill to lower my blood pressure.

5. No, simplemente tiene bloqueados los nervios del carpio, que son los que

   conectan la _____ con el resto de la _____. *No, it only*

   means that the carpal nerves, which connect your wrist to the hand, are blocked.

   ANSWER KEY
   1. cuello, espalda; 2. desagradable; 3. quiere; 4. una pastilla; 5. muñeca, mano

Grammar Builder 1
CONJUGATION OF -ER VERBS AND VER (*TO SEE*)

▶ 12B Grammar Builder 1 (CD 5, Track 22)

Verbs with an -er infinitive ending are also very easy to conjugate. Here are some examples.

correr	to run
beber	to drink
comer	to eat
ver	to see
leer	to read

Let's take a closer look at the verb correr. First, remove the -er ending to get the stem, corr-. Then add the appropriate ending for each subject.

CORRER *(TO RUN)*			
yo corro	I run	nosotros corremos	we run
tú corres	you run (infml.)	vosotros corréis	you run (pl. fml.)
él/ella/usted corre	he/she runs, you run (fml.)	ellos/ellas/ ustedes corren	they run, you run (pl. fml.)

Here are those -er endings once again.

yo	-o	nosotros	-emos
tú	-es	vosotros	-éis
él/ella/usted	-e	ellos/ellas/ustedes	-en

If you take a closer look at the conjugation of -ar and -er verbs, you can see that they are almost identical except for one letter. Here are some more examples of -er verbs.

Ella bebe dos litros de agua a diario.
She drinks two litres of water a day.

Los niños comen dulces.
The children eat sweets.

Now, you may be a little bit puzzled when asked to conjugate the verb ver. Naturally so, because when you take the ending off, you're left with only one letter! Yes, that's actually the stem, and it's conjugated just like correr.

VER *(TO SEE)*			
yo veo	*I see*	nosotros vemos	*we see*
tú ves	*you see (infml.)*	vosotros veis	*you see (pl. fml.)*
él/ella/usted ve	*he/she sees, you see (fml.)*	ellos/ellas/ ustedes ven	*they see, you see (pl. fml.)*

Vemos a nuestros amigos con frecuencia.
We see our friends often.

Sabina y Ana ven muchas películas.
Sabina and Ana see a lot of movies.

Take a look at that first example again. Vemos a nuestros amigos ... Did you notice that little a in between the verb vemos and the phrase nuestros amigos? This is called the a *personal*, and it's used when a direct object is a person. We'll come back to that later on in the course.

⏸

✎ Work Out 1

Choose the verb that best completes the sentence.

1. **Nosotras (beben, bebemos, bebéis) mucha agua.** _____

2. **Ella (lees, leen, lee) un libro.** _____

3. **Tú (corro, corre, corres) por las tardes.** _____

4. **Vosotros (vemos, veis, ven) televisión.** _____

5. Yo no (comes, coméis, como) carne. _____

6. Ustedes (bebéis, beben, bebés) vino tinto. _____

7. Yo (ve, ves, veo) a mi amigo. _____

8. ¿Qué (leo, lee, lees), Ana? _____

ANSWER KEY

1. bebemos; 2. lee; 3. corres; 4. veis; 5. como; 6. beben; 7. veo; 8. lees

Conversation 2

▶ 12C Conversation 2 (CD 5, Track 23 - Spanish Only; Track 24 - Spanish and English)

Isabel is at the pediatrician's office with her little daughter. She's talking to another mother in the waiting room.

Margarita:	Mi hija tiene tres años, ¿y la suya?
Isabel:	Tiene veintidós meses. Se llama Catherina, ¿y la suya?
Margarita:	Sofía. ¿Qué le pasa a Catherina?
Isabel:	Tiene una fiebre muy alta y un brote en todo el cuerpo. No tiene apetito y llora mucho.
Margarita:	Mi hija también tiene una fiebre muy alta.
Isabel:	¿Es este su pediatra de cabecera?
Margarita:	Sí, es muy bueno. Estoy muy contenta. Sobre todo porque le gusta mucho la homeopatía.
Isabel:	Qué bien. No me gusta darle medicinas a Catherina cuando no es absolutamente necesario.
Margarita:	Si, además es un médico que escucha a los padres y tiene mucha paciencia con los niños.
Isabel:	Bueno, ya estoy más tranquila.
Margarita:	No se preocupe. Catherina está en buenas manos.

Margarita:	*My daughter is three years old, and yours?*
Isabel:	*She's twenty-two months. Her name is Catherina. And yours?*

Margarita:	Sofía. What's wrong with Catherina?
Isabel:	She has a very high fever and a rash all over her body. She has no appetite and cries a lot.
Margarita:	My daughter has a high fever, too.
Isabel:	Is this your regular pediatrician?
Margarita:	Yes, he's very good. I am very happy. Especially because he likes homeopathy very much.
Isabel:	That's good. I don't like to give Catherina medicine when it isn't absolutely necessary.
Margarita:	Yes, plus he's a doctor who listens to parents and has a lot of patience with the children.
Isabel:	Well, now I feel better.
Margarita:	Don't worry. Catherina is in good hands.

Take It Further

Homeopathic medicine and other more natural approaches to treating illnesses are becoming the trend in Spanish-speaking countries. In most of Latin America, you'll find that people consider themselves much more in tune with nature and their bodies and prefer natural remedies and herbal teas to conventional Western medicine, which is considered by some to be very aggressive and hard on the body.

Some common herbs are **palo de aceite** (*oily stick*), which is used to treat intestinal problems, rheumatism, colic, and asthma; **cola de caballo** (*horse's tail*), which is used to treat wounds and infections of the gums; **uña de gato** (*cat's claw*), which is used to treat stomach and lung tumors; and **guayaba** (*guava*), which is a fruit whose parts are used to make an infusion to treat diarrhea.

You've probably also heard that in several South American countries, a tea made out of **mate de coca** (*coca leaf*) is a popular beverage. In fact, people living at very high altitudes either drink this tea or chew coca leaves to help fight altitude dizziness and sickness. The effects of this tea are similar to those of coffee. The tea is not considered a drug, and it is also used for medicinal and religious purposes.

✎ Conversation Practice 2

Unscramble the sentences from the dialogue above. The English sentence is unscrambled.

1. ¿/Catherina/pasa/le/a/qué/? *What's wrong with Catherina?* _____

   _____

2. tiene/alta/también/mi/muy/una/hija/fiebre/. *My daughter has a high fever, too.*

   _____

3. gusta/le/sobre todo/homeopatía/mucho/la/porque/. *Especially because he likes*

   homeopathy very much. _____

   _____

4. ya/bueno/más/estoy/tranquila/. *Well, now I feel better.* _____

   _____

5. se/no/preocupe/. *Don't worry.* _____

   _____

ANSWER KEY

1. ¿Qué le pasa a Catherina? 2. Mi hija también tiene una fiebre muy alta. 3. Sobre todo porque le gusta mucho la homeopatía. 4. Bueno, ya estoy más tranquila. 5. No se preocupe.

Grammar Builder 2
CONJUGATION OF -IR VERBS

▶ 12D Grammar Builder 2 (CD 5, Track 25)

The third group of verbs end in -ir in the infinitive.

percibir	to perceive
escribir	to write
vivir	to live
partir	to leave

Here's the -ir conjugation.

ESCRIBIR *(TO WRITE)*			
yo escribo	*I write*	nosotros escribimos	*we write*
tú escribes	*you write (infml.)*	vosotros escribís	*you write (pl. fml.)*
él/ella/usted escribe	*he/she writes, you write (fml.)*	ellos/ellas/ ustedes escriben	*they write, you write (pl. fml.)*

Let's look at the -ir endings one more time.

yo	-o	nosotros	-imos
tú	-es	vosotros	-ís
él/ella/usted	-e	ellos/ellas/ustedes	-en

If you take a closer look, you'll notice that the only difference between -er and -ir verbs is the ending used for nosotros and vosotros. Here are some example sentences with -ir verbs.

Nosotros escribimos muchas cartas.
We write a lot of letters.

Ellos viven en una ciudad grande, pero tú vives en una aldea pequeña.
They live in a big city, but you live in a little village.

Now you've learned how to conjugate all three types of Spanish verbs in the present tense. Don't forget that the Spanish present tense can be translated into English as the simple present (*she goes*), the present progressive or continuous (*she is going*), or the present emphatic (*she does go*). It can also be used to talk about something that will happen in the near future, as in the English *It's 3:00 now, and the train arrives in an hour.*

Here are some useful expressions of time that you can use with the simple present tense.

ahora	*now*
ahora mismo	*right now*
mañana	*tomorrow*
esta noche	*tonight*
siempre	*always*
con frecuencia	*frequently*
a veces	*sometimes*
casi nunca	*seldom, almost never*
nunca	*never*
todos los días	*every day*
todas las semanas	*every week*
una vez por semana	*once a week*
dos veces por semana	*twice a week*

✎ Work Out 2

Translate the following sentences into Spanish.

1. *Right now she has a headache.* _____

   _____

2. *My parents leave tomorrow in the afternoon.* _____

   _____

3. *We live in a small apartment.* _____

   _____

4. *I always drink coffee in the morning.* _____

   _____

5. *She writes emails every day.* _____

   _____

6. *Sometimes we listen to jazz.* _____

   _____

7. *They never eat at night.* _____

   _____

8. *My wife leaves this evening.* _____

   _____

ANSWER KEY

1. Ahora mismo ella tiene dolor de cabeza. 2. Mis padres parten mañana por la tarde. 3. Nosotros vivimos en un apartamento pequeño. 4. Yo siempre bebo café por la mañana. 5. Ella escribe emails todos los días. 6. A veces nosotros escuchamos jazz. 7. Ellos nunca comen por la noche. 8. Mi esposa parte esta noche.

💡 Tip!

Now that you've learned verbs in Spanish, you'll want to find plenty of creative ways to practice using them. The more you use them, the more automatic the verb conjugations will become for you. A simple way to lodge verb conjugations in your mind is repetition—listening to the audio, repeating aloud, reading the forms in the book, and writing them out. There's also a lot of information in the grammar summary on verbs, but for now it's probably best to stick with the present tense. To practice the present tense, make it a goal to learn three to five new and useful verbs every day, and write example sentences for them in your language journal. Tailor this exercise to your life and your routine, and look up any new vocabulary you need. Another activity that will help is to find a photo of people—in a magazine, in an old photo album, online— and write a few sentences describing what they're doing. Stick to regular verbs at first, because we'll cover the irregular ones in small groups as we move along.

✎ Word Recall

Rewrite each sentence given using the subject in parentheses. Make sure that you write the correct form of the -er or -ir verb.

1. Yo corro cinco kilómetros. (Ella) _____

   _____

2. Yo corro cinco kilómetros. (Nosotros) _____

   _____

3. Yo corro cinco kilómetros. (Vosotros) _____

   _____

4. Yo corro cinco kilómetros. (Ellos) _____

   _____

5. **Patricia vive en Sevilla ahora. (Tú)** _____

_____

6. **Patricia vive en Sevilla ahora. (Enrique y Catalina)** _____

_____

7. **Patricia vive en Sevilla ahora. (Yo)** _____

_____

8. **Patricia vive en Sevilla ahora. (Usted)** _____

_____

ANSWER KEY
1. Ella corre cinco kilómetros. 2. Nosotros corremos cinco kilómetros. 3. Vosotros corréis cinco kilómetros. 4. Ellos corren cinco kilómetros. 5. Tú vives en Sevilla ahora. 6. Enrique y Catalina viven en Sevilla ahora. 7. Yo vivo en Sevilla ahora. 8. Usted vive en Sevilla ahora.

How Did You Do?

By now, you should know how to:

☐ Use verbs like *to run, to eat, to see*
(Still unsure? Jump back to page 150.)

☐ Use verbs like *to write, to live, to leave*
(Still unsure? Jump back to page 156.)

☐ Talk about the present tense using time expressions
(Still unsure? Jump back to page 157.)

Don't forget to practice and reinforce what you've learned by visiting **www.livinglanguage.com/languagelab** for flashcards, games, and quizzes for Unit 3!

Unit 3 Essentials

Vocabulary Essentials

PARTS OF THE BODY (HEAD AND NECK)

	head
	face
	hair
	forehead
	ear
	eye
	nose
	cheek
	mouth
	lip
	tongue
	tooth
	molar
	throat
	chin
	neck

[Pg. 120]

PARTS OF THE BODY (BELOW THE NECK)

	the body
	arm
	back
	backbone, spinal column
	shoulder
	elbow
	wrist
	hand
	finger, toe
	stomach
	chest
	leg
	knee
	foot
	heart
	hip

[Pg. 123]

HEALTH EXPRESSIONS

	to have a headache
	to have a sore throat
	to have a fever
	to have a cough
	to have an upset stomach
	to be dizzy

	to have high blood pressure
	to have low blood pressure
	to be nauseated, to have nausea
	to take a blood test
	to take the blood pressure
	to take medication

[Pg. 128]

MORE HEALTH EXPRESSIONS

	What's the problem?
	I have a sore throat and a cough.
	I feel dizzy.
	I have nausea and diarrhea.
	Do you have high blood pressure?
	Have you had any operations?
	Where do you have pain?
	Do you have heart problems?
	Do you have any allergies?
	I'm allergic to penicillin.

[Pg. 137]

DESCRIBING PEOPLE

	to have a long face
	to have a round face
	to be blond
	to be dark skinned

	to be white
	to have black/blue/brown/green eyes
	to have long/short hair
	to be bald
	to be tall
	to be short

[Pg. 134]

-AR VERBS

	to walk
	to talk, to speak
	to touch, to play an instrument
	to listen to
	to taste
	to study

[Pg. 143]

-ER VERBS

	to run
	to drink
	to eat
	to see
	to read

[Pg. 151]

-IR VERBS

	to perceive
	to write
	to live
	to leave

[Pg. 156]

EXPRESSIONS OF FREQUENCY

	now
	right now
	tomorrow
	tonight
	always
	frequently
	sometimes
	seldom, almost never
	never
	every day
	every week
	once a week
	twice a week

[Pg. 157]

Grammar Essentials

POSSESSIVE ADJECTIVES

mi(s)	my
tu(s)	your (infml.)
su(s)	his, her, your (fml.)
nuestro/a(s)	our
vuestro/a(s)	your (infml.)
su(s)	their, your (fml.)

POSSESSION WITH DE + PRONOUN

su + noun; or, noun + de él	his (noun)
su + noun; or, noun + de ella	her (noun)
su + noun; or, noun + de ellos/ellas	their (noun)
su + noun; or, noun + de usted/ustedes	your (noun)

POSSESSIVE PRONOUNS

el mío/la mía, los míos/las mías	mine
el tuyo/la tuya, los tuyos/las tuyas	yours (infml.)
el suyo/la suya, los suyos/las suyas	his, hers, yours (fml.)
el nuestro/la nuestra, los nuestros/las nuestras	ours
el vuestro/la vuestra, los vuestros/las vuestras	yours (infml.)
el suyo/la suya, los suyos/las suyas	theirs, yours (fml.)

-AR **VERB ENDINGS**

yo	-o	nosotros	-amos
tú	-as	vosotros	-áis
él/ella/usted	-a	ellos/ellas/ ustedes	-an

CAMINAR *(TO WALK)*			
yo camino	*I walk*	nosotros caminamos	*we walk*
tú caminas	*you walk (infml.)*	vosotros camináis	*you walk (pl. fml.)*
él/ella/usted camina	*he/she walks, you walk (fml.)*	ellos/ellas/ ustedes caminan	*they walk, you walk (pl. fml.)*

-ER **VERB ENDINGS**

yo	-o	nosotros	-emos
tú	-es	vosotros	-éis
él/ella/usted	-e	ellos/ellas/ ustedes	-en

CORRER *(TO RUN)*			
yo corro	*I run*	nosotros corremos	*we run*
tú corres	*you run (infml.)*	vosotros corréis	*you run (pl. fml.)*
él/ella/usted corre	*he/she runs, you run (fml.)*	ellos/ellas/ ustedes corren	*they run, you run (pl. fml.)*

VER *(TO SEE)*			
yo veo	*I see*	nosotros vemos	*we see*
tú ves	*you see (infml.)*	vosotros veis	*you see (pl. fml.)*
él/ella/usted ve	*he/she sees, you see (fml.)*	ellos/ellas/ustedes ven	*they see, you see (pl. fml.)*

-IR **VERB ENDINGS**

yo	-o	nosotros	-imos
tú	-es	vosotros	-ís
él/ella/usted	-e	ellos/ellas/ustedes	-en

ESCRIBIR *(TO WRITE)*			
yo escribo	*I write*	nosotros escribimos	*we write*
tú escribes	*you write (infml.)*	vosotros escribís	*you write (pl. fml.)*
él/ella/usted escribe	*he/she writes, you write (fml.)*	ellos/ellas/ustedes escriben	*they write, you write (pl. fml.)*

Unit 3 Quiz

A. Let's practice verbs. Write the correct form of the verb in parentheses. But watch out! There are -ar, -er, and -ir verbs combined.

1. Camila _____ en el parque todos los días. (correr)

2. Mis hermanos _____ mucho y son muy atléticos. (caminar)

3. Ustedes _____ en una casa muy bonita. (vivir)

4. En la sala de mi casa, yo _____ mucho. (leer)

5. Mara y Emilio _____ muy bien el español. (escribir)

6. ¿A qué hora _____ tú? (comer)

7. Tú y yo _____ la televisión juntos. (ver)

8. ¿Por qué tú no _____ a tus padres? (escuchar)

B. Give the Spanish name for each part of the human face below. Don't forget to include the definite article.

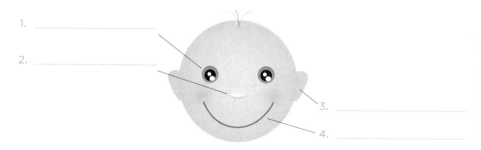

1. _____

2. _____

3. _____

4. _____

C. Select the correct possessive adjective that goes with each body part or object.

1. *our elbows* _____ codos

2. *my shoulder* _____ hombro

3. *our backs* _____ espaldas

4. *his knee* _____ rodilla

5. *their house* _____ casa

6. *your (infml. sing.) leg* _____ pierna

7. *your (fml. sing.) hands* _____ manos

8. *your (fml. pl.) feet* _____ pies

D. Look at the following list of words. One word from each list doesn't quite fit. Which is the odd one out?

1. el diente, el corazón, el estómago, el pecho _____

2. la lengua, la boca, el diente, el cuello _____

3. la mano, la muñeca, la pierna, el dedo _____

4. el pie, la rodilla, la pierna, el codo _____

5. la columna vertebral, la espalda, el cuello, el pie _____

How Did You Do?

Give yourself a point for every correct answer, then use the following key to determine whether or not you're ready to move on:

0–7 points: It's probably best to go back and study the lessons again to make sure you understood everything completely. Take your time; it's not a race! Make sure you spend time reviewing vocabulary with the flashcards and reading through each grammar note carefully.

8–16 points: If the questions you missed were in sections A or B, you may want to review the vocabulary again; if you missed answers mostly in sections C or D, check the unit essentials to make sure you have your conjugations and other grammar basics down.

17–20 points: Feel free to move on to the next unit! You're doing a great job.

 points

Unit 4:

Using the Telephone and Making Appointments

In this unit, you'll learn common vocabulary and phrases used when talking on the phone, including how to make an appointment with someone.

By the end of this unit, you should be able to:

☐ Talk about the telephone and messages

☐ Talk a little bit about computers

☐ Use demonstrative adjectives to express *this book, that teacher*

☐ Use demonstrative pronouns to express *this one, that one*

☐ Talk about leaving a message or sending an e-mail

☐ Make a negative statement

☐ Understand some expressions used on the telephone

☐ Use indefinite pronouns to express *something, anything, either … or*

☐ Ask someone if they'd like to call back or leave a message

☐ Express *to make, to do, to put, to bring,* and *to fall*

☐ Express *to go out* and *to say*

☐ Feel comfortable with the verb *to go*

☐ Distinguish *yes* from *if*

☐ Say what you *want* or *would like*

Lesson 13: Words

By the end of this lesson, you should be able to:

☐ Talk about the telephone and messages

☐ Talk a little bit about computers

☐ Use demonstrative adjectives to express *this book, that teacher*

☐ Use demonstrative pronouns to express *this one, that one*

Word Builder 1

▶ 13A Word Builder 1 (CD 5, Track 26)

el contestador automático	*answering machine*
la llamada	*phone call*
la operadora	*operator*
la guía telefónica	*phone book*
las páginas amarillas	*yellow pages*
la cabina telefónica	*telephone booth*
el mensaje	*message*
el buzón de voz	*voice mail*
la centralita	*switchboard*
eliminar	*to eliminate*
borrar	*to erase*

✎ Word Practice 1

Match the following Spanish words to their English translations.

1. eliminar
2. borrar
3. la operadora
4. el mensaje
5. el buzón de voz
6. la llamada

a. *phone call*
b. *to eliminate*
c. *to erase*
d. *voice mail*
e. *operator*
f. *message*

ANSWER KEY
1. b; 2. c; 3. e; 4. f; 5. d; 6. a

Grammar Builder 1
DEMONSTRATIVE ADJECTIVES

▶ 13B Grammar Builder 1 (CD 5, Track 27)

Demonstratives, or words like *this* and *that*, show or point to places, people, or things. When a demonstrative is used right before a noun, as in *this book*, it's called a demonstrative adjective. In Spanish, demonstrative adjectives must agree in gender and number with the nouns they point to. Also, Spanish distinguishes among three spatial relations, while English recognizes only two. Let's look at each one.

The first set of demonstratives is used to point to things that are relatively close to the speaker. It can be translated as *this* in the singular and *these* in the plural.

este libro	*this book (m. sg.)*
esta casa	*this house (f. sg.)*
estos profesores	*these teachers (m. pl.)*
estas computadoras	*these computers (f. pl.)*

Irregular Verbs **Hacer** (*To Make, To Do*), **Poner**
(*To Put*), **Traer** (*To Bring*), and **Caer** (*To Fall*)

Ir (*To Go*)

Irregular Verbs **Salir** (*To Go
Out*) and **Decir** (*To Say*)

Querer (*To Want, To Love*)

The second set of demonstratives is used to point to things that are farther away
from the speaker but perhaps closer to the listener. The translation is *that* or *those.*

ese niño	that boy (m. sg.)
esa mujer	that woman (f. sg.)
esos cuadernos	those notebooks (m. pl.)
esas llaves	those keys (f. pl.)

Finally, the third set is used to point to things that are relatively far away from
both the speaker and the listener. The most appropriate English translation is *that
(over) there* or *those (over) there.*

aquel edificio	that building there (m. sg.)
aquella oficina	that office over there (f. sg.)
aquellos coches	those cars there (m. pl.)
aquellas calles	those streets over there (f. pl.)

Let's see some more examples in sentences.

Este teléfono no funciona.
This phone doesn't work.

Esa línea está ocupada.
That line is busy.

Aquella cabina telefónica está libre.
That phone booth over there is free.

Ⓘ

✎ Work Out 1

Choose the correct demonstrative adjective to fill in the blank.

1. (Este, Esta, Estos, Estas) _____ llamada es importante.

2. (Aquellos, Aquel, Aquella, Aquellas) _____ oficinas están ocupadas.

3. (Esas, Esa, Ese, Esos) _____ contestador no funciona.

4. (Esas, Esa, Ese, Esos) _____ télefonos son de la oficina de mi tío.

5. (Este, Esta, Estos, Estas) _____ mensajes son para Julián.

6. (Aquellos, Aquel, Aquella, Aquellas) _____ hombre es mi padre.

ANSWER KEY
1. Esta; 2. Aquellas; 3. Ese; 4. Esos; 5. Estos; 6. Aquel

Word Builder 2

▶ 13C Word Builder 2 (CD 5, Track 28)

el fax	fax
el móvil	mobile phone
el celular	cell phone
Internet	internet
la computadora	computer
el teclado	keyboard
la pantalla	screen
la impresora	printer
el ratón	mouse
los audífonos	headphones
la conexión	connection

⏸

✎ Word Practice 2

Match the following Spanish words to their English translations.

1. Internet
2. el ratón
3. el teclado
4. la pantalla
5. la computadora
6. la impresora

a. *internet*
b. *screen*
c. *keyboard*
d. *mouse*
e. *printer*
f. *computer*

ANSWER KEY
1. a; 2. d; 3. c; 4. b; 5. f; 6. e

Grammar Builder 2
DEMONSTRATIVE PRONOUNS

▶ 13D Grammar Builder 2 (CD 5, Track 29)

Words like *this* and *that* not only function as adjectives in English, as in *this book* or *that house*, but can also be used as pronouns, as in *I like this (one) and you like that (one)*. In Spanish, demonstrative pronouns have an accent mark that distinguishes them from demonstrative adjectives.

éste/ésta	this (one)
éstos/éstas	these (ones)
ése/ésa	that (one)
ésos/ésas	those (ones)
aquél/aquélla	that (one) over there
aquéllos/aquéllas	those (ones) over there

Let's take a look at some examples. Notice the difference between demonstrative adjectives, which are used right before nouns, and demonstrative pronouns, which stand on their own in place of nouns.

Unit 4 Lesson 13: Words

177

Este número de fax es el mío y éste es el tuyo.
This fax number is mine and this one is yours.

Esa pantalla es plana y ésa no.
That screen is flat and that one is not.

Aquella computadora es nueva y aquélla no.
That computer is new and that one is not.

There are three neuter demonstrative pronouns that are used to refer to abstract concepts or unspecified objects. They're also used when the speaker doesn't necessarily have a specific noun in mind, so the gender is unknown; the neuter form is used instead.

esto	*this (one, thing)*
eso	*that (one, thing)*
aquello	*that (one, thing) further away*

Here are some examples.

Esto es un desastre.
This is a disaster.

Eso es verdad.
That's true.

Aquello no me gusta.
I don't like that.

Ⓟ

✎ Work Out 2

Choose either the demonstrative adjective or the demonstrative pronoun to complete the sentence.

1. (Ese,Ése) _____ teléfono está ocupado.

2. (Este, Éste) _____ es mi número de celular.

3. (Estos, Éstos) _____ meses son largos.

4. (Esta, Ésta) _____ pantalla es oscura y (aquella, aquélla) _____ es pequeña.

5. (Estas, Éstas) _____ computadoras son costosas.

6. (Esta, Ésta) _____ semana tengo dos reuniones.

7. (Esas, Ésas) _____ son nuestras oficinas.

8. (Ese, Ése) _____ teclado no me gusta.

ANSWER KEY
1. Ese; 2. Éste; 3. Estos; 4. Esta, aquélla; 5. Estas; 6. Esta; 7. Ésas; 8. Ese

---

Take It Further

Demonstrative adjectives can also be used with time expressions, just as they are in English.

esta mañana	*this morning*
esta tarde	*this afternoon*
esta noche	*tonight*
esta semana	*this week*
este día	*this day*
este mes	*this month*

| este año | this year |
| este siglo | this century |

Here are some examples.

Este mes tengo mucho trabajo.
I have a lot of work this month.

Esta tarde tenemos dos reuniones.
We have two meetings this afternoon.

✎ Word Recall

Choose the appropriate demonstrative adjective or pronoun.

1. (Éste/Este/Ésta/Esta) _____ señor es el padre de Paquito.

2. (Éste/Este/Ésta/Esta) _____ es el padre de Paquito.

3. (Éste/Este/Ésta/Esta) _____ señora es la madre de Paquito.

4. (Éste/Este/Ésta/Esta) _____ es la madre de Paquito.

5. (Aquél/Aquel/Aquélla/Aquella) _____ coche es nuevo.

6. (Aquéllos/Aquellos/Aquéllas/Aquellas) _____ coches son nuevos.

7. (Ésas/Esas/Ésos/Esos) _____ cuadernos son para mi clase de español.

8. (Ésas/Esas/Ésos/Esos) _____ plumas son para mi clase de español.

9. (Aquel/Aquél/Aquellos/Aquéllos) _____ edificios son muy altos.

10. (Aquél/Aquél/Aquellos/Aquéllos) _____ son edificios muy altos.

Irregular Verbs **Hacer** (*To Make, To Do*), **Poner**
(*To Put*), **Traer** (*To Bring*), and **Caer** (*To Fall*)

Ir (*To Go*)

Irregular Verbs **Salir** (*To Go
Out*) and **Decir** (*To Say*)

Querer (*To Want, To Love*)

ANSWER KEY
1. Este; 2. Éste; 3. Esta; 4. Ésta; 5. Aquel; 6. Aquellos; 7. Esos; 8. Esas; 9. Aquellos; 10. Aquéllos

How Did You Do?

By now, you should be able to:

☐ Talk about the telephone and messages
(Still unsure? Jump back to page 173.)

☐ Talk a little bit about computers
(Still unsure? Jump back to page 176.)

☐ Use demonstrative adjectives to express *this book, that teacher*
(Still unsure? Jump back to page 174.)

☐ Use demonstrative pronouns to express *this one, that one*
(Still unsure? Jump back to page 177.)

Lesson 14: Phrases

By the end of this lesson, you should be able to:

☐ Talk about leaving a message or sending an e-mail

☐ Make a negative statement

☐ Understand some expressions used on the telephone

☐ Use indefinite pronouns to express *something, anything, either … or*

Phrase Builder 1

▶ 14A Phrase Builder 1 (CD 5, Track 30)

Here are a few verb phrases you'll use when talking on the phone or sending e-mail. They're all regular verbs, except for colgar, which we'll come back to later.

llamar por teléfono	*to make a phone call*
contestar el teléfono	*to answer the phone*
colgar el teléfono	*to hang up the phone*
marcar un número de teléfono	*to dial a phone number*
dejar un mensaje después de oír la señal	*to leave a message after the tone*
enviar un mensaje	*to send a message*
borrar un mensaje	*to erase a message*
copiar un mensaje	*to copy a message*
recibir un fax	*to receive a fax*
hacer una llamada internacional	*to make an international call*
hacer una llamada nacional	*to make a national call*
enviar un correo electrónico	*to send an e-mail*
contestar* un correo electrónico	*to reply to an e-mail*
enviar un archivo	*to send a file*
bajar un archivo	*to download a file*

* Notice that in English, you need a preposition after *reply,* but in Spanish, you can use contestar on its own. This is very similar to what you saw with escuchar (*to listen to*).

�𝄇

✎ Phrase Practice 1

Fill in the missing word or phrase.

1. llamar _____ *to make a phone call*

Irregular Verbs **Hacer** (*To Make, To Do*), **Poner**
(*To Put*), **Traer** (*To Bring*), and **Caer** (*To Fall*)

Ir (*To Go*)

Irregular Verbs **Salir** (*To Go
Out*) and **Decir** (*To Say*)

Querer (*To Want, To Love*)

2. contestar _____ *to answer the phone*

3. _____ el teléfono *to hang up the phone*

4. marcar _____ *to dial a phone number*

5. _____ un correo electrónico *to send an e-mail*

6. _____ un correo electrónico *to reply to an e-mail*

7. _____ un archivo *to send a file*

8. _____ un archivo *to download a file*

ANSWER KEY
1. por teléfono; 2. el teléfono; 3. colgar; 4. un número de teléfono; 5. enviar; 6. contestar; 7. enviar;
8. bajar

Grammar Builder 1
NEGATION

▶ 14B Grammar Builder 1 (CD 5, Track 31)

Making a negative statement in Spanish is very easy—simply place the word no
(*not*) before the verb.

Tengo conexión de Internet en mi casa.
I have an internet connection at home.

No tengo conexión de Internet en mi casa.
I don't have an internet connection at home.

La línea está ocupada.
The line is busy.

La línea no está ocupada.
The line isn't busy.

Hay tono.
There's a dial tone.

No hay tono.
There's no dial tone.

Eres un arquitecto.
You are an architect.

No eres un arquitecto.
You're not an architect.

When the answer to a question is negative, the word no is used twice—once to mean *no*, and once to mean *not*.

¿Está la señora Ruiz en su oficina?
Is Mrs. Ruiz in her office?

No. Ella no está en su oficina.
No. She's not in her office.

¿Tienes tiempo para tomar un café?
Do you have time for a coffee?

No. No tengo tiempo.
No. I don't have time.

Ⅱ

✎ Work Out 1

Make the following statements negative.

1. Éste es mi número de teléfono. _____

2. Las secretarias hablan por teléfono. _____

3. Tus padres tienen una casa pequeña. _____

4. Yo escribo un correo electrónico. _____

5. Tenemos tu número de celular. _____

6. Leo un fax. _____

7. Estas oficinas son muy grandes. _____

8. La línea está ocupada. _____

ANSWER KEY

1. Éste no es mi número de teléfono. 2. Las secretarias no hablan por teléfono. 3. Tus padres no tienen una casa pequeña. 4. Yo no escribo un correo electrónico. 5. No tenemos tu número de celular. 6. No leo un fax. 7. Estas oficinas no son muy grandes. 8. La línea no está ocupada.

Phrase Builder 2

▷ 14C Phrase Builder 2 (CD 5, Track 32)

Here are some phrases you'll use when talking on the phone.

¿Dígame?	Hello? (lit., Tell me?)
¿Aló?	Hello?
Le paso.	I'm putting you through.
La línea está ocupada.	The line is busy.
Está comunicando.	It's ringing.
No hay tono.	There is no dial tone.
No cuelgue, por favor.	Do not hang up, please.
Espere, por favor.	Hold on, please.
poner en espera	to put on hold

⏸

✎ Phrase Practice 2

Translate the following phrases.

1. *Hello? (lit., Tell me?)* _____

2. *Hello?* _____

3. *Do not hang up, please.* _____

4. *Hold on, please.* _____

5. *to put on hold* _____

ANSWER KEY

1. ¿Dígame? 2. ¿Aló? 3. No cuelgue, por favor. 4. Espere, por favor. 5. poner en espera

Irregular Verbs **Hacer** (*To Make, To Do*), **Poner**
(*To Put*), **Traer** (*To Bring*), and **Caer** (*To Fall*)

Ir (*To Go*)

Irregular Verbs **Salir** (*To Go
Out*) and **Decir** (*To Say*)

Querer (*To Want, To Love*)

Grammar Builder 2
INDEFINITE PRONOUNS

▷ 14D Grammar Builder 2 (CD 6, Track 1)

An indefinite pronoun is a pronoun that doesn't refer to anyone in particular.
Here are some indefinite pronouns and other words that will come in handy
in Spanish. Notice that they're all affirmative. We'll look at their negative
counterparts in a moment.

algo	*something*
alguien	*somebody, someone*
algún(-o/-a/-os/-as)	*some, something*
siempre	*always*
también	*also, too*
o … o	*either … or*

Here's how they're used in a sentence.

Hay algo diferente en esta habitación.
There's something different in this room.

Alguien llama por teléfono.
Somebody's calling on the phone.

Algunos teléfonos no funcionan.
Some phones don't work.

Ella siempre escribe emails.
She always writes e-mails.

Nosotros también tocamos el piano.
We also play the piano.

Yo o corro o camino por las mañanas.
I either run or walk in the mornings.

Notice that o ... o is used to introduce two different options, and each o is placed in front of one of the options. In the example above, the two options are actions, so each o is placed before the verb. (Sometimes the first o is omitted.)

Here are their negative counterparts. Ni ... ni functions just like o ... o.

nada	*nothing*
nadie	*nobody, no one*
ningún(-o/-a/-os/-as)	*no, none*
nunca	*never*
tampoco	*neither, not either*
ni ... ni	*neither ... nor*

Negative words can be used alone, preceding the verb.

Jorge nunca come.
Jorge never eats.

Él tampoco canta.
He doesn't sing either.

Nadie habla italiano aquí.
No one here speaks Italian.

Double negation is perfectly correct in Spanish. Usually the word no immediately precedes the verb and another negative word follows the verb.

Intermediate Spanish

Irregular Verbs **Hacer** *(To Make, To Do)*, **Poner**
(To Put), **Traer** *(To Bring)*, and **Caer** *(To Fall)*

Ir *(To Go)*

Irregular Verbs **Salir** *(To Go
Out)* and **Decir** *(To Say)*

Querer *(To Want, To Love)*

No funciona ni el teléfono ni el fax.
Neither the phone nor the fax works.

No hay conexión nunca.
There's never a connection.

No hay nadie en la oficina.
There's nobody in the office./There isn't anyone in the office.

Ⅱ

✎ Work Out 2

Translate the following sentences. When appropriate, use single (instead of double) negation.

1. *I always have a copy of my messages.* _____

   _____

2. *Nobody answers the phone.* _____

   _____

3. *They never erase their messages.* _____

   _____

4. *Someone receives a fax.* _____

   _____

5. *Someone also receives an e-mail.* _____

   _____

6. *He doesn't have a phone or a fax in his office.* _____

_____

ANSWER KEY

1.Siempre tengo una copia de mis mensajes. 2. Nadie contesta el teléfono. 3. Nunca borran sus mensajes. 4. Alguien recibe un fax. 5. Alguien también recibe un correo electrónico. 6. No tiene ni un teléfono ni un fax en su oficina.

Take It Further

Later on in this unit, you'll be learning how to make polite requests. In doing so, the phrase por favor (*please*) comes in very handy. Another phrase that you'll often hear is hágame el favor de (*lit., do me the favor of*). You'll never be wrong to use por favor. However, you might be surprised not to hear the words when asking someone to do something that he or she is expected to do (as when ordering a meal from a server). As in English, your tone of voice can have as much to do with how your request is received as does its grammatical form.

✎ Word Recall

The following are affirmative sentences. Say the opposite by turning each sentence into a negation according to the hints in parentheses.

1. Yo tengo dos reuniones esta semana. (*don't have*) _____

_____

2. La línea está ocupada. (*isn't*) _____

_____

3. Este mes tengo mucho trabajo. (*don't have*) _____

_____

Irregular Verbs **Hacer** (*To Make, To Do*), **Poner**
(*To Put*), **Traer** (*To Bring*), and **Caer** (*To Fall*)   **Ir** (*To Go*)

Irregular Verbs **Salir** (*To Go*   **Querer** (*To Want, To Love*)
Out*) and **Decir** (*To Say*)

4. **Estela y yo hablamos francés.** (*don't speak*) _____

5. **Hay muchas personas en mi oficina.** (*there aren't*) _____

6. **Alguien llama por teléfono.** (*no one*) _____

7. **Ella siempre bebe café.** (*never*) _____

ANSWER KEY

1. Yo no tengo dos reuniones esta semana. 2. La línea no está ocupada. 3. Este mes no tengo mucho trabajo. 4. Estela y yo no hablamos francés . 5. No hay muchas personas en mi oficina. 6. Nadie llama por teléfono. 7. Ella nunca bebe café.

How Did You Do?

By now, you should be able to:

☐ Talk about leaving a message or sending an e-mail
(Still unsure? Jump back to page 182.)

☐ Make a negative statement
(Still unsure? Jump back to page 183.)

☐ Understand some expressions used on the telephone
(Still unsure? Jump back to page 186.)

☐ Use indefinite pronouns to express *something, anything, either ... or*
(Still unsure? Jump back to page 187.)

Lesson 15: Sentences

By the end of this lesson, you should be able to:

☐ Ask someone if they'd like to call back or leave a message

☐ Express *to make, to do, to put, to bring,* and *to fall*

☐ Express *to go out* and *to say*

Sentence Builder 1

▶ 15A Sentence Builder 1 (CD 6, Track 2)

Quisiera hablar con …	*I'd like to talk to …*
Lo siento, tiene un número equivocado.	*Sorry, you have the wrong number.*
¿De parte de quién?	*Who's calling?*
¿Quién lo llama?	*Who's calling?*
¿Con quién hablo?	*Who am I talking to?*
Ahora no está.	*He/She isn't in right now.*
Está ocupado/a.	*He's/She's busy.*
Por favor, llame más tarde.	*Please call later.*
Llame en cinco minutos.	*Please call in five minutes.*
No está en su oficina.	*He/She is not in his/her office.*
Ya salió.	*He/She already left.*
¿Desea dejar un mensaje?	*Would you like to leave a message?*

⏸

Irregular Verbs **Hacer** (*To Make, To Do*), **Poner**
(*To Put*), **Traer** (*To Bring*), and **Caer** (*To Fall*)   Ir (*To Go*)

Irregular Verbs **Salir** (*To Go*   Querer (*To Want, To Love*)
Out*) and **Decir** (*To Say*)

✎ Sentence Practice 1

Translate the following sentences.

1. *I'd like to talk to …* _____

2. *Sorry, you have the wrong number.* _____

3. *Who's calling?* _____

4. *Who am I talking to?* _____

5. *He/She isn't in right now.* _____

6. *He's/She's busy.* _____

7. *Please call later.* _____

ANSWER KEY

1. Quisiera hablar con … 2. Lo siento, tiene un número equivocado. 3. ¿De parte de quién?/¿Quién
lo llama? 4. ¿Con quién hablo? 5. Ahora no está. 6. Está ocupado/a. 7. Por favor, llame más tarde.

Grammar Builder 1
IRREGULAR VERBS HACER (*TO MAKE, TO DO*), PONER (*TO PUT*), TRAER (*TO BRING*), AND CAER (*TO FALL*)

▶ 15B Grammar Builder 1 (CD 6, Track 3)

As you know, there are a few verbs in Spanish that are irregular. Most of the time,
these verbs follow the pattern of endings you learned in Unit 4, but their stems
change a bit when conjugated. For example, you already know the verb tener,
which has a g before the ending for the first person singular (yo tengo), and the e
in its stem changes to ie in several forms (tienes, tiene, tienen).

There are a few other verbs that add g in the first person singular: hacer (*to make, to do*), poner (*to put*), traer (*to bring*), and caer (*to fall*). For all other persons, they are conjugated just like regular -er verbs.

HACER *(TO MAKE, TO DO)*	
yo hago	nosotros/as hacemos
tú haces	vosotros/as hacéis
él/ella/usted hace	ellos/ellas/ustedes hacen

PONER *(TO PUT)*	
yo pongo	nosotros/as ponemos
tú pones	vosotros/as ponéis
él/ella/usted pone	ellos/ellas/ustedes ponen

The verb traer (*to bring*) also takes an i before the g in the yo form.

TRAER *(TO BRING)*	
yo traigo	nosotros/as traemos
tú traes	vosotros/as traéis
él/ella/usted trae	ellos/ellas/ustedes traen

The verb caer (*to fall*) is conjugated just like traer.

CAER *(TO FALL)*	
yo caigo	nosotros/as caemos
tú caes	vosotros/as caéis
él/ella/usted cae	ellos/ellas/ustedes caen

Ⅱ

Irregular Verbs **Hacer** (*To Make, To Do*), **Poner**
(*To Put*), **Traer** (*To Bring*), and **Caer** (*To Fall*)   Ir (*To Go*)

Irregular Verbs **Salir** (*To Go*   **Querer** (*To Want, To Love*)
Out*) and **Decir** (*To Say*)

✎ Work Out 1

Complete the following sentences with the correct form of the verb.

1. Nosotros no _____ llamadas locales. (hacer)

2. Ustedes _____ los contratos. (traer)

3. Ella _____ a María en espera. (poner)

4. Yo _____ llamadas internacionales todos los días. (hacer)

5. Ellas no _____ en la oficina en este momento. (estar)

6. Usted _____ la línea equivocada. (tener)

7. Ella _____ buenas noticias. (traer)

8. Tú _____ ocupado todos los días. (estar)

9. Vosotros _____ la computadora en la oficina. (poner)

10. Yo _____ una reunión el martes. (tener)

ANSWER KEY

1. hacemos; 2. traen; 3. pone; 4. hago; 5. están; 6. tiene; 7. trae; 8. estás; 9. ponéis; 10. tengo

Sentence Builder 2

▶ 15C Sentence Builder 2 (CD 6, Track 4)

¿Quiere esperar un momento?	*Do you want to wait a moment?*
No hay nadie disponible en este momento.	*There's no one available at the moment.*
Por favor, anote mi número de teléfono.	*Please write down my telephone number.*
Necesito hablar con el señor Sánchez lo antes posible.	*I need to speak to Mr. Sánchez as soon as possible.*

Que tenga un buen día.	*Have a nice day.*
Casi no reconozco tu voz.	*I almost don't recognize your voice.*
Tengo los contratos listos, pero falta tu firma.	*I have the contracts ready, but your signature is missing.*
Salgo de viaje ese mismo día.	*I go on a trip that very same day.*
El martes por la mañana me viene bien.	*Tuesday morning suits me fine.*
Tengo una reunión muy temprano.	*I have a meeting very early.*
¿Cuál es su dirección de correo electrónico?	*What's your e-mail address?*
¿Su compañía tiene un sitio web?	*Does your company have a website?*
El informe está en un anexo al correo electrónico.	*The report is in an e-mail attachment.*

(II)

✎ Sentence Practice 2

Fill in the missing words in Spanish.

1. _____ el señor Sánchez lo antes posible.

   I need to speak to Mr. Sánchez as soon as possible.

2. _____ un buen día. *Have a nice day.*

3. El martes por la mañana _____ . *Tuesday morning*

   suits me fine.

4. Tengo _____ muy temprano. *I have a meeting very early.*

5. ¿Cuál es _____ ?

   What's your e-mail address?

6. ¿Su compañía _____ ?

Does your company have a website?

7. El informe está en _____ .

The report is in an e-mail attachment.

ANSWER KEY

1. Necesito hablar con; 2. Que tenga; 3. me viene bien; 4. una reunión; 5. su dirección de correo electrónico; 6. tiene un sitio web; 7. un anexo al correo electrónico

Grammar Builder 2
IRREGULAR VERBS SALIR (*TO GO OUT*) AND DECIR (*TO SAY*)

▶ 15D Grammar Builder 2 (CD 6, Track 5)

Let's look at some more irregular verbs. The verbs salir (*to go out*) and decir (*to say*) are irregular -ir verbs that also have the g in the first person singular.

SALIR *(TO GO OUT)*	
yo salgo	nosotros/as salimos
tú sales	vosotros/as salís
él/ella/usted sale	ellos/ellas/ustedes salen

Notice that decir (*to say*) also has a vowel change from e to i in its stem.

DECIR *(TO SAY)*	
yo digo	nosotros/as decimos
tú dices	vosotros/as decís
él/ella/usted dice	ellos/ellas/ustedes dicen

Yo salgo del trabajo a las tres de la tarde.
I leave work at 3:00 p.m.

Ella dice siempre la verdad.
She always tells the truth.

So far you've learned two verbs that have vowel changes in their stems: tener and decir. In tener, e becomes ie, and in decir, e becomes i. Notice that these changes do not happen in the nosotros/as and vosotros/as forms. You'll learn more about stem changing verbs later, but for now keep in mind that if there is a stem change, it doesn't affect the first and second person plural forms, nosotros/as and vosotros/as.

Ⓘ

✎ Work Out 2

Rewrite the following sentences using the subject pronoun given in parentheses.

1. Yo digo pocas palabras. (nosotros) _____

   _____

2. Tú sales de viaje el domingo. (yo) _____

   _____

3. Ustedes dicen la verdad. (ella) _____

   _____

4. Él sale de su oficina a las tres de la tarde. (tú) _____

   _____

5. Nosotros salimos de nuestra casa a las nueve de la mañana. (vosotros) _____

   _____

6. Ellos no dicen nada. (yo) _____

   _____

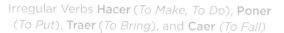

Irregular Verbs **Salir** (*To Go* **Querer** (*To Want, To Love*)
Out) and **Decir** (*To Say*)

ANSWER KEY

1. Nosotros decimos pocas palabras. 2. Yo salgo de viaje el domingo. 3. Ella dice la verdad. 4. Tú sales de tu oficina a las tres de la tarde. 5. Vosotros salís de nuestra casa a las nueve de la mañana. 6. Yo no digo nada.

⚡ Tip!

Don't get too worked up about learning irregular verbs. You'll see that the most frequently used verbs are the ones with the most irregularities—you'll hear them so often that you'll end up learning them very quickly. Also, the most irregular person in the conjugation of verbs is the first person singular, or yo form (*I*). So, even though a verb may be called irregular, it may only mean that the first person singular is irregular and the rest of the conjugation follows a regular pattern, as you saw with some of the verbs in this lesson. If you're a stickler for memorizing irregular forms, though, here are some suggestions. Make flash cards for each new irregular verb, following the two-column format in which the irregular verbs are presented in this lesson. Keep them in your pocket, and when you have a few spare moments, take them out, glance over them, and repeat the forms aloud to yourself. You'll have them memorized pretty quickly.

✎ Word Recall

Let's practice those irregular verbs once again. Rewrite each sentence by using the suggested noun in parentheses.

1. Ella hace muchas llamadas por teléfono. (Tú) _____

_____

2. Ella hace muchas llamadas por teléfono. (Nosotros) _____

_____

3. Ella hace muchas llamadas por teléfono. (Ustedes) _____

_____

4. **Yo siempre digo la verdad. (Tú)** _____

_____

5. **Yo siempre digo la verdad. (Nosotros)** _____

_____

6. **Yo siempre digo la verdad. (Ustedes)** _____

_____

ANSWER KEY

1. Tú haces muchas llamadas por teléfono. 2. Nosotros hacemos muchas llamadas por teléfono.
3. Ustedes hacen muchas llamadas por teléfono. 4. Tú siempre dices la verdad. 5. Nosotros siempre decimos la verdad. 6. Ustedes siempre dicen la verdad.

How Did You Do?

By now, you should be able to:

☐ Ask someone if they'd like to call back or leave a message
(Still unsure? Jump back to page 192.)

☐ Express *to make, to do, to put, to bring,* and *to fall*
(Still unsure? Jump back to page 193.)

☐ Express *to go out* and *to say*
(Still unsure? Jump back to page 197.)

Lesson 16: Conversations

By the end of this lesson, you should be able to:

☐ Feel comfortable with the verb *to go*

☐ Distinguish *yes* from *if*

Irregular Verbs **Hacer** (*To Make, To Do*), **Poner**
(*To Put*), **Traer** (*To Bring*), and **Caer** (*To Fall*)   **Ir** (*To Go*)

Irregular Verbs **Salir** (*To Go
Out*) and **Decir** (*To Say*)   **Querer** (*To Want, To Love*)

☐ Say what you *want* or *would like*

₢ Conversation 1

▶ 16A Conversation 1 (CD 6, Track 6 - Spanish Only; Track 7 - Spanish and English)

Juan Fernández is calling Nova Limitada to speak with Miguel Sánchez. He dials
the switchboard and gets the operator.

Operadora:	Nova Limitada, buenos días, ¿con quién desea hablar?
Juan:	Buenos días. Me llamo Juan Fernández y necesito hablar con el gerente de ventas, el señor Miguel Sánchez.
Operadora:	Le comunico. Un momento por favor.

(after a moment)

Operadora:	La línea está ocupada. ¿Quiere esperar un momento?
Juan:	No, no tengo tiempo. ¿Hay alguien más?
Operadora:	No. Lo siento. En ese departamento no hay nadie disponible en este momento. Todos están en una reunión fuera de la ciudad.
Juan:	Bueno, por favor anote mi número de teléfono. Necesito hablar con el señor Sánchez lo antes posible.
Operadora:	¿Quiere su buzón de voz?
Juan:	Buena idea.
Operadora:	Ya le conecto. Que tenga un buen día.
Juan:	Muchas gracias. Igualmente.

Operator:	*Nova Limitada, good morning; who would you like to speak to?*
Juan:	*Good morning. My name is Juan Fernández, and I need to speak to the sales manager, Mr. Miguel Sánchez.*
Operator:	*I'll put you through. One moment please.*

(after a moment)

Operator:	*The line is busy. Do you want to wait a moment?*
Juan:	*No, I don't have time. Is there anybody else?*
Operator:	*No. I'm sorry. There's no one available in that department at the moment. Everyone is at a meeting out of town.*
Juan:	*Well, please write down my phone number. I need to speak to Mr. Sánchez as soon as possible.*
Operator:	*Do you want his voice mail?*
Juan:	*Good idea.*
Operator:	*I'll put you through right now. Have a nice day.*
Juan:	*Thank you; same to you.*

Take It Further

As briefly mentioned in Lesson 12, when the direct object of a verb is a person, you must introduce it with the preposition a. This a has no real meaning, and when it's followed by the masculine article el, it forms the contraction al.

Invitamos al gerente de ventas.
We're inviting the sales manager.

Traigo a mis amigos.
I'm bringing my friends.

Veo a mis amigos todas las semanas.
I see my friends every week.

Quieren mucho a sus padres.
They love their parents very much.

The only exception is the verb tener. If tener has a person as a direct object, the preposition a is not used.

Irregular Verbs **Hacer** (*To Make, To Do*), **Poner**
(*To Put*), **Traer** (*To Bring*), and **Caer** (*To Fall*)   **Ir** (*To Go*)

Irregular Verbs **Salir** (*To Go
Out*) and **Decir** (*To Say*)   **Querer** (*To Want, To Love*)

Tiene muchos amigos.
She/He has a lot of friends.

Tengo un hermano y una hermana.
I have a brother and a sister.

✎ Conversation Practice 1

Fill in the blanks below with the appropriate word based on the English
translations and the dialogue above.

1. Nova Limitada, buenos días, ¿con quién _____?

   Nova Limitada, good morning; who would you like to speak to?

2. ¿_____ esperar un momento? *Do you want to wait a moment?*

3. ¿Hay _____ más? *Is there anybody else?*

4. En ese departamento no hay _____ disponible en este momento.

   There's no one available in that department at the moment.

5. Todos están en una _____ fuera de la ciudad.

   Everyone is at a meeting out of town.

   ANSWER KEY
   1. desea hablar; 2. Quiere; 3. alguien; 4. nadie; 5. reunión

Grammar Builder 1
IR (TO GO)

▶ 16B Grammar Builder 1 (CD 6, Track 8)

The verb ir (to go) is used in many situations, and it is also an irregular verb.

IR (TO GO)	
yo voy	nosotros/as vamos
tú vas	vosotros/as vais
él/ella/usted va	ellos/ellas/ustedes van

Notice that we generally use the preposition a (to) with the verb ir. And remember that a + the masculine article el forms the contraction al.

Esta tarde voy a mi oficina.
This afternoon I'm going to my office.

Nosotros vamos al cine los fines de semana.
We go to the movies on the weekends.

Ⅱ

✎ Work Out 1

Match the sentences in the left column with the appropriate responses in the right column.

1. ¿Quién lo llama?   a. No, gracias, llamo más tarde.

2. ¿Cuál es su número?   b. Le paso.

3. ¿Desea dejar un mensaje?   c. Lo siento. Ella ya salió.

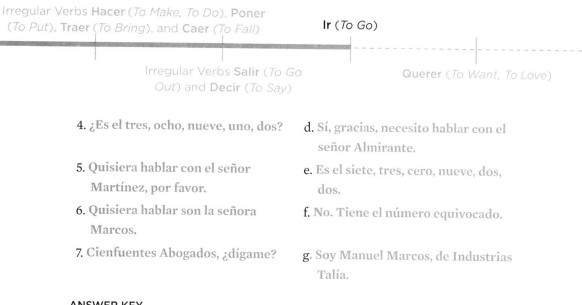

Irregular Verbs **Hacer** (*To Make, To Do*), **Poner** (*To Put*), **Traer** (*To Bring*), and **Caer** (*To Fall*)

Ir (*To Go*)

Irregular Verbs **Salir** (*To Go Out*) and **Decir** (*To Say*)

Querer (*To Want, To Love*)

4. ¿Es el tres, ocho, nueve, uno, dos?

d. Sí, gracias, necesito hablar con el señor Almirante.

5. Quisiera hablar con el señor Martínez, por favor.

e. Es el siete, tres, cero, nueve, dos, dos.

6. Quisiera hablar son la señora Marcos.

f. No. Tiene el número equivocado.

7. Cienfuentes Abogados, ¿dígame?

g. Soy Manuel Marcos, de Industrias Talía.

ANSWER KEY

1. g; 2.e; 3. a; 4. f; 5. b; 6. c; 7. d

Conversation 2

▶ 16C Conversation 2 (CD 6, Track 9 - Spanish Only; Track 10 - Spanish and English)

Later that afternoon, Miguel returns Juan's call.

Secretaria:	Trías y Trías Abogados, buenas tardes.
Miguel:	Buenas tardes. Soy Miguel Sánchez. Necesito hablar con el señor Fernández.
Secretaria:	Le paso.
Juan:	¿Dígame?
Miguel:	¿Con quién hablo?
Juan:	¡Hola, Miguel; soy yo, Juan!
Miguel:	Hola, Juan. Casi no reconozco tu voz. ¿Cómo van las cosas?
Juan:	Pues más o menos. Necesito reunirme contigo urgentemente. Tengo los contratos listos, pero falta tu firma.
Miguel:	¿Qué te parece si nos vemos el miércoles a eso de las nueve?
Juan:	Salgo de viaje ese mismo día. Y el lunes … ¿tienes tiempo?
Miguel:	Pero hombre, si es día festivo. Pero el martes por la mañana me viene bien.
Juan:	Listo. Voy primero a los juzgados y luego a tu oficina.

Miguel:	Tengo una reunión muy temprano ... Si vienes después de las diez, mejor.
Juan:	Perfecto. Entonces, nos vemos el martes.
Miguel:	Hasta luego.

Secretary:	*Trías and Trías Lawyers, good afternoon.*
Miguel:	*Good afternoon. I'm Miguel Sánchez. I need to speak to Mr. Fernández.*
Secretary:	*I'll put you through.*
Juan:	*Hello?*
Miguel:	*Who am I speaking to?*
Juan:	*Hi, Miguel; it's me, Juan!*
Miguel:	*Hi, Juan. I almost don't recognize your voice. How are things?*
Juan:	*Well, so-so. I need to meet with you urgently. I have the contracts ready, but your signature is missing.*
Miguel:	*How about getting together on Wednesday at about nine?*
Juan:	*I leave on a trip that same day. What about Monday ... Do you have time?*
Miguel:	*Come on now, that's a holiday! But Tuesday morning is fine with me.*
Juan:	*Good. I'll first go to court and then to your office.*
Miguel:	*I have a meeting very early. If you come after ten, that's better.*
Juan:	*Perfect. So, see you Tuesday.*
Miguel:	*Till later.*

Take It Further

Don't confuse sí with si. When sí is spelled with an accent mark, it means *yes*; when it is spelled without the accent mark, it means *if*.

Notice that Miguel said: Pero hombre, si es día festivo. The words hombre and si are used as flavoring words, giving emphasis to what Miguel is saying. The

Irregular Verbs **Hacer** (*To Make, To Do*), **Poner**
(*To Put*), **Traer** (*To Bring*), and **Caer** (*To Fall*)   **Ir** (*To Go*)

Irregular Verbs **Salir** (*To Go*   **Querer** (*To Want, To Love*)
Out) and **Decir** (*To Say*)

sentence could be translated in a number of ways to capture the same sentiment,
for example: *Come on now, that's a holiday!*

✎ Conversation Practice 1

Fill in the blanks below with the appropriate word based on the English
translations and the dialogue above.

1. _____ con el señor Fernández. *I need to speak to*

   Mr. Fernández.

2. ¿Con quién _____? *Who am I speaking to?*

3. Pues _____. *Well, so-so.*

4. _____ primero a los juzgados y luego _____. *I'll*

   first go to court and then to your office.

5. Entonces, _____ el martes. *So, see you Tuesday.*

   ANSWER KEY
   1. Necesito hablar; 2. hablo; 3. más o menos; 4. Voy, a tu oficina; 5. nos vemos

Grammar Builder 2
QUERER (TO WANT, TO LOVE)

▶ 16D Grammar Builder 2 (CD 6, Track 11)

When making polite requests you will very often use the verb querer (*to want*).
This is an irregular verb, conjugated as follows.

QUERER (TO WANT)	
yo quiero	nosotros/as queremos

QUERER *(TO WANT)*	
tú quieres	vosotros/as queréis
él/ella/usted quiere	ellos/ellas/ustedes quieren

Querer can be used right before another verb in the infinitive, just as *to want to* is in English.

Quiero una habitación grande, por favor.
I want a big room, please

Quiero hablar con Patricia.
I want to speak to Patricia.

Quiero escribir un correo electrónico.
I want to write an e-mail.

A much nicer and more polite way of making requests is by using the form quisiera (*would like*).

Quisiera una cerveza, por favor.
I would like a beer, please.

Quisiera hablar con Patricia.
I'd like to speak to Patricia.

Quisiera hacer una llamada internacional.
I'd like to make an international call.

Note that this verb is often used to mean *to love*. So, a common way of saying *I love you* is to say Te quiero. Spanish does have the verb amar, which means *to*

Irregular Verbs **Hacer** (*To Make, To Do*), **Poner**
(*To Put*), **Traer** (*To Bring*), and **Caer** (*To Fall*)

Ir (*To Go*)

Irregular Verbs **Salir** (*To Go
Out*) and **Decir** (*To Say*)

Querer (*To Want, To Love*)

love, but it is not used as often, and it is usually used strictly in a romantic way.
Don't forget to use the preposition a if the direct object of querer is a person.

Gloria quiere mucho a su papá.
Gloria loves her daddy very much.

Queremos a nuestros amigos.
We love our friends.

Another verb that can be used to make a polite request is gustar (*to like*). Again,
you would use the form me gustaría (*I would like*).

Me gustaría un café.
I would like a cup of coffee.

Me gustaría llamar por teléfono.
I'd like to make a phone call.

✎ Work Out 2

Translate the following sentences into Spanish.

1. *I would like to speak to the manager, please.* _____

_____

2. *We want a new computer.* _____

_____

3. *I'd like to go to my brother's office.* _____

_____

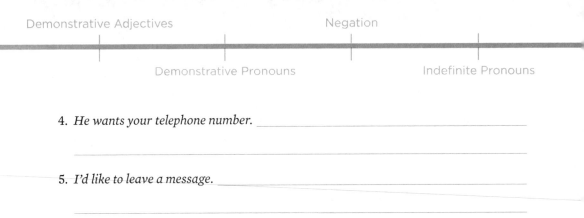

4. *He wants your telephone number.* _____

_____

5. *I'd like to leave a message.* _____

_____

ANSWER KEY

1. Me gustaría/Quisiera hablar con el gerente, por favor. 2. Queremos una computadora nueva.
3. Me gustaría/Quisiera ir a la oficina de mi hermano. 4. Él quiere tu número de teléfono. 5. Me
gustaría/Quisiera dejar un mensaje.

⊕ Culture Note

Every country in the Spanish-speaking world celebrates different national,
religious, and local fiestas or días festivos (*holidays*) depending on heritage and
tradition. For economic reasons, in some countries the government has decided
to move the celebration of religious holidays to the following Monday in order
to avoid the very long puentes (*long weekends, lit., bridges*) that would result in a
holiday being on a Tuesday or Thursday, for example.

You might want to check out the internet for information on holidays like el Día
de los Reyes Magos (*Three Kings Day*), el Día de los Muertos (*All Souls Day*),
la Nochebuena (*Christmas Eve*), la Pascua (*Easter*), or el carnaval (*carnival*) to
learn more about Spanish and Latin American holidays and traditions.

✎ Word Recall

Let's practice some phrases with the verb querer. Make sentences using quisiera
(*I would like to*) followed by the action suggested. For example, *to speak on the
phone:* Quisiera hablar por teléfono

1. *to drink coffee* _____

2. *to speak to my brother* _____

Irregular Verbs **Hacer** (*To Make, To Do*), **Poner**
(*To Put*), **Traer** (*To Bring*), and **Caer** (*To Fall*)

Ir (*To Go*)

Irregular Verbs **Salir** (*To Go
Out*) and **Decir** (*To Say*)

Querer (*To Want, To Love*)

3. *to have more money* _____

4. *to study Spanish* _____

5. *to dance tango* _____

6. *to sleep more* _____

7. *to go to Spain* _____

8. *to walk every day* _____

ANSWER KEY

1. **Quisiera tomar café. 2. Quisiera hablar con mi hermano. 3. Quisiera tener más dinero. 4. Quisiera estudiar español. 5. Quisiera bailar tango. 6. Quisiera dormir más. 7. Quisiera ir a España. 8. Quisiera caminar todos los días.**

How Did You Do?

By now, you should be able to:

☐ Feel comfortable with the verb *to go*
(Still unsure? Jump back to page 204.)

☐ Distinguish *yes* from *if*
(Still unsure? Jump back to page 206.)

☐ Say what you *want* or *would like*
(Still unsure? Jump back to page 207.)

Don't forget to practice and reinforce what you've
learned by visiting **www.livinglanguage.com/
languagelab** for flashcards, games, and quizzes for
Unit 4!

Unit 4 Essentials

Vocabulary Essentials

TELEPHONE VOCABULARY

	answering machine
	phone call
	operator
	phone book
	yellow pages
	telephone booth
	message
	voice mail
	switchboard
	to eliminate
	to erase

[Pg. 173]

TELECOMMUNICATION VOCABULARY

	fax
	mobile phone
	cell phone
	internet
	computer
	keyboard

Intermediate Spanish

	screen
	printer
	mouse
	headphones
	connection

[Pg. 176]

TELECOMMUNICATION VERBS

	to make a phone call
	to answer the phone
	to hang up the phone
	to dial a phone number
	to leave a message after the tone
	to send a message
	to erase a message
	to copy a message
	to receive a fax
	to make an international call
	to make a national/local call
	to send an e-mail
	to reply to an e-mail
	to send a file
	to download a file

[Pg. 182]

TELEPHONE EXPRESSIONS

	Hello? (lit., Tell me?)
	Hello?
	I'm putting you through.
	The line is busy.
	The line is busy.
	There is no dial tone.
	Do not hang up, please.
	Hold on, please.
	to put on hold

[Pg. 186]

MORE TELEPHONE EXPRESSIONS

	I'd like to talk to …
	Sorry, you have the wrong number.
	Who's calling?
	Who's calling?
	Who am I talking to?
	He/She isn't in right now.
	He's/She's busy.
	Please call later.
	Please call in five minutes.
	He/She is not in his/her office.
	He/She already left.
	Would you like to leave a message?

[Pg. 192]

Grammar Essentials

DEMONSTRATIVE ADJECTIVES

este/esta *(m./f.)*	*this*
estos/estas *(m./f.)*	*these*
ese/esa *(m./f.)*	*that*
esos/esas *(m./f.)*	*those*
aquel/aquella *(m./f.)*	*that over there*
aquellos/aquellas *(m./f.)*	*those over there*

DEMONSTRATIVE PRONOUNS

éste/ésta *(m./f.)*, esto *(neuter)*	*this (one)*
éstos/éstas *(m./f.)*	*these (ones)*
ése/ésa *(m./f.)*, eso *(neuter)*	*that (one)*
ésos/ésas *(m./f.)*	*those (ones)*
aquél/aquélla *(m./f.)*, aquello *(neuter)*	*that (one) over there*
aquéllos/aquéllas *(m./f.)*	*those (ones) over there*

NEGATION

To make a negative statement in Spanish, place the word no *(not)* before the verb.

INDEFINITE PRONOUNS

POSITIVE	
algo	*something*
alguien	*somebody, someone*
algún(-o/-a/-os/-as)	*some, something*
siempre	*always*

POSITIVE	
también	*also, too*
o … o	*either … or*

NEGATIVE	
nada	*nothing*
nadie	*nobody, no one*
ningún(-o/-a/-os/-as)	*no, none*
nunca	*never*
tampoco	*neither, not either*
ni … ni	*neither … nor*

IRREGULAR VERBS

CAER *(TO FALL)*	
yo caigo	nosotros/as caemos
tú caes	vosotros/as caéis
él/ella/usted cae	ellos/ellas/ustedes caen

DECIR *(TO SAY)*	
yo digo	nosotros/as decimos
tú dices	vosotros/as decís
él/ella/usted dice	ellos/ellas/ustedes dicen

HACER *(TO MAKE, TO DO)*	
yo hago	nosotros/as hacemos
tú haces	vosotros/as hacéis

HACER *(TO MAKE, TO DO)*

él/ella/usted hace	ellos/ellas/ustedes hacen

IR *(TO GO)*

yo voy	nosotros/as vamos
tú vas	vosotros/as vais
él/ella/usted va	ellos/ellas/ustedes van

PONER *(TO PUT)*

yo pongo	nosotros/as ponemos
tú pones	vosotros/as ponéis
él/ella/usted pone	ellos/ellas/ustedes ponen

QUERER *(TO WANT)*

yo quiero	nosotros/as queremos
tú quieres	vosotros/as queréis
él/ella/usted quiere	ellos/ellas/ustedes quieren

SALIR *(TO GO OUT)*

yo salgo	nosotros/as salimos
tú sales	vosotros/as salís
él/ella/usted sale	ellos/ellas/ustedes salen

TRAER *(TO BRING)*

yo traigo	nosotros/as traemos
tú traes	vosotros/as traéis
él/ella/usted trae	ellos/ellas/ustedes traen

Unit 4 Quiz

A. Let's practice irregular verbs. Write the correct form of the verb in parentheses.

1. Nosotros _____ muchas llamadas internacionales. (hacer)

2. Él _____ la llamada en espera. (poner)

3. Ustedes _____ el pasaporte al aeropuerto. (traer)

4. Vosotros _____ de la oficina tarde. (salir)

5. Yo _____ que tú eres una persona muy simpática. (decir)

6. Tú _____ al trabajo a las ocho de la mañana. (ir)

7. Usted _____ mucho a su familia. (querer)

8. Mario y Lupita _____ dolor de cabeza. (tener)

B. Choose the vocabulary word that best completes the blank.

1. Esta _____ (teléfono/línea) está ocupada.

2. Aquella cabina telefónica está _____ (operadora/libre).

3. Este _____ (mensaje/teléfono) no funciona.

4. Yo necesito marcar el _____ (número/archivo).

5. Quisiera _____ (hablar/hacer) una llamada internacional.

6. Este teléfono no funciona y éste _____ (también/tampoco).

7. Nuestra compañía tiene un _____ (sitio web/computadora) muy interesante.

8. La línea está ocupada y no tiene _____ (tono/tiempo).

C. Say the negative of each of the expressions below:

1. Este teléfono funciona. _____

2. Jorge come siempre. _____

3. Esta semana tengo dos reuniones importantes. _____

_____

4. Hay alguien de Canadá en mi oficina. _____

_____

5. Hay tono. _____

6. Hay conexión siempre. _____

7. Alguien llama por teléfono. _____

8. Yo tengo algo importante en mi computadora. _____

_____

D. Fill out the following chart with the corresponding demonstrative adjective.

	CLOSE TO THE SPEAKER	FAR FROM SPEAKER CLOSE TO THE LISTENER	FAR FROM BOTH
masc. sing.	este muchacho	1. _____ muchacho	2. _____ muchacho
masc. plural	3. _____ muchachos	esos muchachos	4. _____ muchachos
fem. sing.	5. _____ muchacha	6. _____ muchacha	aquella muchacha

	CLOSE TO THE SPEAKER	FAR FROM SPEAKER CLOSE TO THE LISTENER	FAR FROM BOTH
fem. plural	estas muchachas	7. _____ muchachas	8. _____ muchachas

How Did You Do?

Give yourself a point for every correct answer, then use the following key to determine whether or not you're ready to move on:

0–7 points: It's probably best to go back and study the lessons again to make sure you understood everything completely. Take your time; it's not a race! Make sure you spend time reviewing vocabulary with the flashcards and reading through each grammar note carefully.

8–16 points: If the questions you missed were in sections A or B, you may want to review the vocabulary again; if you missed answers mostly in sections C or D, check the unit essentials to make sure you have your conjugations and other grammar basics down.

17–20 points: Feel free to move on to the next unit! You're doing a great job.

 **points**

Unit 5:

Getting Around Town

In this unit, you'll learn how to ask for and give directions. You'll learn a lot of important vocabulary that will help you talk about running errands and getting around cities and towns.

By the end of this unit, you should be able to:

☐ Understand cardinal directions

☐ Distinguish between saber and conocer (*to know*)

☐ Name city landmarks

☐ Say *I can, I must*, and *I have to*

☐ Talk about traffic

☐ Express *to see, to come*, and *to give*

☐ Use phrases like *next to* and *across from* in directions

☐ Use the present progressive to express *I am eating, she is talking*

☐ Give someone directions and ask for directions

☐ Use some common prepositions to describe location

☐ Use some common prepositions of time

☐ Understand how other prepositions are used

☐ Use commands to tell someone to *go, see, work*, or *come*

☐ Understand the differences between para and por

Lesson 17: Words

By the end of this lesson, you should be able to:

☐ Understand cardinal directions

☐ Distinguish between saber and conocer (*to know*)

☐ Name city landmarks

☐ Say *I can*, *I must*, and *I have to*

Word Builder 1

▶ 17A Word Builder 1 (CD 6, Track 12)

norte	*north*
sur	*south*
este/oriente	*east*
oeste/occidente	*west*
izquierda	*left*
derecha	*right*
la carretera/la autopista/la autovía	*highway, freeway*
la salida	*exit*
el peaje	*toll*
el carril/la vía	*lane*
de sentido único	*one-way*
el mapa	*map*
el cruce	*intersection*
las afueras	*outskirts*
el pueblo	*town*

el subterráneo/el metro	subway/metro
el edificio	building
el edificio de apartamentos	apartment building

✎ Word Practice 1

Match the following directional words in Spanish to their English counterparts.

1. derecha   a. *left*

2. sur   b. *right*

3. izquierda   c. *north*

4. oeste   d. *south*

5. este   e. *east*

6. norte   f. *west*

ANSWER KEY
1. b; 2. d; 3. a; 4. f; 5. e; 6. c

Grammar Builder 1
SABER **AND** CONOCER **(TO KNOW)**

▷ 17B Grammar Builder 1 (CD 6, Track 13)

As you may remember from *Essential Spanish*, there are two different verbs that can be translated as *to know*: saber and conocer. They have different meanings and are not interchangeable. Let's start our review of these verbs with saber.

SABER *(TO KNOW)*	
yo sé	nosotros/as sabemos
tú sabes	vosotros/as sabéis
él/ella/usted sabe	ellos/ellas/ustedes saben

Saber and **Conocer** (*To Know*)

Ver (*To See*), Venir (*To Come*),
and **Dar** (*To Give*)

Poder (*Can*), Deber (*Must*),
and **Tener Que** (*To Have To*)

The Present Progressive

Saber means *to know* as in to know a fact, to know something thoroughly, or to know how to do something. It can be followed by a noun like su nombre (*her name*) or la respuesta (*the answer*), by que … (*that* …), donde … (*where* …), and cuando … (*when* …) to introduce facts, or by another verb in the infinitive, in which case it's translated as *to know how to*.

Saben mi nombre.
They know my name.

No sé la respuesta.
I don't know the answer.

Yo sé hablar francés.
I know how to speak French.

Ella sabe mucho sobre geografía.
She knows a lot about geography.

Nosotros sabemos que tienes un secreto.
We know that you have a secret.

Tú sabes dónde está la salida.
You know where the exit is.

Ustedes no saben cuándo parte el tren.
You don't know when the train leaves.

Now let's look again at conocer.

CONOCER *(TO KNOW)*	
yo conozco	nosotros/as conocemos
tú conoces	vosotros/as conocéis

CONOCER *(TO KNOW)*	
él/ella/usted conoce	ellos/ellas/ustedes conocen

Conocer means to know as in to know a person or to be familiar with something—a city, a book, a film, a restaurant, and so on. If the direct object of conocer is a person, don't forget to use the preposition a.

Conocemos a tus padres.
We know your parents.

Pedro conoce un restaurante italiano estupendo.
Pedro knows an excellent Italian restaurant.

Marta no conoce Nueva York.
Marta doesn't know New York./Marta isn't familiar with New York.

Yo conozco a mucha gente famosa.
I know many famous people.

Sometimes conocer can even be used to mean *to meet*, especially in the past tense, which you'll learn a bit later. But for now, learn the following expression.

Gusto en conocerle.
Pleased to meet you.

(II)

✎ Work Out 1

Complete the sentences with the correct form of either saber or conocer:

1. Nosotros no _____ la ciudad de Moscú.

2. Yo _____ bailar salsa.

3. ¿Vosotros _____ historia antigua?

4. Ella no _____ hablar alemán.

5. ¿(Tú) _____ a mi hermana Luisa?

6. Mi familia no _____ a mi esposo.

7. Ella no _____ esquiar.

8. Yo no _____ este restaurante.

ANSWER KEY

1. conocemos; 2. sé; 3. sabéis; 4. sabe; 5. Conoces; 6. conoce; 7. sabe; 8. conozco

Word Builder 2

▶ 17C Word Builder 2 (CD 6, Track 14)

la avenida	*avenue*
la calle	*street*
la cuadra/la manzana	*block*
la esquina	*corner*
la biblioteca	*library*
el restaurante	*restaurant*
la tienda	*store*
el parque	*park*
el banco	*bank*

la iglesia	church
el templo	temple
la mezquita	mosque
la acera/el anden	sidewalk
la panadería	bakery
la carnicería	butcher shop
la cafetería	café/coffee shop
la farmacia	drugstore/pharmacy
el supermercado	supermarket
la tienda de ropa	clothing store
la tienda por departamentos	department store
derecho	straight
el semáforo	traffic light
doblar	to turn
dar la vuelta	to turn around
ir a pie/caminar	to walk
seguir	to follow
el peatón	pedestrian

⓪

✎ Word Practice 2

Match the following words in Spanish to their English counterparts.

1. la tienda de ropa   a. *bakery*

2. el semáforo   b. *café/coffee shop*

3. la acera   c. *butcher shop*

4. la esquina   d. *traffic light*

5. la panadería   e. *corner*

Saber and Conocer (*To Know*)

Ver (*To See*), Venir (*To Come*),
and Dar (*To Give*)

Poder (*Can*), Deber (*Must*),
and Tener Que (*To Have To*)

The Present Progressive

6. la cafetería

7. la carnicería

8. el parque

9. la tienda

10. el peatón

f. *pedestrian*

g. *sidewalk*

h. *store*

i. *clothing store*

j. *park*

ANSWER KEY
1. i; 2. d; 3. g; 4. e; 5. a; 6. b; 7. c; 8. j; 9. h; 10. f

Grammar Builder 2
PODER (*CAN*), DEBER (*MUST*), AND TENER QUE (*TO HAVE TO*)

▶ 17D Grammar Builder 2 (CD 6, Track 15)

The verb poder means *can, to be able to,* or *to have permission to.*

PODER *(CAN)*	
yo puedo	nosotros/as podemos
tú puedes	vosotros/as podéis
él/ella/usted puede	ellos/ellas/ustedes pueden

Just like querer (*to want to*), it's followed by another verb in the infinitive.

¿Puedes esquiar?
Can you ski?

Yo puedo hablar chino.
I'm able to speak Chinese./I can speak Chinese.

¿Podemos usar su teléfono?
May we use your phone?

Aquí no podemos fumar.

We cannot smoke here.

Ella no puede trabajar con música.

She can't work while listening to music.

The verb deber means *must* or *to have to*. Deber is a regular -er verb.

DEBER *(MUST)*	
yo debo	nosotros/as debemos
tú debes	vosotros/as debéis
él/ella/usted debe	ellos/ellas/ustedes deben

Debo estudiar español.

I have to study Spanish.

Debemos entregar este informe hoy.

We have to submit this report today.

Spanish also uses the expression tener que + a verb in the infinitive, which is a bit stronger than using deber.

Tienen que comprar una nueva computadora.

They have to buy a new computer.

Tenéis que hacer las reservaciones de hotel esta tarde.

You have to make the hotel reservations this afternoon.

Ⓘ

Saber and Conocer (*To Know*)

Ver (*To See*), Venir (*To Come*),
and Dar (*To Give*)

Poder (*Can*), Deber (*Must*),
and Tener Que (*To Have To*)

The Present Progressive

✎ Work Out 2

Fill in the blanks with the correct form of the verb in parentheses.

1. _____ ir a la oficina esta tarde. (yo - tener)

2. ¿_____ hacer una llamada internacional? (nosotros - poder)

3. _____ partir a las siete y media. (nosotros - deber)

4. _____ hacer las reservaciones por Internet. (ustedes - poder)

5. _____ doblar a la izquierda. (usted - tener que)

6. _____ hablar con nuestro jefe. (nosotros - tener que)

7. ¿_____ salir temprano de la oficina hoy? (ustedes - poder)

8. _____ traer su pasaporte. (él - deber)

9. _____ hablar por teléfono en este momento. (ella - no poder)

10. _____ partir por la mañana. (usted - tener que)

ANSWER KEY
1. Tengo que; 2. Podemos; 3. Debemos; 4. Pueden; 5. Tiene que; 6. Tenemos que; 7. Pueden; 8. Debe; 9. No puede; 10. Tiene que

Take It Further

Here are a few expressions you'll often hear using saber and conocer.

no saber ni jota de algo
to not have a clue about something

¿Quién sabe?
Who knows?

¡Yo qué sé!
How do I know!?/How should I know!?

conocer palmo a palmo
to know like the back (lit., palm) of one's hand

No sé.
I don't know.

conocer de vista
to know by sight

dar a conocer
to make known

Conozco la ciudad de Nueva York palmo a plamo.
I know New York like the back of my hand.

Ella no sabe ni jota de álgebra.
She has no clue about algebra.

Conocemos a tu esposo de vista.
We know your husband by sight.

Saber and Conocer (*To Know*)

Ver (*To See*), Venir (*To Come*),
and Dar (*To Give*)

Poder (*Can*), Deber (*Must*),
and **Tener Que** (*To Have To*)

The Present Progressive

✎ Word Recall

Fill in the blanks with the correct form of the verb in parentheses.

1. Tú _____ escuchar con atención. (deber)

2. Tú _____ escuchar con atención. (poder)

3. Tú _____ escuchar con atención. (saber)

4. Tú _____ escuchar con atención (tener que)

5. Yo _____ tocar la guitarra eléctrica. (deber)

6. Yo _____ tocar la guitarra eléctrica. (poder)

7. Yo _____ tocar la guitarra eléctrica. (saber)

8. Yo _____ tocar la guitarra eléctrica. (tener que)

ANSWER KEY
1. debes; 2. puedes; 3. sabes; 4. tienes que; 5. debo; 6. puedo; 7. sé; 8. tengo que

How Did You Do?

By now, you should be able to:

☐ Understand cardinal directions
(Still unsure? Jump back to page 222.)

☐ Distinguish between saber and conocer (*to know*)
(Still unsure? Jump back to page 223.)

☐ Name city landmarks
(Still unsure? Jump back to page 226.)

☐ Say *I can, I must,* and *I have to*
(Still unsure? Jump back to page 228.)

Lesson 18: Phrases

By the end of this lesson, you should be able to:

☐ Talk about traffic

☐ Express *to see, to come,* and *to give*

☐ Use phrases like *next to* and *across from* in directions

☐ Use the present progressive to express *I am eating, she is talking*

Phrase Builder 1

▶ 18A Phrase Builder 1 (CD 6, Track 16)

Here are some phrases you can use when traveling by car.

¡Pare!/¡Alto!	*Stop!*
el embotellamiento	*traffic jam*
apagar las luces	*to turn off the lights*
pagar el peaje	*to pay the toll*
abrocharse el cinturón de seguridad	*to buckle up*
poner el pie en el freno	*to hit the brakes*
exceder el límite de velocidad	*to exceed the speed limit*
saltarse el semáforo	*to go through a light*
ir en dirección opuesta	*to go in the opposite direction*
reducir la velocidad	*to slow down*
pagar una multa	*to pay a fine*

Saber and Conocer (To Know)

Ver (To See), Venir (To Come),
and Dar (To Give)

Poder (Can), Deber (Must),
and Tener Que (To Have To)

The Present Progressive

✎ Phrase Practice 1

Fill in the appropriate Spanish verb in the following phrases.

1. _____ las luces *to turn off the lights*

2. _____ el peaje *to pay the toll*

3. _____ el cinturón de seguridad *to buckle up*

4. _____ el pie en el freno *to hit the brakes*

5. _____ el límite de velocidad *to exceed the speed limit*

6. _____ el semáforo *to go through a light*

7. _____ en dirección opuesta *to go in the opposite direction*

8. _____ la velocidad *to slow down*

9. _____ una multa *to pay a fine*

ANSWER KEY
1. apagar; 2. pagar; 3. abrocharse; 4. poner; 5. exceder; 6. saltarse; 7. ir; 8. reducir; 9. pagar

Grammar Builder 1
VER (TO SEE), VENIR (TO COME), AND DAR (TO GIVE)

▶ 18B Grammar Builder 1 (CD 6, Track 17)

In this section, we'll take a look at two more irregular verbs, venir (*to come*) and dar (*to give*). But first let's start with a review of ver, which you saw in Lesson 12.

VER (TO SEE)	
yo veo	nosotros/as vemos
tú ves	vosotros/as veis
él/ella/usted ve	ellos/ellas/ustedes ven

Ver means *to see*, but it is also used to mean *to watch*—for example, to watch TV, a play, a sports event, or a movie. You will also often hear Spanish speakers using the expression a ver, which literally means *let's see*.

A ella le gusta ver películas de horror.
She likes to watch horror movies.

Nosotros vemos televisión todas las noches.
We watch TV every evening.

A ver, la calle Alcalá está a dos cuadras de aquí.
Let's see, Alcalá Street is two blocks from here.

Veis/Ven un partido de tenis.
You are watching a tennis match.

The verb venir (*to come*) is an irregular verb.

VENIR *(TO COME)*	
yo vengo	nosotros/as venimos
tú vienes	vosotros/as venís
él/ella/usted viene	ellos/ellas/ustedes vienen

Notice that it's often used with the preposition de—take a look.

Ellos vienen de Brasil.
They come from Brazil.

Nosotros venimos de trabajar.
We're coming from work.

¿Vienes del supermercado?

Are you coming from the supermarket?

The verb dar (*to give*) is also an irregular verb.

DAR (*TO GIVE*)	
yo doy	nosotros/as damos
tú das	vosotros/as dais
él/ella/usted da	ellos/ellas/ustedes dan

Dar is used in a variety of common expressions.

dar (las) gracias	to give thanks
dar a luz	to give birth
dar con algo	to find something
dar de narices	to fall flat on one's face (lit., nose)
dar la hora	to tell time
dar la mano	to shake hands

Ella no quiere dar a luz en el hospital.

She doesn't want to give birth in the hospital.

El reloj da la hora exacta.

The clock shows/gives the exact time.

No me gusta dar la mano a personas extrañas.

I don't like to shake hands with strangers.

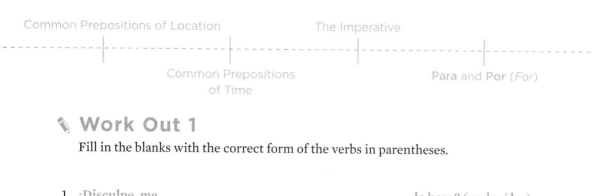

✎ Work Out 1

Fill in the blanks with the correct form of the verbs in parentheses.

1. ¿Disculpe, me _____ la hora? (poder/dar)

2. Mis abuelos _____ en el tren de las once. (venir)

3. Yo _____ una comedia esta noche. (querer/ver)

4. En su país las personas no _____ la mano. (dar)

5. No me _____ televisión. (gustar/ver)

6. Los padres _____ regalos a sus hijos en Navidad. (dar)

7. Yo _____ de la universidad. (venir)

8. Ellos _____ un partido de fútbol. (ver)

ANSWER KEY
1. puede dar; 2. vienen; 3. quiero ver; 4. dan; 5. gusta ver; 6. dan; 7. vengo; 8. ven

Phrase Builder 2

▶ 18C Phrase Builder 2 (CD 6, Track 18)

The following phrases will help you get around town and ask for directions.

cruzar la calle	*to cross the street*
caminar dos cuadras/manzanas	*to walk two blocks*
al lado de	*next to*
enfrente de	*in front of*
a mano izquierda	*on the left-hand side*
a mano derecha	*on the right-hand side*
en la esquina	*at the corner*
a la vuelta de la esquina	*around the corner*

Poder (*Can*), Deber (*Must*),
and Tener Que (*To Have To*)

The Present Progressive

| por el anden (por la acera) | *on the sidewalk* |
| por el callejón | *through the alley* |

Phrase Practice 2

Match the Spanish phrase to its English counterpart.

1. enfrente de
2. a la vuelta de la esquina
3. a mano derecha
4. en la esquina
5. al lado de
6. a mano izquierda

a. *next to*
b. *in front of*
c. *on the left-hand side*
d. *on the right-hand side*
e. *at the corner*
f. *around the corner*

ANSWER KEY
1. b; 2. f; 3. d; 4. e; 5.a; 6. c

Grammar Builder 2
THE PRESENT PROGRESSIVE

18D Grammar Builder 2 (CD 6, Track 19)

We've seen a lot of verbs in the simple present tense. But Spanish, like English, also has a present progressive tense, which expresses actions happening at the very moment you are speaking. The formation is similar to English: use the verb estar (*to be*) followed by the present participle, which is like the -*ing* form of the verb in English. The present participle is formed as follows.

For -ar verbs, take off the -ar and add -ando to the stem.

For -er and -ir verbs, take off the -er or -ir and add -iendo to the stem.

Estoy caminando por el callejón.
I'm walking through the alley.

Estás hablando por teléfono.
You're talking on the phone.

Está comiendo churros.
He/She is eating churros.

¿Usted está viendo televisión?
Are you watching TV?

Estamos dando las gracias.
We're giving thanks.

Estáis conociendo la ciudad.
You're getting to know the city.

No están escribiendo cartas.
They/You aren't writing letters.

There are, of course, a few irregular verbs that you will learn as we go along, and those irregularities may include the present participle. Here are the present participles of the irregular verbs we have seen so far.

VERB		PRESENT PARTICIPLE	
traer	*to bring*	trayendo	*bringing*
decir	*to say*	diciendo	*saying*
ir	*to go*	yendo	*going*
venir	*to come*	viniendo	*coming*
poder	*to be able to*	pudiendo	*being able to*

Saber and Conocer (*To Know*)

Ver (*To See*), Venir (*To Come*),
and Dar (*To Give*)

Poder (*Can*), Deber (*Must*),
and Tener Que (*To Have To*)

The Present Progressive

Unlike English, Spanish does not use this tense to express a future action. It is only used to talk about an action that is happening at the moment of speech. Here are a few time expressions you're likely to use with this tense.

ahora	*now*
ahora mismo	*right now*
en este momento	*at this moment*

✎ Work Out 2

Change the verbs in the following sentences from the simple present to the present progressive.

1. Cantamos en el coro de la iglesia. _____

2. Él envía un fax. _____

3. Ustedes dicen pocas palabras. _____

4. Visito la ciudad de Nueva York. _____

5. Ellos salen de la oficina. _____

6. Vosotros habláis con vuestro jefe. _____

7. ¿Lees el periódico? _____

_____

8. Él toma café. _____

_____

ANSWER KEY
1. Estamos cantando en el coro de la iglesia. 2. Él está enviando un fax. 3. Ustedes están diciendo pocas palabras. 4. Estoy visitando la ciudad de Nueva York. 5. Ellos están saliendo de la oficina. 6. Vosotros estáis hablando con vuestro jefe. 7. ¿Estás leyendo el periódico? 8. Él está tomando café.

Take It Further

Muletillas or frases de relleno (*filler words*) are used when the speaker doesn't know what to say next or is looking for a word. These phrases are the equivalents of the English filler words *well, um, you know, err,* and so on. Spanish speakers prefer to use words like este, pues, a ver, por así decir, es decir, vamos, or bueno. There is some regional variation in the use of Spanish filler phrases. People from Argentina, for example, are known around the world for using the word che at the beginning of their sentences, and Spaniards tend to use vamos fairly often. In many regions, the word mira or mire (*look*) is used to start a sentence.

Mire, el teatro queda a dos cuadras.
Look, the theater is two blocks away.

A ver, cruce la calle y doble a la derecha.
Let's see, cross the street and turn right.

Pues, es muy fácil.
Well, it's very easy.

✎ Word Recall

Form the present progressive with the subject and verb suggested.

1. Yo – hablar _____

2. Yo - beber _____

3. Yo - vivir _____

4. Yo - comer _____

5. Nosotros - bailar _____

6. Nosotros – poner _____

7. Nosotros - decir _____

8. Nosotros – traer _____

ANSWER KEY

1. Yo estoy hablando. 2. Yo estoy bebiendo. 3. Yo estoy viviendo. 4. Yo estoy comiendo. 5. Nosotros estamos bailando. 6. Nosotros estamos poniendo. 7. Nosotros estamos diciendo. 8. Nosotros estamos trayendo.

How Did You Do?

By now, you should be able to:

☐ Talk about traffic
(Still unsure? Jump back to page 233.)

☐ Express *to see*, *to come*, and *to give*
(Still unsure? Jump back to page 234.)

☐ Use phrases like *next to* and *across from* in directions
(Still unsure? Jump back to page 237.)

☐ Use the present progressive to express *I am eating*, *she is talking*
(Still unsure? Jump back to page 238.)

Lesson 19: Sentences

By the end of this lessson, you should be able to:

☐ Give someone directions and ask for directions

☐ Use some common prepositions to describe location

☐ Use some common prepositions of time

☐ Understand how other prepositions are used

Sentence Builder 1

▶ 19A Sentence Builder 1 (CD 6, Track 20)

Siga derecho hasta …	Go straight till …
Le agradezco mucho su ayuda.	Thanks a lot for your help. (lit., I thank you much for your help.)
¿Sabe cómo llegar a … ?	Do you know how to get to … ?
Aquí en el mapa está muy claro.	Here on the map, it is very clear.
Buen viaje.	Have a good trip.
Siga por el carril de la derecha.	Stay in the right lane.
A más o menos dos kilómetros hay un peaje.	At more or less two kilometers, there is a toll.
Tome la rampa en dirección …	Take the ramp towards …

✎ Sentence Practice 1

Fill in the blanks in the following sentences with the appropriate word or phrase.

1. _____ hasta ... *Go straight till ...*

2. _____ su ayuda. *Thanks for (lit., I thank you for) your help.*

3. ¿Sabe _____ ...? *Do you know how to get to ...?*

4. **Aquí en el mapa está** _____. *Here on the map, it is very clear.*

5. _____. *Have a good trip.*

6. _____ de la derecha. *Stay in the right lane.*

7. _____ hay un peaje. *At more or less two kilometers, there is a toll.*

8. **Tome la rampa** _____ ... *Take the ramp towards ...*

ANSWER KEY

1. **Siga derecho**; 2. **Le agradezco mucho**; 3. **cómo llegar a**; 4. **muy claro**; 5. **Buen viaje**; 6. **Siga por el carril**; 7. **A más o menos dos kilómetros**; 8. **en dirección**

Grammar Builder 1
COMMON PREPOSITIONS OF LOCATION

⊙ 19B Grammar Builder 1 (CD 6, Track 21)

Prepositions are those little words we use to connect other words in order to show spatial, temporal, or other kinds of relationships. Examples of prepositions are *on*, *in*, and *at*. In Spanish, prepositions function almost the same way as in

English, but their precise usage often has to be memorized. Let's first take a look at prepositions that show spatial relationships.

en	*in, on*
entre	*between*
delante de	*in front of*
enfrente de	*in front of*
detrás de	*behind*
debajo de	*underneath*
encima de	*on top of*
sobre	*above*
contra	*against*
cerca de	*close to*
lejos de	*far away from*
dentro de	*inside of*
fuera de	*outside of*

When showing spatial relationships, either estar or hay (*there is/are*) is typically used. Take a look at how the above prepositions are used in a sentence.

Madrid está en España.
Madrid is in Spain.

Antonio está sentado entre Marta y Alejandra.
Antonio is seated between Marta and Alejandra.

El teatro está delante de mi oficina.
The theater is in front of my office.

Hay un edificio alto enfrente de nuestra casa.
There's a tall building in front of our house.

Saber and Conocer (*To Know*)

Ver (*To See*), Venir (*To Come*),
and Dar (*To Give*)

Poder (*Can*), Deber (*Must*),
and Tener Que (*To Have To*)

The Present Progressive

La tienda está detrás del museo.
The shop is behind the museum.

Hay un gato debajo de la mesa.
There's a cat underneath the table.

El/La computador/a está encima del escritorio.
The computer is on top of the desk.

Hay dos lámparas sobre la cama.
There are two lamps above the bed.

El armario está contra la pared.
The closet is against the wall.

La universidad está cerca de aquí.
The university is close to here.

Su oficina está lejos de su casa.
His office is far away from his house.

Los huevos están dentro de la nevera.
The eggs are inside the refrigerator.

El museo está fuera de la ciudad.
The museum is outside of the city.

⏸

✎ Work Out 1

Replace each of the underlined prepositions with one that means the opposite.
For example, if you see debajo de (*underneath*), change it to encima de (*on top of*).

1. Delante del armario hay una puerta. _____

_____

2. Los turistas están dentro del museo. _____

_____

3. Mi familia vive lejos de mi casa. _____

_____

4. Enfrente de su casa hay un bar. _____

_____

5. El niño está debajo de la cama. _____

_____

6. Cerca de mi casa está la universidad. _____

_____

7. Los archivos están detrás de esos libros. _____

_____

8. Los documentos están dentro del sobre. _____

_____

ANSWER KEY

1. Detrás del armario hay una puerta. 2. Los turistas están fuera del museo. 3. Mi familia vive cerca de mi casa. 4. Detrás de su casa hay un bar. 5. El niño está encima de la cama. 6. Lejos de mi casa está la universidad. 7. Los archivos están enfrente de esos libros. 8. Los documentos están fuera del sobre.

Saber and Conocer (*To Know*)

Ver (*To See*), Venir (*To Come*),
and Dar (*To Give*)

Poder (*Can*), Deber (*Must*),
and Tener Que (*To Have To*)

The Present Progressive

Sentence Builder 2

▶ 19C Sentence Builder 2 (CD 6, Track 22)

El teatro está a mano izquierda.	*The theater is on the left-hand side.*
Seguid derecho por esta calle.	*Go straight down this street.*
¿Me puede decir cómo llegar a … ?	*Can you tell me how to get to … ?*
La entrada para visitantes está en la parte de atrás.	*The visitors' entrance is in back*
Queremos tomarnos un café para coger fuerzas.	*We want to have a cup of coffee to wake us up a bit (lit., to get some strength).*
En la esquina de la plaza hay un café.	*On the corner of the plaza there's a coffee place.*
Vamos, es muy fácil.	*Let's see—it's very easy.*
Ahí queda el teatro de la ópera.	*That's where the opera theater is located.*

⒤

✎ Sentence Practice 2

Fill in the blanks below with the appropriate word or phrase.

1. _____ a mano izquierda. *The theater is on the left-hand side.*

2. Seguid derecho _____. *Go straight down this street.*

3. ¿_____ cómo llegar a … ? *Can you tell me how to get to … ?*

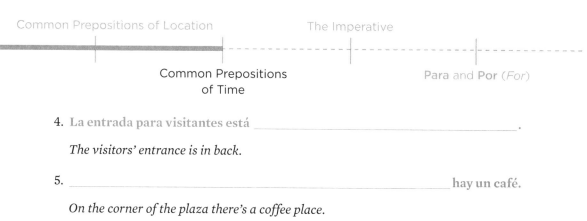
4. La entrada para visitantes está _____.

The visitors' entrance is in back.

5. _____ hay un café.

On the corner of the plaza there's a coffee place.

ANSWER KEY

1. El teatro está; 2. por esta calle; 3. Me puede decir; 4. en la parte de atrás; 5. En la esquina de la plaza

Grammar Builder 2
COMMON PREPOSITIONS OF TIME

▶ 19D Grammar Builder 2 (CD 6, Track 23)

Now let's look at some prepositions and phrasal prepositions of time.

antes de	*before*
después de	*after*
desde	*since, from*
durante	*during*
hasta	*until, till*

Antes de salir, leo el periódico.
Before leaving, I read the newspaper.

Después del trabajo, hacemos deporte.
After work, we play sports.

Desde esta mañana estoy trabajando en este proyecto.
I've been working (lit., I am working) on this project since this morning.

Desde este edificio podemos ver toda la ciudad.
From this building, we can see the entire city.

Están de vacaciones desde enero hasta abril.

They are on vacation from January till April.

Generalmente tomo una siesta durante el día.

I usually take a nap during the day.

¡Hasta mañana!

See you tomorrow!/Until tomorrow!

Take It Further

19E Take It Further (CD 6, Track 24)

Here are other common prepositions, some of which you already know.

a	to, at
con	with
de	of
hacia	toward
sin	without
sobre	about/on top of

The preposition a has several uses. First, it's a common preposition of motion.

Vamos a Caracas.

We're going to Caracas.

Ellos viajan a Chile todos los veranos.

They travel to Chile every summer.

In the last unit, you learned about the preposition a when it introduces a direct object that is a person. A is also used to introduce an indirect object, like the English *to*.

Ella da su comida a los pobres.
She gives her food to the poor.

Enviamos muchos mensajes a nuestros amigos.
We send many messages to our friends.

A is also used after certain verbs, such as aprender and comenzar.

Tengo que aprender a escribir a máquina.
I need to learn how to type.

Tengo que comenzar a estudiar com más frecuencia.
I need to start studying more often.

Some verbs are followed by de before an infinitive. Here are a few examples of common expressions using de + an infinitive.

acabar de hacer algo	to have just done something
tratar de hacer algo	to try to do something
cesar de hacer algo	to stop doing something

Juan acaba de salir de la oficina.
Juan just left the office.

Ella trata de aprender a esquiar.
She tries to learn how to ski.

Mi hija no cesa de llorar.
My daughter doesn't stop crying.

Finally, here are examples of how to use hacia, sin, and sobre:

Ellos van hacia Madrid.
They are going towards Madrid.

Me gusta el café sin azúcar.
I like coffee without sugar.

El libro es sobre turismo en España.
The book is about tourism in Spain.

✎ Work Out 2

Choose the preposition that best completes the sentence:

1. No queremos ir de viaje _____ nuestros hijos. (sobre, sin, a)

2. El mapa es _____ Carlos. (de, hacia, a)

3. _____ hoy estoy haciendo dieta. (hasta, antes de, desde)

4. _____ partir, quiero ir a la catedral otra vez. (después de, antes de, durante)

5. _____ la mañana bebo mucho café. (durante, sin, a)

6. Aprender _____ hablar otro idioma no es fácil. (de, a, con)

7. Tenemos que comenzar _____ preparar la presentación. (a, con, de)

8. El mensaje es _____ algo personal. (de, sobre, a)

ANSWER KEY

1. sin; 2. de; 3. Desde; 4. Antes de; 5. Durante; 6. a; 7. a; 8. sobre

 **Tip!**

When you're learning another language, it's not always easy to meet native speakers. But it's important to give yourself the chance to hear native speakers, even if you can't interact with them. Listening to the radio provides one opportunity to do that. Here are a few links that will help you find different radio stations in Spanish. The phrase that you should look for is escucha en vivo (listen direct/live):

www.radiocentro.com.mx (Mexico)
www.continental.com.ar (Argentina)
www.caracol.com.co (Colombia)
www.rtve.es/rne/envivo.htm (Spain)

Newspapers are also a great way to practice Spanish. A single site that will direct you to a huge number of newspapers from around the world, including, of course, Spanish-speaking countries, is **www.onlinenewspapers.com**. Just select the country that you're interested in.

Of course, you won't be able to follow everything that you read or hear at this point, but a good strategy is to look for stories that you're already familiar with, perhaps from English-language media. Alternatively, focus on a very small piece of real Spanish, maybe a paragraph or a very short audio clip, and read or listen along with a dictionary as many times as it takes to really become familiar with it. Just be patient, and be adventurous. You'll be surprised at how easy it is to practice your new language online!

✎ Word Recall

A. Give the opposite of the following prepositions:

1. antes de _____

2. lejos de _____

3. encima de _____

4. delante de _____

B. Now choose the preposition that best completes the sentence:

1. California está _____ (en/encima de) México.

2. Yo voy al parque _____ (a/con) mi amigo.

3. Yo voy al gimnasio _____ (lejos de/durante) la tarde.

4. Mi casa está _____ (entre/fuera) la casa de la familia López y la casa de la familia Pérez.

ANSWER KEY
A. 1. después de; 2. cerca de; 3. debajo de; 4. detrás de
B. 1. encima de; 2. con; 3. durante; 4. entre

How Did You Do?

By now, you should be able to:

☐ Give someone directions and ask for directions
(Still unsure? Jump back to page 243.)

☐ Use some common prepositions to describe location
(Still unsure? Jump back to page 244.)

☐ Use some common prepositions of time
(Still unsure? Jump back to page 249.)

☐ Understand how other prepositions are used
(Still unsure? Jump back to page 250.)

Lesson 20: Conversations

By the end of this lesson, you should be able to:

☐ Use commands to tell someone to go, see, work, or come

☐ Understand the differences between para and por

Conversation 1

▶ 20A Conversation 1 (CD 6, Track 25 - Spanish Only; Track 26 - Spanish and English)

Alfonso and Luisa are on their honeymoon in Madrid. Today they're going to visit the palace of El Escorial, in the foothills of the Sierra de Guadarrama to the northwest of Madrid. Alfonso is asking the hotel receptionist for driving directions.

Recepcionista:	Este … ¿Sabe cómo llegar a la Gran Vía?
Alfonso:	Sí, claro que sí. Hasta ahí no me pierdo.
Recepcionista:	Bien. Pues siga derecho por la Gran Vía, luego tome la Avenida de la Victoria. Siga derecho hasta la salida número seis.
Alfonso:	Aquí tengo un mapa. A ver … sí, aquí está: salida seis, autovía del Noreste, ¿verdad?
Recepcionista:	Exactamente. Siga por ahí hasta la salida dieciocho. Siga por el carril de la derecha y tome la rampa en dirección Las Rosas/El Escorial.
Alfonso:	Pues, es muy fácil. Aquí en el mapa está muy claro.
Recepcionista:	A más o menos dos kilómetros hay un peaje.
Alfonso:	¿Cuánto hay que pagar?
Recepcionista:	Mire … No sé. Pero no es mucho. Cuando pase el peaje, doble a la izquierda. El Escorial no está muy lejos de ahí.
Alfonso:	Bueno, le agradezco mucho su ayuda.

| Recepcionista: | De nada. Buen viaje. |
| Alfonso: | Gracias. |

Hotel clerk:	Well … Do you know how to get to the Gran Vía?
Alfonso:	Yes, of course. Up to there I won't get lost.
Hotel clerk:	Good. Then, go straight along the Gran Vía, then take the Avenida de la Victoria. Go straight until exit number 6.
Alfonso:	I have a map here. Let's see … yes, here it is: Exit 6, Northeast highway, is that right?
Hotel clerk:	Exactly. Go down through there until exit 18. Take the right lane up the ramp towards "Las Rosas/El Escorial."
Alfonso:	Well, it's very easy. Here on the map, it is very clear.
Hotel clerk:	At about two kilometers, there's a toll.
Alfonso:	How much is it?
Hotel clerk:	Hmm, I don't know. But it's not much. Once you pass the toll, make a left turn. The Escorial is not far from there.
Alfonso:	Well, thank you very much for your help.
Hotel clerk:	Not at all. Have a good trip.
Alfonso:	Thank you.

🌐 Culture Note

The Royal Monastery of San Lorenzo del Escorial was built between 1563 and 1584 for Felipe II and is traditionally believed to have been built in honor of St. Lawrence. Its severe and non-ornamental style became one of the most influential in Spain. The palace is a monastery, a museum, a library, and the burial place of Spanish sovereigns. The complex is a UNESCO world heritage site.

There are many myths about the Sierra de Guadarrama, the mountains to the northwest of Madrid. One such myth, known as La Sima de los Pastores (*the Shepherd's Chasm*), tells of a hidden treasure buried in one of the mountains. It is believed that a certain Rafael Corraliza, who was in charge of the financial

affairs of the monastery, decided one day to run off to Portugal with the treasure. He took a route that he thought would be less guarded towards the town of Robledondo. It was already dark, and when he reached the area known as Sima de los Pastores, he was swallowed by the earth, treasure and all. It is said that St. Lawrence had something to do with this, and with time, the abyss was covered with rocks and leaves to prevent something similar from ever happening again.

✎ Conversation Practice 1

Fill in the blanks below with the appropriate word based on the English translation and the dialogue above.

1. **Pues por la Gran Vía,** _____ **la Avenida de la Victoria.**

   Then, go straight along the Gran Vía, then take the Avenida de la Victoria.

2. **Siga derecho** _____ **la salida número seis.** *Go straight until exit number 6.*

3. **Aquí en** _____ **está muy claro.** *Here on the map, it is very clear.*

4. **Cuando pase el peaje,** _____.

   Once you pass the toll, make a left turn.

5. **El Escorial no está muy** _____ **de ahí.** *The Escorial is not far from there.*

   ANSWER KEY

   1. luego tome; 2. hasta; 3. el mapa; 4. doble a la izquierda; 5. lejos

Grammar Builder 1
THE IMPERATIVE

▶ 20B Grammar Builder 1 (CD 6, Track 27)

Let's look at the imperative, or command form, which you would use, for instance, when giving directions.

Because there are different ways of expressing *you* in Spanish, there are different command forms, informal and formal, corresponding to **tú**, **usted**, **vosotros**, and **ustedes**. For the **tú** (infml.) command forms, just take the final -s off the present **tú** form of a regular verb. For example, from **tú hablas** (*you speak*), the imperative is **habla** (*speak*). In the same way, **comer** (*to eat*) becomes **come** (*eat*) and **escribir** (*to write*) becomes **escribe** (*write*). There are, of course, some irregular verbs. Here are a few.

salir (*to leave, to go out*)	**sal** (*leave, go out*)
decir (*to say, to tell*)	**di** (*say, tell*)
venir (*to come*)	**ven** (*come*)
hacer (*to do, to make*)	**haz** (*do, make*)
tener (*to have*)	**ten** (*have*)
poner (*to put*)	**pon** (*put*)
ver (*to see*)	**ve** (*see*)
ir (*to go*)	**ve** (*go*)

The command with **vosotros** (also informal) is even easier. Just take the infinitive form of the verb, drop the final -r, and add a -d. This works for all verbs. So **hablar** becomes **hablad**, **comer** becomes **comed**, **escribir** becomes **escribid**, **decir** becomes **decid**, **poner** becomes **poned**, and so on.

Let's now take a look at how to make formal commands with **usted** and **ustedes**. Take the present form of the first person singular (**yo**) of the verb, drop the final -o, and add -e or -en for -ar verbs, and add -a or -an for -er and -ir verbs.

TRABAJAR *(TO WORK)*	
(usted) trabaje	*work (sg.)*
(ustedes) trabajen	*work (pl.)*

COMER *(TO EAT)*	
(usted) coma	*eat (sg.)*
(ustedes) coman	*eat (pl.)*

ESCRIBIR *(TO WRITE)*	
(usted) escriba	*write (sg.)*
(ustedes) escriban	*write (pl.)*

As usual, there are a few irregular verbs.

saber *(to know)*	sepa, sepan
ser *(to be)*	sea, sean
ir *(to go)*	vaya, vayan
dar *(to give)*	dé, den
estar *(to be)*	esté, estén

Ⓘ

✎ Work Out 1

Rephrase each sentence as a command.

1. Tienes que llamar a mi secretaria. _____

   _____

2. Tenéis que partir a las seis de la mañana. _____

   _____

3. Tienen que hacer las reservaciones por Internet. _____

   _____

4. Tienes que caminar dos cuadras y doblar a la derecha. _____

_____

5. Tiene que enviar el informe hoy por la tarde. _____

_____

6. Tenéis que decir la verdad. _____

_____

7. Tienes que contestar el mensaje. _____

_____

8. Tenéis que seguir derecho por esta calle. _____

_____

9. Tiene que llamar a Marta a las diez en punto. _____

_____

10. Tienen que regresar temprano. _____

_____

ANSWER KEY

1. Llama a mi secretaria. 2. Partid a las seis de la mañana. 3. Hagan las reservaciones por Internet.
4. Camina dos cuadras y dobla a la derecha. 5. Envíe el informe hoy por la tarde. 6. Decid la verdad.
7. Contesta el mensaje. 8. Seguid derecho por esta calle. 9. Llame a Marta a las diez en punto.
10. Regresen temprano.

Conversation 2

20C Conversation 2 (CD 6, Track 28 - Spanish Only; Track 29 - Spanish and English)

Alfonso and Luisa are now at la Puerta del Sol in Madrid. They are lost, and Luisa is asking a woman on the street for directions to el Palacio Real.

Luisa:	Disculpe, ¿nos puede decir cómo llegar al Palacio Real?
Señora:	Vamos, es muy fácil. Está a unas pocas cuadras de aquí. Seguid derecho por esta calle que se llama Calle del Arenal hasta llegar a la plaza.
Luisa:	Ahí queda el teatro de la ópera, ¿no?
Señora:	Sí, el teatro está a mano izquierda. Tenéis que seguir por ahí e inmediatamente doblar a mano derecha y continuar por una calle muy pequeña ... no recuerdo el nombre.
Luisa:	No importa. Podemos preguntar a alguien.
Señora:	Desde allí se puede ver la Plaza de Oriente. El palacio está en frente. Y la entrada para visitantes está en la parte de atrás.
Luisa:	Muchas gracias.
Señora:	Si queréis tomar un café para coger fuerzas, hay una cafetería que está muy bien en la esquina de la plaza a mano izquierda.
Luisa:	Con este frío, creo que un chocolate con churros es mejor idea.
Señora:	¡Vamos, en este lugar los churros son deliciosos!

Luisa:	*Excuse me, could you please tell us how to get to the Royal Palace?*
Woman:	*It's very easy. It's a few blocks away from here. Go straight down this street, which is called Calle del Arenal, until you reach the square.*
Luisa:	*The opera theater is there, isn't it?*
Woman:	*Yes, the theater is on the left-hand side. You have to go through there and immediately turn right and go along a very short street ... I don't remember its name.*
Luisa:	*It doesn't matter. We can ask someone.*

Woman:	From there, you can see the Plaza de Oriente. The palace is in front. And the visitors' entrance is in back.
Luisa:	Many thanks.
Woman:	If you'd like to have a coffee to pick yourself up (lit., regain strength) to go on, there's a café on the corner on the left-hand side that is pretty good.
Luisa:	It's so cold, I think a chocolate with churros is a better idea.
Woman:	Well, at this place, the churros are delicious!

⊕ Culture Note

La Puerta del Sol (the Gateway of the Sun) is Madrid's center square, one of the busiest points and one of the city's most popular meeting places. The square marks the site of the original eastern entrance to the city through a gatehouse in a castle. These have long since disappeared, and in their place there has been a succession of churches. In the late nineteenth century, the area was turned into a square, becoming the center of café society. Shaped like a half-moon, the square features a red brick building with a clock tower, which is the focus of the city's New Year's Eve celebration. Crowds fill the square on that day, and at midnight, people swallow a single grape with each toll of the bell. According to tradition, this is supposed to bring good luck throughout the year.

The Palacio Real (Royal Palace) is no longer used as a residence for the royal family, who live instead in the Palacio de la Zarzuela, a more modest palace outside Madrid. The Royal Palace, lavish and built to impress, is used for state occasions. Construction lasted twenty-six years, and its decor reflects the exuberant tastes of two Bourbon kings: Charles III and Charles IV.

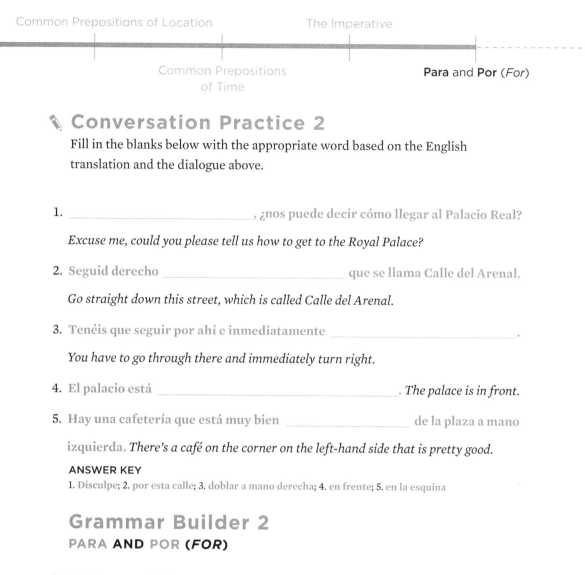

✎ Conversation Practice 2

Fill in the blanks below with the appropriate word based on the English translation and the dialogue above.

1. _____, ¿nos puede decir cómo llegar al Palacio Real?

   Excuse me, could you please tell us how to get to the Royal Palace?

2. Seguid derecho _____ que se llama Calle del Arenal.

   Go straight down this street, which is called Calle del Arenal.

3. Tenéis que seguir por ahí e inmediatamente _____.

   You have to go through there and immediately turn right.

4. El palacio está _____. *The palace is in front.*

5. Hay una cafetería que está muy bien _____ de la plaza a mano

   izquierda. *There's a café on the corner on the left-hand side that is pretty good.*

   ANSWER KEY
   1. Disculpe; 2. por esta calle; 3. doblar a mano derecha; 4. en frente; 5. en la esquina

Grammar Builder 2
PARA **AND** POR **(*FOR*)**

▶ 20D Grammar Builder 2 (CD 6, Track 30)

You've probably already seen the prepositions para and por in the dialogues. Both of them are usually translated into English as *for*, but they have different uses.

Para indicates a purpose (*in order to*), an intention (*intended for*), a limit in time (*by/until a certain time*), or a destination (*towards*). Note that when used to show an intention, para is followed by a verb in the infinitive. Here are a few examples.

Saber and Conocer (*To Know*)

Ver (*To See*), Venir (*To Come*),
and Dar (*To Give*)

Poder (*Can*), Deber (*Must*),
and Tener Que (*To Have To*)

The Present Progressive

Esta carta es para Julián.
This letter is for Julián.

Este nuevo programa es para hacer diseños gráficos.
This new program is for making graphic designs.

Necesitamos el informe para mañana a las nueve en punto.
We need the report by tomorrow morning at nine o'clock.

Voy para Cuernavaca.
I'm going to Cuernavaca.

On the other hand, **por** is used to indicate cause or reason (*because of, due to*), a length of time (*for*), or to indicate exchange (*in place of, in exchange for*). It can also mean *through.*

El viaje está cancelado por la tormenta.
The trip is canceled because of the storm.

Necesito cambiar unos dólares por pesos.
I need to exchange some dollars for pesos.

El hombre salió por esa puerta.
The man left through that door.

Pasamos por Miami de camino a Chile.
We went through Miami on our way to Chile.

Queremos una habitación por diez noches.
We want a room for ten nights.

✎ Work Out 2

Take a look at the following sentences and decide what preposition you would use in Spanish.

1. Puedes cambiar el suéter _____ otro en una talla más grande.

   (*You can exchange the sweater for another one in a bigger size.*)

2. Tenemos que terminar el proyecto _____ la próxima semana.

   (*We have to finish the project by next week.*)

3. El regalo es _____ su hermana. (*The present is for her sister.*)

4. Ella está mirando _____ la ventana. (*She is looking through the window.*)

5. Ella está ahorrando _____ comprar una casa.

   (*She is saving in order to buy a house.*)

6. Ellos están partiendo _____ Londres. (*They are leaving for London.*)

7. _____ su retraso, no podemos empezar la conferencia.

   (*Because of his delay, we cannot begin the conference.*)

8. Queremos alquilar el apartamento _____ tres años.

   (*We want to rent the apartment for three years.*)

ANSWER KEY
1. por; 2. para; 3. para; 4. por; 5. para; 6. para; 7. Por; 8. por

---

Take It Further

Learning por and para is, again, a question of practice and being very patient with yourself. Just remember that it is not a big deal if you get these prepositions wrong. Most people will appreciate your effort and won't mind the mistakes you make.

To help you a bit, here are some colloquial expressions that you will often hear using por. Try to familiarize yourself with them, and experiment with using them from time to time.

¡Por Dios!	*For God's sake!*
¡Por fin!	*At last!*
por lo visto	*apparently*
por eso	*for this reason*
por lo tanto	*therefore*
por desgracia	*unfortunately*
por una parte	*on the one hand*
por otra parte	*on the other hand*
por supuesto	*of course*
por casualidad	*by chance*

Por lo visto el vuelo está retrasado.
Apparently, the flight is delayed.

Nos encontramos con María por casualidad.
We bumped into María by chance.

Por desgracia no podemos viajar mañana.
Unfortunately, we can't travel tomorrow.

✎ Word Recall

The following sentences are informal commands in the tú form. Turn them into formal commands by using the usted form.

1. Habla español ahora. _____

2. Toma una siesta. _____

3. Camina hasta mi casa. _____

4. Trabaja más. _____

5. Escribe en la computadora. _____

6. Bebe más vino. _____

ANSWER KEY

1. Hable español ahora. 2. Tome una siesta. 3. Camine hasta mi casa. 4. Trabaje más. 5. Escriba en la computadora. 6. Beba más vino.

How Did You Do?

By now, you should be able to:

☐ Use commands to tell someone to *go*, *see*, *work*, or *come*
(Still unsure? Jump back to page 257.)

☐ Understand the differences between para and por
(Still unsure? Jump back to page 263.)

Don't forget to practice and reinforce what you've learned by visiting **www.livinglanguage.com/languagelab** for flashcards, games, and quizzes for Unit 5!

Unit 5 Essentials

Vocabulary Essentials

DIRECTIONAL VOCABULARY

	north
	south
	east
	west
	left
	right

[Pg. 222]

DRIVING VOCABULARY

	highway, freeway
	exit
	toll
	lane
	one-way
	map
	intersection

[Pg. 222]

OTHER WORDS AROUND TOWN

	outskirts
	town
	subway/metro
	building
	apartment building

[Pg. 222]

TOWN FEATURES

	avenue
	street
	block
	corner
	traffic light
	pedestrian

[Pg. 226]

PLACES AROUND TOWN

	library
	restaurant
	store
	park
	bank
	church
	temple
	mosque

	sidewalk
	bakery
	butcher shop
	café/coffee shop
	drugstore/pharmacy
	supermarket
	clothing store
	department store

[Pg. 226]

VERBS AND ADJECTIVES FOR GETTING AROUND TOWN

	straight
	to turn
	to turn around
	to walk
	to follow

[Pg. 227]

DRIVING EXPRESSIONS

	Stop!
	traffic jam
	to turn off the lights
	to pay the toll
	to buckle up
	to hit the brakes
	to exceed the speed limit

	to go through a light
	to go in the opposite direction
	to slow down
	to pay a fine

[Pg. 233]

EXPRESSIONS USING DAR

	to give thanks
	to give birth
	to find something
	to fall flat on one's face (lit., nose)
	to tell time
	to shake hands

[Pg. 236]

DIRECTIONAL EXPRESSIONS

	to cross the street
	to walk two blocks
	next to
	in front of
	on the left-hand side
	on the right-hand side
	at the corner
	around the corner
	on the sidewalk
	through the alley

[Pg. 237]

MORE DIRECTIONAL EXPRESSIONS

	Go straight till …
	Thanks for (lit., I thank you for) your help.
	Do you know how to get to … ?
	Here on the map, it is very clear.
	Have a good trip.
	Stay in the right lane.
	At more or less two kilometers, there is a toll.
	Take the ramp towards …
	The theater is on the left-hand side.
	Go straight down this street.
	Can you tell me how to get to … ?
	The visitors' entrance is in back.

[Pg. 243, Pg. 248]

EXPRESSIONS USING POR

	For God's sake!
	At last!
	apparently
	for this reason
	therefore
	unfortunately
	on the one hand
	on the other hand
	of course

	by chance

[Pg. 266]

Grammar Essentials

THE PRESENT PROGRESSIVE

The present progressive is formed as follows in Spanish:

estar (*to be*) + present participle

To form the present participle:

For -ar verbs, take off the -ar and add -ando to the stem.

For -er and -ir verbs, take off the -er or -ir and add -iendo to the stem.

IRREGULAR PRESENT PARTICIPLES

VERB	PRESENT PARTICIPLE
traer (*to bring*)	trayendo
decir (*to say*)	diciendo
ir (*to go*)	yendo
venir (*to come*)	viniendo
poder (*to be able to*)	pudiendo

COMMON PREPOSITIONS OF LOCATION

en	*in, on*
entre	*between*
delante de	*in front of*
enfrente de	*in front of*
detrás de	*behind*
debajo de	*underneath*
encima de	*on top of*

sobre	above
contra	against
cerca de	close to
lejos de	far away from
dentro de	inside of
fuera de	outside of

COMMON PREPOSITIONS OF TIME

antes de	before
después de	after
desde	since, from
durante	during
hasta	until, till

OTHER COMMON PREPOSITIONS

a	to, at
con	with
de	of
hacia	toward
sin	without
sobre	about/on top of

THE IMPERATIVE

	FAMILIAR	SINGULAR POLITE	PLURAL POLITE
comer (to eat)	(tú) come	(usted) coma	(ustedes) coman
dar (to give)	da	dé	den

	FAMILIAR	SINGULAR POLITE	PLURAL POLITE
decir *(to say, to tell)*	di	diga	digan
escribir *(to write)*	escribe	escriba	escriban
estar *(to be)*	está	esté	estén
hacer *(to do, to make)*	haz	haga	hagan
ir *(to go)*	ve	vaya	vayan
poner *(to put)*	pon	ponga	pongan
saber *(to know)*	sabe	sepa	sepan
salir *(to leave, to go out)*	sal	salga	salgan
ser *(to be)*	sé	sea	sean
tener *(to have)*	ten	tenga	tengan
trabajar *(to work)*	trabaja	trabaje	trabajen
venir *(to come)*	ven	venga	vengan
ver *(to see)*	ve	vea	vean

PARA **AND** POR

1. Para indicates a purpose (*in order to*), an intention (*intended for*), a limit in time (*by/until a certain time*), a length of time (*for*), or a destination (*towards*). When used to show intention, para is followed by a verb in the infinitive.

2. Por is used to indicate cause or reason (*because of, due to*), or to indicate exchange (*in place of, in exchange for*). It can also mean *through*.

VERBS

CONOCER *(TO KNOW A PERSON OR TO BE FAMILIAR WITH SOMETHING)*	
yo conozco	nosotros/as conocemos
tú conoces	vosotros/as conocéis
él/ella/usted conoce	ellos/ellas/ustedes conocen

DAR (TO GIVE)

yo doy	nosotros/as damos
tú das	vosotros/as dais
él/ella/usted da	ellos/ellas/ustedes dan

DEBER (MUST)

yo debo	nosotros/as debemos
tú debes	vosotros/as debéis
él/ella/usted debe	ellos/ellas/ustedes deben

PODER (CAN)

yo puedo	nosotros/as podemos
tú puedes	vosotros/as podéis
él/ella/usted puede	ellos/ellas/ustedes pueden

SABER (TO KNOW A FACT, TO KNOW HOW TO DO SOMETHING)

yo sé	nosotros/as sabemos
tú sabes	vosotros/as sabéis
él/ella/usted sabe	ellos/ellas/ustedes saben

VENIR (TO COME)

yo vengo	nosotros/as venimos
tú vienes	vosotros/as venís
él/ella/usted viene	ellos/ellas/ustedes vienen

Unit 5 Quiz

A. Match the column on the left with its appropriate English counterpart on the right.

1. el peaje   a. *right*

2. la derecha   b. *corner*

3. las afueras   c. *sidewalk*

4. la biblioteca   d. *toll*

5. la esquina   e. *lights*

6. las luces   f. *butcher shop*

7. la carnicería   g. *outskirts*

8. la acera   h. *library*

B. Form the present progressive of the following sentences.

1. Mi amiga Brenda habla español. _____

_____

2. Yo como churros. _____

_____

3. Nosotros damos las gracias. _____

_____

4. Usted ve la televisión con su familia. _____

_____

5. Ustedes pagan el peaje. _____

_____

6. Ernesto y yo apagamos las luces. _____

_____

7. Mis amigos esquían muy bien. _____

_____

8. Su hija cruza la calle. _____

_____

C. Translate each of the following sentences.

1. *The theater is in front of the bakery.* _____

_____

2. *There's a museum next to the library.* _____

_____

3. *The bank is at the corner.* _____

_____

4. *The pharmacy is behind the supermarket.* _____

_____

5. *There's a book under the table.* _____

_____

D. Choose the vocabulary word that best fits each sentence.

1. El opuesto del norte es el _____ (este/sur).

2. El opuesto de la izquierda es la _____ (derecha/salida).

3. Tú vives en una ciudad grande pero yo vivo en un _____

   (pueblo/cruce) pequeño.

4. Yo _____ (sé/conozco) el nombre del artista.

5. Yo _____ (sé/conozco) al tío de Pepe.

6. La casa está en la _____ (iglesia/esquina).

7. Yo compro ropa en _____ (el parque/la tienda).

8. La comida es muy buena en ese _____ (restaurante/banco).

How Did You Do?

Give yourself a point for every correct answer, then use the following key to determine whether or not you're ready to move on:

0-7 points: It's probably best to go back and study the lessons again to make sure you understood everything completely. Take your time; it's not a race! Make sure you spend time reviewing vocabulary with the flashcards and reading through each grammar note carefully.

8-16 points: If the questions you missed were in sections A or B, you may want to review the vocabulary again; if you missed answers mostly in sections C or D, check the unit essentials to make sure you have your conjugations and other grammar basics down.

17-20 points: Feel free to move on to the next level! You're doing a great job.

 points

Pronunciation Guide

If you've ever had trouble with English spelling, or if you've ever come across an unfamiliar word and had no idea how to pronounce it, you'll be happy to know that neither of these things is likely to be an issue in Spanish. Spanish spelling is phonetic, meaning that things are pronounced the way they're written. The rules for stress—which SYL-la-ble gets the EM-pha-sis—are very regular in Spanish, and any irregularities are marked in spelling with an accent mark. We'll cover all of that little by little, but let's get started with an overview of Spanish pronunciation.

1. VOWELS

Each vowel in Spanish is pronounced clearly and distinctly, and each vowel has one and only one pronunciation. A vowel may be written with an accent, as in sí or América, but this never changes the pronunciation of that vowel. It may mark stress, as in América, or it may only serve to distinguish between two words, as in sí (*yes*) and si (*if*). Let's look at each vowel, starting with simple vowels.

a	like *a* in *father*	a, amigo, la, las, pan, habla, Santiago
e	like *ay* in *day*, but cut off before the *ee*	él, de, en, padre, tren, este, Mercedes
i	like *i* in *police*	mí, amiga, hiciste, cinco, Chile, Sevilla
o	like *o* in *no*, but cut off before the *oo*	no, dos, hombre, costar, ocho, teléfono, Colombia
u	like *u* in *rule*	uno, tú, mucho, azúcar, Honduras, puro

Vowels can also appear in pairs, which are called diphthongs. A diphthong is usually a combination of a weaker vowel (i or u) and a more prominent one.

ai, ay	like *i* in *bide*	aire, hay, traigo, ¡ay!

au	like *ou* in *house*	restaurante, autobús, automóvil, Mauricio
ei, ey	like *ay* in *day*	seis, ley, treinta, rey
ia, ya	like *ya* in *yard*	gracias, comercial, estudiar, ya
ie, ye	like *ye* in *yet*	pie, quiero, tiene, yerba, abyecto
io, yo	like *yo* in *yoga*	yo, acción, despacio, estudio
iu, yu	like *u* in *united*	ciudad, yuca, yugo, yunta
oi, oy	like *oy* in *toy*	estoy, hoy, oiga, voy
ua	like *wa* in *want*	cuatro, Juan, ¿cuál?, ¿cuánto?
ue	like *we* in *west*	nueve, fuego, puerta, cuesta, bueno
uo	like *wo* in *woe*	continuo, antiguo, mutuo, superfluo
ui, uy	like *we* in *week*	muy, ruido, cuidado, huir

2. CONSONANTS

b	like *b* in *boy* at the beginning of a word	bueno, brazo, bajo, barca, bocadillo
b	between vowels for some speakers, as above, but the lips don't touch	Cuba, haber, beber, cobayo, deber, ubicar
c	like *k* in *kite* before consonants, a, o, and u	Cristóbal, cosa, casa, cuánto, cuál, truco

c	like *s* in *sea* before e and i	cerca, servicio, cierto, fácil, posición
ch	like *ch* in *choose*	charlar, chico, muchacho, ocho, mucho
d	at the beginning of a word or after n, like *d* in *day*, but with the tongue touching the back of the upper teeth	día, despegar, durante, cuándo, donde, mando
d	between vowels, like *th* in *thin*	media, nada, todo, poder, freiduría, prometido
f	like *f* in *father*	familia, Francisco, Federico, formulario
g	like *g* in *go* before consonants, a, o, and u	grande, Gloria, gustar, gusano, goloso, ganar, vengo
g	like the strong *h* in *hope* before e or i	general, Gibraltar, girar, rígido, urgente
gü	like *gw* in *Gwen*	vergüenza, lengüeta, cigüeña
h	silent	hablo, hay, hubo, ahora, hombre, deshonroso
j	like the strong *h* in *hope*	julio, jabón, mejor, José, tarjeta, jefe, trujar
ll	like *y* in *yes*	llamo, pollo, llama, llover, allí, llaves, trulla
m	like *m* in *met*	mismo, Marco, mano, Manuel, pluma, mandar

n	like *n* in *not*	nunca, no, Nicaragua, Argentina, nombre
ñ	like *ni* in *onion*	español, mañana, muñeca, ñame, gañir
p	like *p* in *pear*	para, pueblo, postre, Panamá, Perú
qu	like *k* in *kite*	que, querer, paquete, saquen, quemar, quizás
r	at the beginning of a word, a trilled sound made with the tongue against the ridge behind the upper teeth	rico, rubio, Ramón, Rosa, rincón, red, risa
r	otherwise like the tapped *d* in *ladder*	América, pero, quisiera, aire, libre, brazo, caro
rr	like word-initial r, a trilled sound made with the tongue against the ridge behind the upper teeth	perro, carro, tierra, horror, irritar, terrible
s	like *s* in *see* (never like *z* in *zone*)	casa, sucio, San Salvador, soltero, vasto, rosa
t	like *t* in *take*, but with the tongue touching the back of the upper teeth	tocar, fruta, tú, teclado, traje, tener
v	like *b* in *boy* at the beginning of a word	vaso, veinte, vivir, vivo, veramente
y	like *y* in *yes*; on its own, like *ee* in *teen*	ayer, ayudo, Bayamo, poyo

z	like *s* in *see*	zona, diez, luz, marzo, azul, azúcar

3. STRESS

There are three simple rules to keep in mind when it comes to stress. First, if a word ends in any consonant other than -n or -s, the last syllable receives the stress.

cuidad, capaz, notabilidad, navegar, familiar, refrigerador

Second, if a word ends in a vowel or in -n or -s, the penultimate (second-to-last) syllable receives the stress.

amigo, hablan, derechos, cubierto, portorriqueño, examen, libros

Note that diphthongs with the weak vowels i or u count as one syllable, so the stress will regularly fall before them.

academia, continuo, manubrio, sanitario, justicia

Combinations with two strong vowels count as two syllables.

tarea, menudeo, banqueteo, barbacoa

Any time stress doesn't follow these rules, an accent is used.

inglés, teléfono, tomó, práctico, drogaría, todavía, título, farmacéutico, petróleo, revés, apagón

4. REGIONAL SPANISH PRONUNCIATION

The Spanish pronunciation that you'll learn in this course is standard Latin American Spanish. There are certainly some local differences in pronunciation that you will probably come across, the most commonly known being the difference between Latin American and European Spanish. The major difference in pronunciation is that the sound *th*, as in *thin*, is much more common in Spain. In Latin America, this sound is typically only found in *d* when it comes between vowels.

media, nada, todo, poder, puedo

These words are pronounced with a *th* in Spain, too. But in Spain, c before i or e and z is also pronounced like *th* in *thin*.

cerca, servicio, cierto, fácil, docena, diez, voz, luz, marzo, azul, razón

There are some noticeable differences in local varieties of Spanish found in Latin America and Spain, as well. You don't need to worry about imitating these differences; the standard pronunciation you'll learn in this course will serve you perfectly well. But you may notice, for example, that in some countries or regions the combination ll is pronounced like the *lli* in *million*, the *j* in *juice*, the *sh* in *show*, or the *s* in *pleasure*. The semivowel y may have a similar range of pronunciation. In some countries, particularly in the Caribbean, final s may be dropped altogether, if not the entire last syllable! You may even hear r pronounced as something similar to l. There's certainly nothing wrong with any of these variations, although as a student, you'll probably find it useful to concentrate on the standard pronunciation offered in this course first.

Intermediate Spanish

Grammar Summary

Keep in mind that there are always at least some exceptions to every grammar rule.

1. ARTICLES

	DEFINITE		INDEFINITE	
	Singular	Plural	Singular	Plural
Masculine	el	los	un	unos
Feminine	la	las	una	unas

Note: El is used before a feminine noun beginning with stressed a (or ha). The article lo is used before parts of speech other than nouns when they are used as nouns. Unos (unas) is often used to mean *some* or *a few*.

2. CONTRACTIONS

de + el = del (*from/of the*)
a + el = al (*to the*)

3. PLURALS

a. Nouns ending in an unstressed vowel or diphthong add -s.
b. Nouns ending in a stressed vowel or diphthong add -es.
c. Nouns ending in a consonant add -es.
d. Nouns ending in -z change the z to c and then add -es.

4. POSSESSION

Possession is shown by the preposition de: el libro de Juan (*Juan's book*).

5. ADJECTIVES

Adjectives agree with the nouns they modify in both gender and number.

a. If the masculine singular ending is -o, the feminine singular is -a, the masculine plural is -os, and the feminine plural is -as.

b. If the masculine singular ending is not -o, there is no change in the feminine singular, and both genders are -es in the plural.

6. COMPARISON

The regular comparative is formed with más (*more*) or menos (*less*), and the regular superlative is formed with the definite article + más (*the most*) or menos (*the least*).

7. PRONOUNS

	SUBJECT	DIRECT OBJECT	INDIRECT OBJECT	PREPOSITIONAL	REFLEXIVE
1st sg.	yo	me	me	mí	me
2nd sg.	tú	te	te	ti	te
3rd m. sg.	él	lo	le	él	se
3rd f. sg.	ella	la	le	ella	se
2nd sg., fml.	usted	lo/la	le	usted	se
1st pl.	nosotros/ nosotras	nos	nos	nosotros	nos
2nd pl.	vosotros/ vosotras	os	os	vosotros	os
3rd m. pl.	ellos	los	les	ellos	se

Intermediate Spanish

	SUBJECT	DIRECT OBJECT	INDIRECT OBJECT	PREPOSITIONAL	REFLEXIVE
3rd f. pl.	ellas	las	les	ellas	se
2nd pl., fml.	ustedes	los/las	les	ustedes	se

8. QUESTION WORDS

¿Qué?	What?	¿Cuál? ¿Cuáles?	What?/ Which one?
¿Por qué?	Why?	¿Quién? ¿Quiénes?	Who?
¿Cómo?	How?	¿Dónde?	Where?
¿Cuánto? ¿Cuánta? ¿Cuántos? ¿Cuántas?	How much?/How many?	¿Cuándo?	When?

9. ADVERBS

Spanish -mente corresponds to -ly in English. It is added to the feminine form of the adjective.

10. DEMONSTRATIVES

ADJECTIVES		PRONOUNS			
Masculine	Feminine	Masculine	Feminine	Neuter	
este	esta	éste	ésta	esto	*this*
ese	esa	ése	ésa	eso	*that*
aquel	aquella	aquél	aquélla	aquello	*that (farther removed)*
estos	estas	éstos	éstas	estos	*these*
esos	esas	ésos	ésas	esos	*those*
aquellos	aquellas	aquéllos	aquéllas	aquellos	*those (farther removed)*

11. *IF* SENTENCES

IF THE MAIN CLAUSE HAS A VERB IN THE:	THE SI *(IF)* CLAUSE HAS A VERB IN THE:
Present	*Present/Future*
Future	*Present*
Imperfect	*Imperfect*
Preterite	*Preterite*
Conditional	*Imperfect Subjunctive (-ra or -se)*
Past Conditional	*Past Perfect Subjunctive (hubiera or hubiese)*

If the subject of the main clause and the subject of the *if* clause are the same, it's possible to replace a verb in the subjunctive with an infinitive. In this case si is replaced by de.

12. SUBJUNCTIVE

The subjunctive is used:

a. with verbs of desire, request, suggestion, permission, approval and disapproval, judgment, opinion, uncertainty, emotion, surprise, fear, denial, and so on. It is often used in a dependent clause introduced by que (*that*).

b. in affirmative or negative commands in the polite form, in negative commands in the familiar form, in *let's* suggestions, and in indirect or third person commands with *let* (*him/her/them*).

c. in si (*if*) conditional clauses that are unreal or contrary to fact.

d. after impersonal verbs that do not express certainty.

e. after certain conjunctions that never introduce statements of accomplished fact (antes de que, aunque, como si, etc.). Other conjunctions may or may not introduce a statement of accomplished fact. When they do, they take the indicative; otherwise they take the subjunctive (a menos que, a pesar de que, etc.).

f. to refer to indefinites like ningún (*no*) or alguien (*someone*) when there's a doubt about that person's existence.

g. after compounds with -quiera (*-ever*): quienquiera (*whoever*), dondequiera (*wherever*), cualquier (*whatever, whichever*).

comer
to eat

yo	nosotros/as
tú	vosotros/as
él/ella/usted	ellos/ellas/ustedes

Present		Present Progressive	
como	comemos	estoy comiendo	estamos comiendo
comes	coméis	estás comiendo	estáis comiendo
come	comen	está comiendo	están comiendo

Preterite		Imperfect	
comí	comimos	comía	comíamos
comiste	comisteis	comías	comíais
comió	comieron	comía	comían

Future		Conditional	
comeré	comeremos	comería	comeríamos
comerás	comeréis	comerías	comeríais
comerá	comerán	comería	comerían

Imperative		Subjunctive	
		coma	comamos
come	comed	comas	comáis
coma		coma	coman

conducir
to drive

yo	nosotros/as
tú	vosotros/as
él/ella/usted	ellos/ellas/ustedes

Present

conduzco	conducimos
conduces	conducís
conduce	conducen

Present Progressive

estoy conduciendo	estamos conduciendo
estás conduciendo	estáis conduciendo
está conduciendo	están conduciendo

Preterite

conduje	condujimos
condujiste	condujisteis
condujo	condujeron

Imperfect

conducía	conducíamos
conducías	conducíais
conducía	conducían

Future

conduciré	conduciremos
conducirás	conduciréis
conducirá	conducirán

Conditional

conduciría	conduciríamos
conducirías	conduciríais
conduciría	conducirían

Imperative

conduce	conducid
conduzca	

Subjunctive

conduzca	conduzcamos
conduzcas	conduzcáis
conduzca	conduzcan

conocer
to know

yo	nosotros/as
tú	vosotros/as
él/ella/usted	ellos/ellas/ustedes

Present

conozco	conocemos
conoces	conocéis
conoce	conocen

Present Progressive

estoy conociendo	estamos conociendo
estás conociendo	estáis conociendo
está conociendo	están conociendo

Preterite

conocí	conocimos
conociste	conocisteis
conoció	conocieron

Imperfect

conocía	conocíamos
conocías	conocíais
conocía	conocían

Future

conoceré	conoceremos
conocerás	conoceréis
conocerá	conocerán

Conditional

conocería	conoceríamos
conocerías	conoceríais
conocería	conocerían

Imperative

conoce	conoced
conozca	

Subjunctive

conozca	conozcamos
conozcas	conozcáis
conozca	conozcan

dar
to give

yo	nosotros/as
tú	vosotros/as
él/ella/usted	ellos/ellas/ustedes

Present		Present Progressive	
doy	damos	estoy dando	estamos dando
das	dais	estás dando	estáis dando
da	dan	está dando	están dando

Preterite		Imperfect	
di	dimos	daba	dábamos
diste	disteis	dabas	dabais
dio	dieron	daba	daban

Future		Conditional	
daré	daremos	daría	daríamos
darás	daréis	darías	daríais
dará	darán	daría	darían

Imperative		Subjunctive	
		dé	demos
da	dad	des	deis
dé		dé	den

deber
to have to, must

yo	nosotros/as
tú	vosotros/as
él/ella/usted	ellos/ellas/ustedes

Present

debo	debemos
debes	debéis
debe	deben

Present Progressive

estoy debiendo	estamos debiendo
estás debiendo	estáis debiendo
está debiendo	están debiendo

Preterite

debí	debimos
debiste	debisteis
debió	debieron

Imperfect

debía	debíamos
debías	debíais
debía	debían

Future

deberé	deberemos
deberás	deberéis
deberá	deberán

Conditional

debería	deberíamos
deberías	deberíais
debería	deberían

Imperative

debe	debed
deba	

Subjunctive

deba	debamos
debas	debáis
deba	deban

escoger
to choose

yo	nosotros/as
tú	vosotros/as
él/ella/usted	ellos/ellas/ustedes

Present

escojo	escogemos
escoges	escogéis
escoge	escogen

Present Progressive

estoy escogiendo	estamos escogiendo
estás escogiendo	estáis escogiendo
está escogiendo	están escogiendo

Preterite

escogí	escogimos
escogiste	escogisteis
escogió	escogieron

Imperfect

escogía	escogíamos
escogías	escogíais
escogía	escogían

Future

escogeré	escogeremos
escogerás	escogeréis
escogerá	escogerán

Conditional

escogería	escogeríamos
escogerías	escogeríais
escogería	escogerían

Imperative

escoge	escoged
escoja	

Subjunctive

escoja	escojamos
escojas	escojáis
escoja	escojan

estar
to be

yo	nosotros/as
tú	vosotros/as
él/ella/usted	ellos/ellas/ustedes

Present

estoy	estamos
estás	estáis
está	están

Present Progressive

estoy estando	estamos estando
estás estando	estáis estando
está estando	están estando

Preterite

estuve	estuvimos
estuviste	estuvisteis
estuvo	estuvieron

Imperfect

estaba	estábamos
estabas	estábais
estaba	estaban

Future

estaré	estaremos
estarás	estaréis
estará	estarán

Conditional

estaría	estaríamos
estarías	estaríais
estaría	estarían

Imperative

está	estad
esté	

Subjunctive

esté	estemos
estés	estéis
esté	estén

hablar
to speak, to talk

yo	nosotros/as
tú	vosotros/as
él/ella/usted	ellos/ellas/ustedes

Present

hablo	hablamos
hablas	habláis
habla	hablan

Present Progressive

estoy hablando	estamos hablando
estás hablando	estáis hablando
está hablando	están hablando

Preterite

hablé	hablamos
hablaste	hablasteis
habló	hablaron

Imperfect

hablaba	hablábamos
hablabas	hablabais
hablaba	hablaban

Future

hablaré	hablaremos
hablarás	hablaréis
hablará	hablarán

Conditional

hablaría	hablaríamos
hablarías	hablaríais
hablaría	hablarían

Imperative

habla	hablad
hable	

Subjunctive

hable	hablemos
hables	habléis
hable	hablen

hacer
to do, to make

yo	nosotros/as
tú	vosotros/as
él/ella/usted	ellos/ellas/ustedes

Present		Present Progressive	
hago	hacemos	estoy haciendo	estamos haciendo
haces	hacéis	estás haciendo	estáis haciendo
hace	hacen	está haciendo	están haciendo

Preterite		Imperfect	
hice	hicimos	hacía	hacíamos
hiciste	hicisteis	hacías	hacíais
hizo	hicieron	hacía	hacían

Future		Conditional	
haré	haremos	haría	haríamos
harás	haréis	harías	haríais
hará	harán	haría	harían

Imperative		Subjunctive	
		haga	hagamos
haz	haced	hagas	hagáis
haga		haga	hagan

ir
to go

yo	nosotros/as
tú	vosotros/as
él/ella/usted	ellos/ellas/ustedes

Present

voy	vamos
vas	vais
va	van

Present Progressive

estoy yendo	estamos yendo
estás yendo	estáis yendo
está yendo	están yendo

Preterite

fui	fuimos
fuiste	fuisteis
fue	fueron

Imperfect

iba	íbamos
ibas	ibais
iba	iban

Future

iré	iremos
irás	iréis
irá	irán

Conditional

iría	iríamos
irías	iríais
iría	irían

Imperative

ve	id
vaya	

Subjunctive

vaya	vayamos
vayas	vayáis
vaya	vayan

pedir
to ask for

yo	nosotros/as
tú	vosotros/as
él/ella/usted	ellos/ellas/ustedes

Present		Present Progressive	
pido	pedimos	estoy pidiendo	estamos pidiendo
pides	pedís	estás pidiendo	estáis pidiendo
pide	piden	está pidiendo	están pidiendo

Preterite		Imperfect	
pedí	pedimos	pedía	pedíamos
pediste	pedisteis	pedías	pedíais
pidió	pidieron	pedía	pedían

Future		Conditional	
pediré	pediremos	pediría	pediríamos
pedirás	pediréis	pedirías	pediríais
pedirá	pedirán	pediría	pedirían

Imperative		Subjunctive	
		pida	pidamos
pide	pedid	pidas	pidáis
pida		pida	pidan

pensar
to think

yo	nosotros/as
tú	vosotros/as
él/ella/usted	ellos/ellas/ustedes

Present

pienso	pensamos
piensas	pensáis
piensa	piensan

Present Progressive

estoy pensando	estamos pensando
estás pensando	estáis pensando
está pensando	están pensando

Preterite

pensé	pensamos
pensaste	pensasteis
pensó	pensaron

Imperfect

pensaba	pensábamos
pensabas	pensabais
pensaba	pensaban

Future

pensaré	pensaremos
pensarás	pensaréis
pensará	pensarán

Conditional

pensaría	pensaríamos
pensarías	pensaríais
pensaría	pensarían

Imperative

piensa	pensad
piense	

Subjunctive

piense	pensemos
pienses	penséis
piense	piensen

poder
to be able to, can

yo	nosotros/as
tú	vosotros/as
él/ella/usted	ellos/ellas/ustedes

Present		Present Progressive	
puedo	podemos	estoy pudiendo	estamos pudiendo
puedes	podéis	estás pudiendo	estáis pudiendo
puede	pueden	está pudiendo	están pudiendo

Preterite		Imperfect	
pude	pudimos	podía	podíamos
pudiste	pudisteis	podías	podíais
pudo	pudieron	podía	podían

Future		Conditional	
podré	podremos	podría	podríamos
podrás	podréis	podrías	podríais
podrá	podrán	podría	podrían

Imperative		Subjunctive	
		pueda	podamos
puede	poded	puedas	podáis
pueda		pueda	puedan

poner
to put

yo	nosotros/as
tú	vosotros/as
él/ella/usted	ellos/ellas/ustedes

Present

pongo	ponemos
pones	ponéis
pone	ponen

Present Progressive

estoy poniendo	estamos poniendo
estás poniendo	estáis poniendo
está poniendo	están poniendo

Preterite

puse	pusimos
pusiste	pusisteis
puso	pusieron

Imperfect

ponía	poníamos
ponías	poníais
ponía	ponían

Future

pondré	pondremos
pondrás	pondréis
pondrá	pondrían

Conditional

pondría	pondríamos
pondrías	pondríais
pondría	pondrían

Imperative

pon	poned
ponga	

Subjunctive

ponga	pongamos
pongas	pongáis
ponga	pongan

querer
to want

yo	nosotros/as
tú	vosotros/as
él/ella/usted	ellos/ellas/ustedes

Present

quiero	queremos
quieres	queréis
quiere	quieren

Present Progressive

estoy queriendo	estamos queriendo
estás queriendo	estáis queriendo
está queriendo	están queriendo

Preterite

quise	quisimos
quisiste	quisisteis
quiso	quisieron

Imperfect

quería	queríamos
querías	queríais
quería	querían

Future

querré	querremos
querrás	querréis
querrá	querrán

Conditional

querría	querríamos
querrías	querríais
querría	querrían

Imperative

quiere	quered
quiera	

Subjunctive

quiera	queramos
quieras	queráis
quiera	quieran

saber
to know

yo	nosotros/as
tú	vosotros/as
él/ella/usted	ellos/ellas/ustedes

Present		Present Progressive	
sé	sabemos	estoy sabiendo	estamos sabiendo
sabes	sabéis	estás sabiendo	estáis sabiendo
sabe	saben	está sabiendo	están sabiendo

Preterite		Imperfect	
supe	supimos	sabía	sabíamos
supiste	supisteis	sabías	sabíais
supo	supieron	sabía	sabían

Future		Conditional	
sabré	sabremos	sabría	sabríamos
sabrás	sabréis	sabrías	sabríais
sabrá	sabrán	sabría	sabrían

Imperative		Subjunctive	
		sepa	sepamos
sabe	sabed	sepas	sepáis
sepa		sepa	sepan

salir
to go out

yo	nosotros/as
tú	vosotros/as
él/ella/usted	ellos/ellas/ustedes

Present		Present Progressive	
salgo	salimos	estoy saliendo	estamos saliendo
sales	salís	estás saliendo	estáis saliendo
sale	salen	está saliendo	están saliendo

Preterite		Imperfect	
salí	salimos	salía	salíamos
saliste	salisteis	salías	salíais
salió	salieron	salía	salían

Future		Conditional	
saldré	saldremos	saldría	saldríamos
saldrás	saldréis	saldrías	saldríais
saldrá	saldrán	saldría	saldrían

Imperative		Subjunctive	
		salga	salgamos
sal	salid	salgas	salgáis
salga		salga	salgan

ser
to be

yo	nosotros/as
tú	vosotros/as
él/ella/usted	ellos/ellas/ustedes

Present

soy	somos
eres	sois
es	son

Present Progressive

estoy siendo	estamos siendo
estás siendo	estáis siendo
está siendo	están siendo

Preterite

fui	fuimos
fuiste	fuisteis
fue	fueron

Imperfect

era	éramos
eras	erais
era	eran

Future

seré	seremos
serás	seréis
será	serán

Conditional

sería	seríamos
serías	seríais
sería	serían

Imperative

sé	sed
sea	

Subjunctive

sea	seamos
seas	seáis
sea	sean

tener
to have

yo	nosotros/as
tú	vosotros/as
él/ella/usted	ellos/ellas/ustedes

Present		Present Progressive	
tengo	tenemos	estoy teniendo	estamos teniendo
tienes	tenéis	estás teniendo	estáis teniendo
tiene	tienen	está teniendo	están teniendo

Preterite		Imperfect	
tuve	tuvimos	tenía	teníamos
tuviste	tuvisteis	tenías	teníais
tuvo	tuvieron	tenía	tenían

Future		Conditional	
tendré	tendremos	tendría	tendríamos
tendrás	tendréis	tendrías	tendríais
tendrá	tendrán	tendría	tendrían

Imperative		Subjunctive	
		tenga	tengamos
ten	tened	tengas	tengáis
tenga		tenga	tengan

traer
to bring

yo	nosotros/as
tú	vosotros/as
él/ella/usted	ellos/ellas/ustedes

Present		Present Progressive	
traigo	traemos	estoy trayendo	estamos trayendo
traes	traéis	estás trayendo	estáis trayendo
trae	traen	está trayendo	están trayendo

Preterite		Imperfect	
traje	trajimos	traía	traíamos
trajiste	trajisteis	traías	traíais
trajo	trajeron	traía	traían

Future		Conditional	
traeré	traeremos	traería	traeríamos
traerás	traeréis	traerías	traeríais
traerá	traerán	traería	traerían

Imperative		Subjunctive	
		traiga	traigamos
trae	traed	traigas	traigáis
traiga		traiga	traigan

venir
to come

yo	nosotros/as
tú	vosotros/as
él/ella/usted	ellos/ellas/ustedes

Present		Present Progressive	
vengo	venimos	estoy viniendo	estamos viniendo
vienes	venís	estás viniendo	estáis viniendo
viene	vienen	está viniendo	están viniendo

Preterite		Imperfect	
vine	vinimos	venía	veníamos
viniste	vinisteis	venías	veníais
vino	vinieron	venía	venían

Future		Conditional	
vendré	vendremos	vendría	vendríamos
vendrás	vendréis	vendrías	vendríais
vendrá	vendrán	vendría	vendrían

Imperative		Subjunctive	
		venga	vengamos
ven	venid	vengas	vengáis
venga		venga	vengan

ver
to see

yo	nosotros/as
tú	vosotros/as
él/ella/usted	ellos/ellas/ustedes

Present

veo	vemos
ves	veis
ve	ven

Present Progressive

estoy viendo	estamos viendo
estás viendo	estáis viendo
está viendo	están viendo

Preterite

vi	vimos
viste	visteis
vio	vieron

Imperfect

veía	veíamos
veías	veíais
veía	veían

Future

veré	veremos
verás	veréis
verá	verán

Conditional

vería	veríamos
verías	veríais
vería	verían

Imperative

ve	ved
vea	

Subjunctive

vea	veamos
veas	veáis
vea	vean

vivir
to live

yo	nosotros/as
tú	vosotros/as
él/ella/usted	ellos/ellas/ustedes

Present		Present Progressive	
vivo	vivimos	estoy viviendo	estamos viviendo
vives	vivís	estás viviendo	estáis viviendo
vive	viven	está viviendo	están viviendo

Preterite		Imperfect	
viví	vivimos	vivía	vivíamos
viviste	vivisteis	vivías	vivíais
vivió	vivieron	vivía	vivían

Future		Conditional	
viviré	viviremos	viviría	viviríamos
vivirás	viviréis	vivirías	viviríais
vivirá	vivirán	viviría	vivirían

Imperative		Subjunctive	
		viva	vivamos
vive	vivid	vivas	viváis
viva		viva	vivan

Glossary

Note that the following abbreviations will be used in this glossary: (m.) = masculine, (f.) = feminine, (sg.) = singular, (pl.) = plural, (fml.) = formal/polite, (infml.) = informal/familiar. If a word has two grammatical genders, (m./f.) or (f./m.) is used.

Spanish-English

A

a *to, at*
  a las cinco *at five (o'clock)*
  ¿A qué hora es? *At what time is it?*
  A ver ... *Let's see ...*
  de ... a ... *from ... through ...*
abdomen (m.) *abdomen*
abogado/abogada (m./f.) *lawyer*
abonado/abonada (m./f.) *subscriber*
  línea (f.) de abonado digital (DSL) *DSL*
abrigo (m.) *overcoat*
abril (m.) *April*
abrir *to open*
  abrir la puerta *to open the door*
abrochar *to fasten*
  abrocharse el cinturón de seguridad *to buckle up*
absolutamente *absolutely*
absoluto/absoluta (m./f.) *absolute*
  en absoluto *absolutely not*
absurdo/absurda (m./f.) *absurd*
abuela (f.) *grandmother*
abuelo (m.) *grandfather*
  abuelos (pl.) *grandfathers, grandparents*
aburrido/aburrida (m./f.) *bored, boring*
aburrir *to bore*
aburrirse *to be bored, to get bored*
  Me aburre/aburren ... (sg./pl.) *I'm bored by ...*
acabar *to finish*
  acabar de ... *to have just ... (done something)*
academia (f.) *school, academy*
académico/académica (m./f.) *academic*
accidente (m.) *accident*
aceite (m.) *oil*

aceptar *to accept*
acera (f.) *sidewalk*
aconsejar *to advise*
  aconsejar que ... *to advise that/to ...*
acostarse *to go to bed*
actor (m.) *actor*
actriz (f.) *actress*
actualmente *at the present time*
acuerdo (m.) *agreement*
  De acuerdo. *All right.*
acupuntura (f.) *acupuncture*
además *moreover*
Adiós. *Good-bye.*
adjuntar *to attach*
  adjuntar un documento *to attach a file*
adjunto/adjunta (m./f.) *enclosed*
  documento (m.) adjunto *attachment*
adolescente (m.) *adolescent, teenager*
adulto/adulta (m./f.) *adult*
aerolínea (f.) *airline*
aeropuerto (m.) *airport*
afeitar *to shave*
  navaja (f.) de afeitar *razor*
afeitarse *to shave (oneself)*
afición (f.) *hobby*
aficionado/aficionada (m./f.) *fan*
afuera *outside*
afueras (f. pl.) *outskirts*
agencia (f.) *agency*
agente (m./f.) *agent*
agitado/agitada (m./f.) *agitated, rough*
agosto (m.) *August*
agradable (m./f.) *pleasant*
agradecer *to be thankful*
  Le agradezco su ayuda. *Thank you for your help.*
agrio/agria (m./f.) *sour*
agua (f.) *water*

agua mineral *mineral water*
el agua *the water*
las aguas *the waters*
aguacate (m.) *avocado*
aguja (f.) *needle*
ahí *there*
ahora *now*
  ahora mismo *right now*
ahorrar *to save*
ahumado/ahumada (m./f.) *smoked*
ajedrez (m.) *chess*
ajustado/ajustada (m./f.) *tight*
al (a + el) *to the* (m.)/*at the* (m.)
albornoz (m.) *robe*
alcalde (m.) *mayor*
alcaldía (f.) *municipal building*
alcoba (f.) *bedroom, room*
aldea (f.) *village*
alegrarse *to be glad*
  alegrarse de que … *to be glad that …*
alegre (m./f.) *happy*
alemán (m.) *German (language)*
alemán/alemana (m./f.) *German*
alergia (f.) *allergy*
alérgico/alérgica (m./f.) *allergic*
alfombra (f.) *carpet*
álgebra (f.) *algebra*
algo *something, somewhat*
  ¿Algo más? *Anything else?*
algodón (m.) *cotton*
alguien *somebody, someone*
  alguien más *somebody else*
algún/alguno/alguna (before m. sg. nouns/
  m. sg./f. sg.) *some, something*
algunos/algunas (m. pl./f. pl.) *some, something*
allí *there*
almorzar *to have lunch*
almuerzo (m.) *lunch*
¿Aló? *Hello? (on the phone)*
alquilar *to rent*
alto (m.) *stop, height*
  ¡Alto! *Stop!*
alto/alta (m./f.) *tall, high*
  tener la tensión alta *to have high blood
    pressure*
alumno/alumna (m./f.) *student*
amanecer (m.) *dawn*
  al amanecer *at dawn*

amar *to love*
amargo/amarga (m./f.) *bitter, sour*
amarillo/amarilla (m./f.) *yellow*
  páginas (f. pl.) amarillas *yellow pages*
americana (f.) *jacket*
americano/americana (m./f.) *American*
amigo/amiga (m./f.) *friend*
amueblado/amueblada (m./f.) *furnished*
anaranjado/anaranjada (m./f.) *orange (color)*
ancho/ancha (m./f.) *wide, baggy*
andar *to walk*
andén (m.) *sidewalk, platform*
  por el andén *on the sidewalk*
anexo (m.) *attachment*
  anexo al correo electrónico *e-mail
    attachment*
angosto/angosta (m./f.) *narrow*
anillo (m.) *ring*
año (m.) *year*
  año pasado *last year*
  año que viene *next year*
  año entrante *next year*
  ¿Cuántos años tiene? *How old are you
    (sg. fml.)/is he/is she?*
  este año *this year*
  los años cincuenta *the fifties*
  segundo año *second year*
  tercer año *third year*
  tener … años *to be … years old*
anoche *last night*
anotar *to record, to write down*
  anotar un gol *to score a goal*
antes *before*
  antes de … *before …*
  lo antes posible *as soon as possible*
antigüedad (f.) *antique*
  tienda (f.) de antigüedades *antique store*
antigüedades (f. pl.) *antiques*
antiguo/antigua (m./f.) *old*
antipático/antipática (m./f.) *unfriendly*
apagar *to turn off*
  apagar las luces *to turn off the lights*
aparador (m.) *cupboard*
apartamento (m.) *apartment*
apetito (m.) *appetite*
apostar *to bet*
  apuesto a que … *to bet that …*
aprender *to learn*

aprender a … *to learn how to …*
Estoy aprendiendo español. *I'm learning Spanish.*
aprobar *to pass*
aprobar un curso *to pass a course*
aprobar un examen *to pass a test*
apuesta (f.) *bet*
apuro (m.) *difficult situation*
aquel/aquella (m. sg./f. sg.) *that (far from the speaker and the listener)*
aquél/aquélla (m. sg./f. sg.) *that (one) over there (far from the speaker and the listener)*
aquello (neuter) *that (one, thing) over there (far from the speaker and the listener)*
aquellos/aquellas (m. pl./f. pl.) *those (far from the speaker and the listener)*
aquéllos/aquéllas (m. pl./f. pl.) *those (ones) over there (far from the speaker and the listener)*
aquí *here*
Aquí está … *Here is …*
Aquí tiene. *Here you are.*
árbol (m.) *tree*
archivo (m.) *file*
área (m.) *area*
arena (f.) *sand*
Argentina (f.) *Argentina*
argentino/argentina (m./f.) *Argentinian*
armario (m.) *closet, filing cabinet*
arquitecto/arquitecta (m./f.) *architect*
arquitectura (f.) *architecture*
arroz (m.) *rice*
arte (m.) *art*
artesanía (f.) *craft*
artista (m./f.) *artist*
asar *to grill*
bien asada *well-done*
así *so*
Así es. *That's right.*
Así que … *So …*
por así decir *so to speak*
asignatura (f.) *subject, course*
asistente (m./f.) *assistant*
asistir *to attend, to be present*
astronauta (m./f.) *astronaut*
atardecer (m.) *dusk*
al atardecer *at dusk*
atención (f.) *attention*
atender *to attend to, to serve, to take care of*

atentamente *carefully*
atleta (m./f.) *athlete*
atlético/atlética (m./f.) *athletic*
atracción (f.) *attraction*
atractivo/atractiva (m./f.) *attractive*
atrás *behind, back*
atún (m.) *tuna*
audífonos (m. pl.) *headphones*
aula (m.) *classroom*
auto (m.) *car*
autobús (m.) *bus*
recorrido (m.) por autobús *tour bus*
automático/automática (m./f.) *automatic*
contestador (m.) automático *answering machine*
automóvil (m.) *car*
autopista (f.) *highway, freeway*
autor/autora (m./f. less common) *author*
autovía (f.) *highway, freeway*
avenida (f.) *avenue*
aventura (f.) *adventure*
películas (pl.) de aventuras *adventure films*
avión (m.) *airplane*
ayer *yesterday*
ayuda (f.) *help*
Le agradezco su ayuda. *Thank you for your help.*
ayudar *to help*
¿Puede ayudarme? *Can you help me?*
ayuntamiento (m.) *city hall*
azúcar (m.) *sugar*
azul (m.) claro *the color light blue*
azul (m./f.) *blue*
azul claro *light blue*
azul marino *navy blue*
azul oscuro *dark blue*
ser de sangre azul *to have blue blood (lit., to be of blue blood)*

B

bailar *to dance*
baile (m.) *dancing*
bajar *to lower, to download*
bajo *under, below*
bajo/baja (m./f.) *short*
tener la tensión baja *to have low blood pressure*
balcón (m.) *balcony*

balón (m.) *ball*
baloncesto (m.) *basketball*
bañador (m.) *bathing trunks*
banana (f.) *banana*
bañarse *to take a bath, to bathe*
banco (m.) *bank*
banda (f.) *band*
bañera (f.) *bathtub*
baño (m.) *bathroom*
  traje (m.) de baño *bathing suit*
banquero/banquera (m./f.) *banker*
bar (m.) *bar*
barato/barata (m./f.) *cheap*
barbería (f.) *barbershop*
barbilla (f.) *chin*
barrio (m.) *neighborhood*
base (f.) *base*
bastante *quite, enough, quite a lot*
bata (f.) *robe*
batidora (f.) *blender*
bebé (m./f.) *baby*
beber *to drink*
bebida (f.) *drink*
bebito/bebita (m./f.) *little baby*
beca (f.) *scholarship*
béisbol (m.) *baseball*
  partido (m.) de béisbol *baseball game*
beneficio (m.) *benefit*
besar *to kiss*
biblioteca (f.) *library*
bicicleta (f.) *bicycle*
bien *well*
  Estoy bien. *I'm fine.*
  Que esté bien. *May you be well.*
  Que estés bien. *Take care.*
  ¡Qué bien! *How nice!*
Bienvenido./Bienvenida. (m./f.) *Welcome.* (to a man/to a woman)
billar (m.) *pool, billiards*
billete (m.) *ticket*
biología (f.) *biology*
blanco/blanca (m./f.) *white*
  ir de punta en blanco *to be dressed to the nines (lit., to go from the tip in white)*
  vino (m.) blanco *white wine*
bloquear *to block*
blusa (f.) *blouse*
bobo/boba (m./f.) *fool, idiot*

boca (f.) *mouth*
boleto (m.) *ticket*
bolígrafo (m.) *pen*
Bolivia (f.) *Bolivia*
boliviano/boliviana (m./f.) *Bolivian*
bolsa (f.) *bag, sack*
bolso (m.) *handbag*
bombachas (f. pl.) *women's underwear*
bonito/bonita (m./f.) *nice, pretty*
bordo (m.) *board*
  a bordo *on board*
  Bienvenidos a bordo. *Welcome aboard.*
borracho/borracha (m./f.) *drunk*
borrar *to erase*
bosque (m.) *forest*
bote (m.) *carton*
botella (f.) *bottle*
botiquín (m.) *medicine cabinet*
bragas (f. pl.) *women's underwear*
Brasil (m.) *Brazil*
brasileño/brasileña (m./f.) *Brazilian* (noun)
brasilero/brasilera (m./f.) *Brazilian* (adjective)
brazo (m.) *arm*
brote (m.) *rash*
buceo (m.) *diving*
buen/bueno/buena (before m. sg. nouns/m./f.) *good*
  Buenas noches. *Good evening./Good night.*
  Buenas tardes. *Good afternoon.*
  Buenos días. *Good morning.*
  ¡Buen provecho! *Enjoy the meal!*
  ¡Buen trabajo! *Good job!*
  El tiempo es bueno. *The weather is good.*
  Es bueno que … *It's good that …*
  Hace muy buen tiempo. *It's beautiful.*
  Nochebuena (f.) *Christmas Eve*
bufanda (f.) *scarf*
buscar *to look for, to pick up*
buzón (m.) *mailbox*
  buzón de voz *voice mail*

C

caballero (m.) *gentleman*
caballo (m.) *horse*
cabecera (f.) *head*
  pediatra (m./f.) de cabecera *regular pediatrician*
cabeza (f.) *head*

pararse de cabeza *to go crazy, to go out of one's mind*

perder la cabeza *to lose one's head*

tener dolor de cabeza *to have a headache*

tener la cabeza fría *to keep a cool head*

cabina (f.) *booth, cabin*

  cabina telefónica *telephone booth*

cable (m.) *cable*

cada (m./f.) *each, every*

cadera (f.) *hip*

caer *to fall*

café (m.) *coffee*

café (m./f.) *coffee-colored*

cafetera (f.) *coffeemaker*

cafetería (f.) *café, coffee shop, cafeteria, diner*

caja (f.) *cash register, box*

cajetilla (f.) *packet*

  cajetilla de cigarrillos *pack of cigarettes*

cajón (m.) *drawer*

calcetines (m. pl.) *socks*

caliente (m./f.) *hot*

calificaciones (f. pl.) *grades*

calle (f.) *street*

  luz (f.) de la calle *streetlight*

callejón (m.) *alley*

calor (m.) *heat*

  Hace calor. *It's hot.*

  tener calor *to be hot, to be warm*

calvo/calva (m./f.) *bald*

calzar *to wear (shoes)*

  ¿Qué número calza? *What shoe size do you wear?*

calzoncillos (m. pl.) *men's underpants*

calzoncitos (m. pl.) *women's underwear*

calzones (m. pl.) *men's undergarments*

cama (f.) *bed*

cámara (f.) *camera*

camarera (f.) *waitress*

camarero (m.) *waiter*

camarón (m.) *shrimp*

cambiar *to change, to exchange*

cambio (m.) *change*

caminar *to walk*

camino (m.) *way, path*

camisa (f.) *shirt*

camiseta (f.) *T-shirt, undershirt*

camisilla (f.) *undershirt*

campeón/campeona (m./f.) *champion*

campeonato (m.) *championship*

camping (m.) *camping*

  ir de camping *to go camping*

campo (m.) *field, camp*

Canadá (m.) *Canada*

canadiense (m./f.) *Canadian*

canal (m.) *channel*

cancelar *to cancel*

canción (f.) *song*

candidato/candidata (m./f.) *candidate*

cansado/cansada (m./f.) *tired*

cansancio (m.) *fatigue*

  tener cansancio *to be tired*

cantante (m./f.) *singer*

cantar *to sing*

capacidad (f.) *capacity*

cara (f.) *face*

  dar la cara *to face the circumstances*

  ser caradura *to be shameless*

carbón (m.) *coal*

cárcel (f.) *prison*

carnaval (m.) *carnival*

carne (f.) *meat, beef*

  carne de cerdo (f.) *pork*

carnicería (f.) *butcher shop*

caro/cara (m./f.) *expensive*

carpeta (f.) *file*

carpintero/carpintera (m./f.) *carpenter*

carpio (m.) *carpus*

  síndrome (m.) del túnel del carpio *carpal tunnel syndrome*

carrera (f.) *major, university course*

carretera (f.) *highway, freeway*

carril (m.) *lane*

  Siga por el carril de la derecha. *Stay in the right lane.*

carro (m.) *car*

carta (f.) *menu, letter*

  cartas (f. pl.) *playing cards*

cartelera (f.) *billboard, list of plays*

  cartelera de cine *movie listing*

cartera (f.) *wallet, handbag*

cartón (m.) *carton, cardboard*

casa (f.) *house*

casado/casada (m./f.) *married*

casarse *to get married*

  casarse con *to marry (someone)*

casi *almost*

casi nunca *seldom, almost never*
caso (m.) *case*
casualidad (f.) *chance, coincidence*
  por casualidad *by chance*
catedral (f.) *cathedral*
catorce *fourteen*
caza (f.) *hunting*
CD (m.) *CD*
  CD rom (m.) *CD-ROM*
  lector (m.) de CD *CD player*
  lector (m.) de CD rom *CD-ROM drive*
cebolla (f.) *onion*
ceja (f.) *eyebrow*
celeste (m./f.) *sky blue*
celoso/celosa (m./f.) *jealous*
celular (m.) *cell phone*
cena (f.) *dinner*
cenar *to eat dinner*
centralita (f.) *switchboard*
centro (m.) *center*
  centro comercial *shopping mall*
  centro de información *information center*
cerca *close, near*
  cerca de … *close to/near …*
cerdo (m.) *pork*
  carne (f.) de cerdo *pork*
cerdo/cerda (m./f.) *pig*
  carne (f.) de cerdo *pork*
cerebro (m.) *brain*
cero *zero*
cerrar *to close*
cerro (m.) *hill*
cerveza (f.) *beer*
cesar *to stop*
  cesar de … *to stop … (doing something)*
césped (m.) *lawn, grass*
champaña (m.) *champagne*
champú (m.) *shampoo*
chanchito/chanchita (m./f.) *piglet*
Chao. *Bye.*
chaqueta (f.) *jacket*
charcutería (f.) *delicatessen*
charla (f.) *chat*
  espacio (m.) para charla *chat room*
chat (m.) *chat room*
che *hey (filler word, Argentina)*
cheque (m.) *check*
chica (f.) *girl*

chico (m.) *boy*
Chile (m.) *Chile*
chileno/chilena (m./f.) *Chilean*
chinelas (f. pl.) *slippers*
chino (m.) *Chinese (language)*
chiste (m.) *joke*
  contar un chiste verde *to tell an obscene joke (lit., to tell a green joke)*
chocolate (m.) *chocolate*
chuleta (f.) *chop*
  chuleta de cordero *lamb chop*
ciclismo (m.) *biking, cycling*
cielo (m.) *sky*
cien/ciento (before a noun/before a number except mil) *one hundred*
  cien personas *one hundred people*
  cien por ciento *one hundred percent*
  ciento tres dólares *one hundred and three dollars*
  por ciento *percent*
ciencia (f.) *science*
cierto/cierta (m./f.) *true*
  No es cierto que … *It is not true that …*
cigarrillo (m.) *cigarette*
  cajetilla (f.) de cigarrillos *pack of cigarettes*
cinco *five*
  a las cinco *at five (o'clock)*
  cuarenta y cinco *forty-five*
cincuenta *fifty*
cine (m.) *movie*
cinturón (m.) *belt*
  abrocharse el cinturón de seguridad *to buckle up*
circo (m.) *circus*
cita (f.) *appointment*
ciudad (f.) *city, town*
claramente *clearly*
claro *clearly*
  ¡Claro que sí! *Of course!*
  Sí, claro. *Yes, of course.*
claro/clara (m./f.) *light*
  azul (m./f.) claro *light blue*
clase (f.) *class, kind*
  toda clase *all kinds*
clásico/clásica (m./f.) *classic*
  música (f.) clásica *classical music*
cliente (m./f.) *customer*
clínica (f.) *clinic*

farmacia (f.) clínica   *clinical pharmacy*
club (m.)   *club*
coca (f.)   *coca*
coche (m.)   *car*
cocina (f.)   *kitchen, stove, cooking*
cocinar   *to cook*
código (m.)   *code*
codo (m.)   *elbow*
coger   *to catch, to pick up, to take*
　coger fuerzas (f. pl.)   *to regain strength*
　coger un examen   *to take a test*
coincidencia (f.)   *coincidence*
　¡Qué coincidencia!   *What a coincidence!*
cola (f.)   *tail, line*
　hacer una cola   *to stand in line*
colección (f.)   *collection*
coleccionar   *to collect*
colega/colega (m./f.)   *colleague*
colegio (m.)   *elementary/secondary school*
colgar   *to hang*
　colgar el teléfono   *to hang up the phone*
colina (f.)   *hill*
collar (m.)   *necklace*
Colombia (f.)   *Colombia*
colombiano/colombiana (m./f.)   *Colombian*
colonia (f.)   *cologne*
color (m.)   *color*
　¿De qué color es … ?   *What color is … ?*
　ver todo color de rosa   *to be an optimist, to*
　　wear rose colored glasses
colorado/colorada (m./f.)   *red*
　ponerse colorado   *to be embarrassed (lit., to*
　　turn red)
columna (f.)   *column*
　columna vertebral   *backbone, spinal column*
coma (f.)   *comma*
combinar   *to combine, to match*
　combinar con …   *to go with …*
comedia (f.)   *comedy*
comedor (m.)   *dining room*
comenzar   *to start, to begin*
　comenzar a …   *to start … (doing something)*
comer   *to eat*
comercial (m./f.)   *commercial*
　centro (m.) comercial   *shopping mall*
comida (f.)   *food, dinner*
como   *as, like*
　como ya sabes   *as you already know*

cómo   *how* (question)
　¿Cómo?   *What?/Pardon me?*
　¿Cómo estás (tú)?   *How are you?* (infml.)
　¿Cómo estás de tiempo?   *Do you have time?/*
　　How are you doing for time?
　¿Cómo está usted?   *How are you?* (fml.)
　¿Cómo se llama usted?   *What's your*
　　name? (fml.)
　¿Cómo te llamas?   *What's your name?* (infml.)
　¿Cómo te trata la vida?   *How's life treating*
　　you?
　¿Cómo va todo?   *How is everything going?*
　¿Sabe cómo … ?   *Do you know how to … ?*
cómodo/cómoda (m./f.)   *comfortable*
compañía (f.)   *company*
completamente   *completely*
completar   *to complete*
completo/completa (m./f.)   *full*
　a tiempo completo   *full-time*
compra (f.)   *purchase*
　ir de compras   *to go shopping*
comprar   *to buy, to shop*
　comprar en rebaja   *to buy on sale*
comprender   *to understand*
computadora (f.)   *computer*
comunicar   *to communicate*
　Está comunicando.   *The line is busy.*
con   *with, to*
concierto (m.)   *concert*
condimentado/condimentada (m./f.)   *spicy*
conducir   *to drive*
conectar   *to connect*
conexión (f.)   *connection*
conferencia (f.)   *conference, meeting, lecture*
　sala (f.) de conferencias   *meeting room*
conjunto (m.)   *band (music)*
conocer   *to know (people, places), to meet*
　conocer de vista   *to know by sight*
　conocer palmo a palmo   *to know like the back*
　　of one's hand
　dar a conocer   *to make known*
　Gusto en conocerlo/la.   *Pleased to meet you.*
　　(to a man/to a woman)
consultar   *to look up, to consult*
consultorio (m.)   *office*
　consultorio del médico   *doctor's office*
contable (m./f.)   *accountant*
contar   *to count, to tell*

contar un chiste verde to tell an obscene joke
(lit., to tell a green joke)
contento/contenta (m./f.) happy
contestador (m.) (automático) answering
machine
contestar to reply to, to answer
contestar el teléfono to answer the phone
contigo with you
continuar to continue
Continúa recto. Continue straight.
contra against
contrato (m.) contract
contribución (f.) contribution
copa (f.) wineglass
copa de vino glass of wine
copia (f.) copy
copiar to copy
corazón (m.) heart
corbata (f.) tie
cordero/cordera (m./f.) lamb
chuleta (f.) de cordero lamb chop
coro (m.) choir
correo (m.) post office
correo electrónico (correo-e) e-mail
dirección (f.) de correo electrónico e-mail
address
correr to run
cortado/cortada (m./f.) sour
cortina (f.) curtain
corto/corta (m./f.) short
cosa (f.) thing
¿Cómo van las cosas? How are things?
cosquilleo (m.) tingling feeling
costar to cost
¿Cuánto cuesta? How much does it cost?
costoso/costosa (m./f.) expensive
costura (f.) sewing
crédito (m.) loan, credit
tarjeta (f.) de crédito credit card
creer to believe, to think
Creo que sí. I think so.
no creer que … not to believe that …
¿No crees? Don't you think?
crema (f.) creme
crema de afeitar shaving cream
crío/cría (m./f.) kid
cruce (m.) intersection
cruzar to cross

cuaderno (m.) notebook
cuadra (f.) block
Está a dos cuadras de aquí. It's two blocks
from here.
cuadro (m.) painting, picture, square
a cuadros plaid
cual/cuales (sg./pl.) which (relative pronoun), as
cuál/cuáles (sg./pl.) which, what (question)
cualificación (f.) qualification, skill
cualificado/cualificada (m./f.) qualified
cualquier any
cuando when (relative adverb)
cuándo when (question)
cuanto/cuanta/cuantos/cuantas (m. sg./f. sg./
m. pl./f. pl.) as much, as many
en cuanto a … regarding …
cuánto/cuánta/cuántos/cuántas (m. sg./f. sg./
m. pl./f. pl.) how much, how many
¿Cuántos años tiene? How old are you (sg.
fml.)/is he/is she?
¿Cuánto cuesta? How much does it cost?
¿Cuánto es? How much is it?
cuarenta forty
cuarenta y cinco forty-five
cuarto (m.) quarter, room, bedroom
a las seis menos cuarto at a quarter to six
a las seis y cuarto at a quarter past six
término (m.) tres cuartos medium (cooked
meat)
cuatro four
cuatrocientos/cuatrocientas (m./f.) four
hundred
cuchara (f.) spoon
cuchillo (m.) knife
cuello (m.) neck
cuenco (m.) bowl
cuenta (f.) bill, check, account
tener en cuenta to take into account
pagar la cuenta to check out
cuero (m.) leather
cuerpo (m.) body
cuerpo humano human body
cuestionario (m.) questionnaire
cuñada (f.) sister-in-law
cuñado (m.) brother-in-law
currículum (m.) curriculum
currículum vítae résumé, CV
curso (m.) course

cuyo/cuya/cuyos/cuyas (m. sg./f. sg./m. pl./f. pl.) *whose, of which* (relative pronoun)

D

dar *to give, to show*
dar a conocer *to make known*
dar a luz *to give birth*
dar con *to find (something)*
dar de narices *to fall flat on one's face*
dar la cara *to face the circumstances*
dar la hora *to tell time*
dar la mano *to shake hands*
dar la vuelta *to turn around*
dar (las) gracias *to give thanks*
de *of, from, about*
de … a … *from … through …*
¿De dónde eres? *Where are you from?*
de la madrugada *in the early morning (before daybreak)*
de la mañana *in the morning*
de la noche *in the evening, at night*
de la tarde *in the afternoon*
De nada. *You're welcome.*
¿De qué color es … ? *What color is … ?*
debajo *underneath*
debajo de … *underneath …*
deber *must, to owe*
débil (m./f.) *weak*
década (f.) *decade*
decidir *to decide*
decir *to tell, to say*
¿Cómo se dice " … " en … ? *How do you say " … " in … ?*
¿Díga(me)? *Hello? (on the phone)*
No me digas. *Really?*
por así decir *so to speak*
¿Qué quiere decir eso? *What does that mean?*
decisión (f.) *decision*
dedicar *to dedicate*
dedo (m.) *finger*
dedo del pie *toe*
dejar *to leave*
dejar un mensaje después de oír la señal *to leave a message after the tone*
del (de + el) *of the* (m.), *from the* (m.), *about the* (m.)
delante *in front*
delante de … *in front of …*
delgado/delgada (m./f.) *thin*

delicioso/deliciosa (m./f.) *delicious*
delito (m.) *crime*
demasiado/demasiada (m./f.) *too much, too many*
dentista (m./f.) *dentist*
dentro *inside*
dentro de … *inside of …*
departamento (m.) *department*
tienda (f.) por departamentos *department store*
depender *to depend*
depender de … *to depend on …*
dependiente/dependienta (m./f.) *store clerk*
deporte (m.) *sport*
deportista (m./f.) *person who plays sports*
deportivo/deportiva (m./f.) *athletic*
zapatillas (f. pl.) deportivas *sneakers, tennis shoes*
derecha (f.) *right side*
a la derecha *on the right*
Gira a la derecha. *Turn right.*
derecho *straight*
Siga derecho. *Go straight.*
derecho (m.) *law, right, duty*
derechos (pl.) de matrícula *tuition*
derecho/derecha (m./f.) *right-side*
a mano derecha *on the right-hand side*
desafortunadamente *unfortunately*
desagradable (m./f.) *unpleasant*
desarrollar *to develop*
desastre (m.) *disaster*
desayuno (m.) *breakfast*
descansar *to rest*
desconocer *not to know*
descremado/descremada (m./f.) *skimmed*
leche (f.) descremada *skim milk*
describir *to describe*
descripción (f.) *description*
descuento (m.) *discount*
hacer un descuento *to give a discount*
treinta por ciento de descuento *thirty percent off*
desde *since, from*
desear *to want, to wish*
desear que … *to wish that …*
¿Qué desea? *What would you like?*
desgracia (f.) *misfortune*
por desgracia *unfortunately*

Glossary

deshabillé (m.) *robe*
desierto (m.) *desert*
desodorante (m.) *deodorant*
despacho (m.) *office*
despacio *slowly*
  Hable más despacio, por favor. *Speak more*
    slowly, please.
despedirse *to say good-bye*
despertarse *to wake up, to get up*
después *afterwards*
  después de … *after …*
detalle (m.) *detail*
detergente (m.) *detergent*
  detergente de ropa *laundry detergent*
  detergente de vajilla *dishwashing detergent*
detestar *to detest*
detrás *behind*
  detrás de … *behind …*
día (m.) *day*
  Buenos días. *Good morning.*
  día festivo *holiday*
  dos días a la semana *twice a week*
  este día *this day*
  hoy en día *nowadays*
  Que tenga un buen día. *Have a nice day.*
  todo el día *all day*
  todos los días *every day*
diario (m.) *diary*
  llevar un diario *to keep a diary*
diario/diaria (m./f.) *daily*
diarrea (f.) *diarrhea*
diciembre (m.) *December*
diecinueve *nineteen*
dieciocho *eighteen*
dieciséis *sixteen*
diecisiete *seventeen*
diente (m.) *tooth*
diez *ten*
  a las ocho y diez *at eight ten (8:10)*
  diez mil *ten thousand*
  diez y seis *sixteen*
  diez y siete *seventeen*
  diez y ocho *eighteen*
  diez y nueve *nineteen*
diferencia (f.) *difference*
diferente (m./f.) *different*
difícil (m./f.) *difficult*
digital (m./f.) *digital*

línea (f.) de suscriptor/abonado digital
  (DSL) *DSL*
diligentemente *diligently*
dinero (m.) *money*
Dios (m.) *God*
  ¡Por Dios! *For God's sake!*
diploma (m.) *diploma*
dirección (f.) *address, direction*
  dirección de correo electrónico *e-mail*
    address
dirigir *to direct*
disco (m.) *disk, record*
  disco de vinilo *vinyl record, LP*
disculpa (f.) *excuse, apology*
disculpar *to excuse*
  Disculpa./Disculpe. *Excuse me.* (infml./fml.)
discutir *to discuss*
diseño (m.) *design*
Disneylandia *Disneyland*
disponible (m./f.) *available*
diversión (f.) *amusement*
  parque (m.) de diversiones *amusement park*
divertido/divertida (m./f.) *fun*
divertirse *to have fun*
divorciado/divorciada (m./f.) *divorced*
divorciarse *to get a divorce*
  divorciarse de … *to divorce (someone)*
doblar *to turn*
doce *twelve*
doctor/doctora (m./f.) *doctor*
documental (m.) *documentary*
documento (m.) *document, file*
  documento adjunto *attachment*
dólar (m.) *dollar*
dolor (m.) *pain*
  tener dolor de cabeza *to have a headache*
  tener dolor de garganta *to have a sore throat*
dominar *to dominate, to master*
  Domino el francés. *I speak French fluently.*
domingo (m.) *Sunday*
don (m.) *Mr.*
doña (f.) *Mrs.*
donde *where* (relative adverb)
dónde *where* (question)
  ¿De dónde eres? *Where are you from?*
dorado/dorada (m./f.) *gold (color)*
dormir *to sleep*
dormitorio (m.) *bedroom*

dos *two*
  dos días a la semana *twice a week*
doscientos/doscientas (m./f.) *two hundred*
dotado/dotada (m./f.) *talented*
drama (m.) *drama*
dramático/dramática (m./f.) *dramatic*
  obra (f.) dramática *drama*
ducha (f.) *shower*
ducharse *to take a shower/bath*
dudar *to doubt*
  dudar que … *to doubt that …*
dulce (m.) *sweet, pastry*
dulce (m./f.) *sweet*
durante *during*
duro/dura (m./f.) *hard*
  ser caradura *to be shameless*
DVD (m.) *DVD*
  lector (m.) de DVD *DVD player*

E

economía (f.) *economics*
económico/económica (m./f.) *economical, low-cost*
  precio (m.) económico *reasonable price*
Ecuador (m.) *Ecuador*
ecuatoriano/ecuatoriana (m./f.) *Ecuadorian*
edad (f.) *age*
edificio (m.) *building*
efectivamente *actually*
efectivo (m.) *cash*
  pagar en efectivo *to pay cash*
eficientemente *efficiently*
ejercicio (m.) *exercise*
el *the* (m. sg.)
  el de ella *hers*
  el de ellas *theirs* (f. pl.)
  el de ellos *theirs* (m. pl./mixed group)
  el de él *his*
  el de usted *yours* (sg. fml.)
  el de ustedes *yours* (pl.)
él *he*
  el de él (m. sg.) *his*
  la de él (f. sg.) *his*
eléctrico/eléctrica (m./f.) *electric, electrical*
electricista/electricista (m./f.) *electrician*
electrodoméstico (m.) *electrical appliance*
  tienda (f.) de electrodomésticos *electronics store*

electrónico/electrónica (m./f.) *electronic*
  correo (m.) electrónico *e-mail*
  dirección (f.) de correo electrónico *e-mail address*
elefante (m.) *elephant*
elegante (m./f.) *elegant*
elegir *to choose*
eliminar *to delete, to eliminate*
ella *she*
  el de ella (m. sg.) *hers*
  la de ella (f. sg.) *hers*
ellas *they* (f. pl.)
  el de ellas (m. sg.) *theirs* (f. pl.)
  la de ellas (f. sg.) *theirs* (f. pl.)
ellos *they* (m. pl./mixed group)
  el de ellos (m. sg.) *theirs* (m. pl./mixed group)
  la de ellos (m. sg.) *theirs* (m. pl./mixed group)
embarazada (f.) *pregnant*
embotellamiento (m.) *traffic jam*
emocionante (m./f.) *exciting*
empatado/empatada (m./f.) *tied*
  quedar empatados *to be tied*
empatar *to draw, to tie*
empezar *to begin*
empleado/empleada (m./f.) *employee*
empleo (m.) *job, employment*
en *in, at, by (means), on*
enamorado/enamorada (m./f.) *in love*
encantar *to enchant*
  Encantado./Encantada. *Pleased to meet you.*
  (said by a man/said by a woman)
  Me encanta/encantan … (sg./pl.) *I really like …*
  ¡Me encantaría! *I'd love to!*
encanto (m.) *charm*
encima *above*
  encima de … *above …*
  y encima … *and on top of that …*
encontrar *to meet up with, to find*
  encontrarse con … *to meet … (somebody)*
enero (m.) *January*
enfadarse *to get angry*
  enfadarse de que … *to be angry that …*
enfermedad (f.) *illness, disease*
enfermo/enferma (m./f.) *sick*
enfrente *opposite*
  enfrente de … *across from … , in front of …*
enhorabuena (f.) *congratulations*

enorme (m./f.) *huge*

ensalada (f.) *salad*

entender *to understand*

enterizo/enteriza (m./f.) *one-piece*

entero/entera (m./f.) *whole*
  leche (f.) entera *whole milk*

entonces *then*
  Hasta entonces. *Until then.*

entrada (f.) *entrance, ticket, appetizer*

entrante (m./f.) *coming*
  mes (m.) entrante *next month*

entrar *to enter*

entre *between*
  entre ... y ... *between ... and ...*

entregar *to submit*

entrenador/entrenadora (m./f.) *coach*

entretenimiento (m.) *entertainment*

entrevista (f.) *interview*
  programa (m.) de entrevistas *talk show*

entrevistar *to interview*

enviar *to send*

equipo (m.) *team*

equitación (f.) *horseback riding*

equivocado/equivocada (m./f.) *wrong*
  número (m.) equivocado *wrong number*

escaleras (f. pl.) *stairs*

escaparate (m.) *display window*
  ir de escaparates *to go window-shopping*

escoba (f.) *broom*

escoger *to choose*

escondidas (f. pl.) *hide-and-seek*

escotado/escotada (m./f.) *low-cut*

escribir *to write*

escritor/escritora (m./f.) *writer*

escritorio (m.) *desk, study*

escuchar *to listen to*

escuela (f.) *school*

escultura (f.) *sculpture*

ese/esa (m. sg./f. sg.) *that (near the listener)*

ése/ésa (m. sg./f. sg.) *that (one) (near the listener)*

eso (neuter) *that (one, thing) (near the listener)*
  a eso de *about, around*
  a eso de las nueve *at about nine o'clock*
  por eso *for this reason*

esos/esas (m. pl./f. pl.) *those (near the listener)*

ésos/ésas (m. pl./f. pl.) *those (ones) (near the listener)*

espacio (m.) *space*

espacio para charla *chat room*

espalda (f.) *back*

España (f.) *Spain*

español (m.) *Spanish (language)*
  Estoy aprendiendo español. *I'm learning Spanish.*
  Hablo un poco de español. *I speak a little Spanish.*

español/española (m./f.) *Spanish*

espantoso/espantosa (m./f.) *scary*

especialidad (f.) *specialty, major*

especialización (f.) *specialization, master's degree*

especializarse *to specialize*
  especializarse en ... *to major in ...*

espectador/espectadora (m./f.) *spectator*

espejo (m.) *mirror*

espera (f.) *wait*
  poner en espera *to put on hold*

esperar *to hope, to wait*
  esperar que ... *to hope that ...*
  Espere, por favor. *Hold on, please.*
  ¡Yo espero que sí! *I hope so!*

espeso/espesa (m./f.) *thick*

espía (m./f.) *spy*

esposa (f.) *wife*

esposo (m.) *husband*

esquiar *to ski*

esquina (f.) *corner*
  a la vuelta de la esquina *around the corner*

estación (f.) *station*
  estación de ferrocarril *train station*
  estación de tren *train station*

estación (f.) *season*

estadio (m.) *stadium*

estado (m.) *state*
  los Estados Unidos *the United States*

estadounidense (m./f.) *American*

estampado/estampada (m./f.) *with a pattern, patterned*

estampilla (f.) *postage stamp*

estanque (m.) *pond*

estante (m.) *shelf, bookshelf*

estar *to be*
  Aquí está ... *Here is ...*
  ¿Cómo estás (tú)? *How are you?* (infml.)
  ¿Cómo estás de tiempo? *Do you have time?/ How are you doing for time?*

¿Cómo está usted? *How are you?* (fml.)
Está granizando. *It's hailing.*
Está lloviendo. *It's raining.*
Está nevando. *It's snowing.*
Está nublado. *It's cloudy.*
estar en buenas manos *to be in good hands*
estar mal *to be not doing well*
Estoy aprendiendo español. *I'm learning Spanish.*
Estoy bien. *I'm fine.*
No está mal. *It's not bad.*
Que esté bien. *May you be well.*
Que estés bien. *Take care.*
este (m.) *east*
este/esta (m. sg./f. sg.) *this (near the speaker)*
  esta noche (f.) *this evening, tonight*
éste/ésta (m. sg./f. sg.) *this (one) (near the speaker)*
estilo (m.) *style*
esto (neuter) *this (one, thing) (near the speaker)*
estómago (m.) *stomach*
  tener mal de estómago *to have an upset stomach*
estos/estas (m. pl./f. pl.) *these (near the speaker)*
éstos/éstas (m. pl./f. pl.) *these (ones) (near the speaker)*
estrecho/estrecha (m./f.) *narrow*
estrella (f.) *star*
estrenar *to use for the first time*
estresante (m./f.) *stressing, stressful*
estudiante/estudiante (m./f.) *student*
estudiar *to study*
estudio (m.) *study, office*
  estudios (pl.) *studies*
estupendo/estupenda (m./f.) *fine, wonderful, marvelous*
  ¡Estupendo! *Great!*
etiqueta (f.) *tag, label*
  etiqueta con el precio *price tag*
ex *ex-*
exacto/exacta (m./f.) *exact*
  Exacto. *Exactly.*
examen (m.) *test*
  aprobar un examen *to pass a test*
  hacer un examen, presentarse a un examen *to take a test*
  hacerse un examen de sangre *to take a blood test*

suspender un examen *to fail a test*
exceder *to exceed*
excelente (m./f.) *excellent*
excepción (f.) *exception*
excursionismo (m.) *hiking*
  hacer excursionismo *to go hiking*
exigente (m./f.) *demanding*
exigir *to demand*
éxito (m.) *success*
experiencia (f.) *experience*
explicación (f.) *explanation*
exterior (m.) *outside*
extra (m./f.) *extra*
  horas (f. pl.) extras *extra hours, overtime*
extranjero/extranjera (m./f.) *foreign, foreigner*
extraño/extraña (m./f.) *strange*
  persona (f.) extraña *strange person*
extraordinario/extraordinaria (m./f.) *extraordinary*
extrovertido/extrovertida (m./f.) *extroverted*

F

fábrica (f.) *factory*
fácil (m./f.) *easy*
fácilmente *easily*
facultad (f.) *department (at college/university)*
falda (f.) *skirt*
faltar *to miss, to be lacking, to be necessary*
fama (f.) *fame*
familia (f.) *family*
familiar (m./f.) *(of) family, familiar*
famoso/famosa (m./f.) *famous*
fantástico/fantástica (m./f.) *fantastic*
farmacéutico/farmacéutico (m./f.) *pharmacist*
farmacia (f.) *drugstore, pharmacy*
  farmacia clínica *clinical pharmacy*
farola (f.) *lamppost*
favor (m.) *favor*
  Hágame el favor de … *Do me the favor of …*
  Por favor. *Please.*
favorito/favorita (m./f.) *favorite*
fax (m.) *fax machine*
febrero (m.) *February*
fecha (f.) *date*
felicitar *to congratulate*
  ¡Felicitaciones! *Congratulations!*
feliz (m./f.) *happy*
felizmente *happily*

feo/fea (m./f.) *ugly*
ferrocarril (m.) *railroad, train*
  estación (f.) de ferrocarril *train station*
festivo/festiva (m./f.) *festive*
  día (m.) festivo *holiday*
fiebre (f.) *fever*
  tener fiebre *to have a fever*
fiesta (f.) *party, holiday*
fijo/fija (m./f.) *fixed, permanent*
  trabajo (m.) fijo *steady job*
fila (f.) *line*
  hacer una fila *to stand in line*
filatelia (f.) *stamp collecting*
filosofía (f.) *philosophy*
fin (m.) *end*
  fin de semana *weekend*
  por fin *finally, at last*
final (m.) *end*
finanzas (f. pl.) *finance*
firma (f.) *signature*
física (f.) *physics*
flor (f.) *flower*
folleto (m.) *brochure*
fontanero/fontanera (m./f.) *plumber*
forma (f.) *way, manner*
fósil (m.) *fossil*
foto (f.) *picture, photograph*
  hacer una foto *to take a picture*
fotografía (f.) *photography*
francés (m.) *French (language)*
francés/francesa (m./f.) *French*
frasco (m.) *jar, bottle*
frase (f.) *phrase*
frecuencia (f.) *frequency*
  con frecuencia *frequently, often*
frecuente (m./f.) *frequent*
frecuentemente *frequently*
fregadero (m.) *(kitchen) sink*
freno (m.) *brake (automobile)*
  poner el pie en el freno *to hit the brakes*
frente (f.) *forehead*
fríjol (m.) *bean*
frío (m.) *cold temperature/sensation*
  Hace frío. *It's cold.*
  tener frío *to be cold*
frío/fría (m./f.) *cold*
  tener la cabeza fría *to keep a cool head*
frito/frita (m./f.) *fried*

fruta (f.) *fruit*
fuera *outside*
  fuera de … *outside of …*
fuerte (m./f.) *strong*
fuerza (f.) *strength*
  coger fuerzas (f. pl.) *to regain strength*
fumar *to smoke*
funcionar *to work, to function*
fútbol (m.) *soccer*
  fútbol americano *football*
futuro (m.) *future*

G

gabardina (f.) *raincoat*
gafas (f. pl.) *eyeglasses*
  gafas de sol *sunglasses*
galería (f.) *gallery*
galleta (f.) *cookie*
gamba (f.) *shrimp*
gamuza (f.) *suede*
gana (f.) *wish, desire*
  tener ganas de … *to feel like …*
ganar *to earn, to win*
  ¡Ojalá que ganen! *I hope they win!*
ganga (f.) *bargain*
garaje (m.) *garage*
garganta (f.) *throat*
  tener dolor de garganta *to have a sore throat*
gasolinera (f.) *gas station*
gasto (m.) *expense*
gato (m.) *cat*
gel (m.) *gel*
generalmente *generally*
generoso/generosa (m./f.) *generous*
gente (f.) *people*
geografía (f.) *geography*
gerente (m.) *manager*
gimnasia (f.) *gymnastics*
gimnasio (m.) *gymnasium*
girar *to turn*
  Gira a la derecha. *Turn right.*
  Gira a la izquierda. *Turn left.*
gol (m.) *goal*
  anotar/hacer/marcar un gol *to score a goal*
gordo/gorda (m./f.) *fat, big*
gracia (f.) *grace, appeal*
  dar (las) gracias *to give thanks*
  gracias (pl.) *thanks*

Gracias. *Thank you.*

Muchas gracias. *Thanks a lot.*

gracioso/graciosa (m./f.) *funny*

grado (m.) *degree*

graduarse *to graduate*

gráfico/gráfica (m./f.) *graphic*

gramo (m.) *gram*

gran/grande (before sg. nouns/all other cases) *big, large, great*

granizar *to hail*

Está granizando. *It's hailing.*

granjero/granjera (m./f.) *farmer*

gratis *free*

grave (m./f.) *serious*

gris (m.) *the color gray*

gris (m./f.) *gray*

gritar *to shout, to scream*

grito (m.) *cry, scream*

último grito *the very latest*

guantes (m. pl.) *gloves*

guardar *to save, to keep*

guayaba (f.) *guava*

guía (f.) *(guide) book*

guía telefónica *phone book*

guitarra (f.) *guitar*

tocar la guitarra *to play the guitar*

gustar *to please*

gustar que … *to like (it) that …*

Me gusta/gustan … (sg./pl.) *I like …*

Me gustaría … *I'd like …*

gusto (m.) *pleasure, taste*

Gusto en conocerlo/la. *Pleased to meet you.* (to a man/to a woman)

Mucho gusto. *It's a pleasure.*

H

haber *to have*

¿Cómo te ha ido? *How have you been?*

Hay … *There is …/There are …*

Hay que … *It is necessary to …*

No hay nada que … *There's nothing that …*

No hay nadie que … *There's no one who/that …*

No hay ningún … que … *There's no … that/who …*

¿Qué hay? *What's up?/What's going on?*

habitación (f.) *room, bedroom*

hablar *to speak, to talk*

hablar con …. *to speak to …*

¿Hablas inglés? *Do you speak English?* (infml.)

¿Habla usted inglés? *Do you speak English?* (fml.)

Hable más despacio, por favor. *Speak more slowly, please.*

Hablo un poco de español. *I speak a little Spanish.*

hacer *to do, to make*

Hace calor. *It's hot.*

Hace frío. *It's cold.*

Hace muy buen tiempo. *It's beautiful.*

hacer a la medida *to custom sew*

hacer deporte *to play sports*

hacer una cola/fila *to stand in line*

hacer un descuento *to give a discount*

hacer excursionismo *to go hiking*

hacer senderismo *to go hiking*

hacer una foto *to take a picture*

hacer una llamada internacional/local/nacional *to make an international/local/national call*

hacerse un examen de sangre *to take a blood test*

Hace sol. *It's sunny.*

Hace viento. *It's windy.*

Hágame el favor de … *Do me the favor of …*

Se me hace tarde. *I'm late.*

hacha (f.) *axe*

hacia *toward*

hambre (f.) *hunger*

tener hambre *to be hungry*

hasta *until, even*

Hasta entonces. *Till then.*

Hasta luego. *I'll see you later.*

Hasta mañana. *Until tomorrow./See you tomorrow.*

Hasta más tarde. *Until later.*

Hasta pronto. *See you soon.*

hecho/hecha (m./f.) *made, done*

heladería (f.) *ice cream parlor*

helado (m.) *ice cream*

heredar *to inherit*

hermana (f.) *sister*

hermano (m.) *brother*

hermanos (pl.) *brothers, brothers and sisters, siblings*

hielo (m.) *ice*

hierba (f.) *herb*
higiénico/higiénica (m./f.) *hygienic*
  papel (m.) higiénico *toilet paper*
hija (f.) *daughter*
hijastra (f.) *stepdaughter*
hijastro (m.) *stepson*
hijo (m.) *son*
  hijos (pl.) *sons, children (sons and daughters)*
hincha (m./f.) *fan, supporter*
hincharse *to swell*
historia (f.) *history*
historial (m.) *background, record*
  historial de trabajo *résumé*
hockey (m.) *hockey*
hoja (f.) *sheet (of paper)*
  hoja de vida *résumé*
Hola. *Hello.*
hombre (m.) *man*
  hombre de negocios *businessman*
hombro (m.) *shoulder*
homeopatía (f.) *homeopathy*
honesto/honesta (m./f.) *honest*
honorarios (m. pl.) *fees*
hora (f.) *time, hour*
  ¿A qué hora es? *At what time is it?*
  dar la hora *to tell time*
  horas (f. pl.) extras *extra hours, overtime*
  ¿Qué hora es? *What time is it?*
  ¿Qué horas son? *What time is it?*
  ¿Qué hora tiene? *What time do you have?*
horario (m.) *schedule*
horno (m.) *oven*
horror (m.) *horror*
hospital (m.) *hospital*
hostal (m.) *youth hostel*
hotel (m.) *hotel*
hoy *today*
  hoy en día *nowadays*
hueso (m.) *bone*
huevo (m.) *egg*
humano/humana (m./f.) *human*
  cuerpo (m.) humano *human body*
huracán (m.) *hurricane*

I

ida (f.) *outbound journey*
idea (f.) *idea*
ideal (m./f.) *ideal*

idioma (m.) *language*
iglesia (f.) *church*
igual (m./f.) *equal*
  … es igual a … *… equals (=) …*
igualmente *also, likewise*
  Igualmente. *The same to you.*
imaginar *to imagine*
impedir *to prevent*
importante (m./f.) *important*
importar *to matter*
  No importa. *It doesn't matter.*
imposible (m./f.) *impossible*
  Es imposible que … *It is impossible that …*
impresionante (m./f.) *impressive*
impresora (f.) *printer*
impuesto (m.) *tax*
  planilla (f.) de impuestos *tax return*
incentivo (m.) *incentive*
incluir *to include*
  ¿Está incluido el servicio? *Is service included?*
incómodo/incómoda (m./f.) *uncomfortable*
infantil (m./f.) *children's*
  sicología (f.) infantil *child psychology*
información (f.) *information*
  centro (m.) de información *information center*
informal (m./f.) *casual*
informe (m.) *report*
ingeniería (f.) *engineering*
  ingeniería mecánica *mechanical engineering*
ingeniero/ingeniera (m./f.) *engineer*
Inglaterra (f.) *England*
inglés (m.) *English (language)*
  ¿Hablas inglés? *Do you speak English?* (infml.)
  ¿Habla usted inglés? *Do you speak English?* (fml.)
inglés/inglesa (m./f.) *English*
ingrediente (m.) *ingredient*
ingreso (m.) *earnings*
inmediatamente *immediately*
inmediato/inmediata (m./f.) *immediate*
  de inmediato *immediately*
inodoro (m.) *toilet*
insistir *to insist*
  insistir en que … *to insist that …*
instantáneo/instantánea (m./f.) *instantaneous*
  mensaje (m.) instantáneo *instant message*

inteligente (m./f.) *intelligent, smart*
intercambiar *to exchange*
interés (m.) *interest*
  tener interés en … *to be interested in …*
  visitar los lugares de interés *to go sightseeing*
interesante (m./f.) *interesting*
interesar *to interest*
  Me interesa/interesan … (sg./pl.) *I'm
    interested in …*
intermedio/intermedia (m./f.) *intermediate*
internacional (m./f.) *international*
  llamada (f.) internacional *international call*
Internet *internet*
  por Internet *online*
intersección (f.) *intersection*
investigación (f.) *research, investigation*
  trabajo (m.) de investigación *research paper*
invierno (m.) *winter*
invitación (f.) *invitation*
invitado/invitada (m./f.) *guest*
invitar *to invite*
ir *to go*
  ¿Cómo te ha ido? *How have you been?*
  ¿Cómo van las cosas? *How are things?*
  ir a … *to go to (a place), to be going to (do)*
  ir a pie/caminar *to walk*
  ir de camping *to go camping*
  ir de compras *to go shopping*
  ir de escaparates *to go window-shopping*
  ir de punta en blanco *to be dressed to the
    nines (lit., to go from the tip in white)*
ira (f.) *anger*
  estar rojo de la ira *to be very angry (lit., to be
    red with fury)*
italiano (m.) *Italian (language)*
italiano/italiana (m./f.) *Italian*
izquierda (f.) *left side*
  a la izquierda *on the left*
  Gira a la izquierda. *Turn left.*
izquierdo/izquierda (m./f.) *left*
  a mano izquierda *on the left-hand side*

J

jabón (m.) *soap*
jamón (m.) *ham*
jardín (m.) *garden*
jazz (m.) *jazz*
jeans (m. pl.) *jeans*

jefe/jefa (m./f.) *boss*
jersey (m.) *sweater*
jornada (f.) *working day*
jornal (m.) *wage*
jota (f.) *the letter j*
  no saber ni jota de … *to not have a clue
    about …*
joven (m./f.) *young*
jubilado/jubilada (m./f.) *retired, retired person*
juego (m.) *game*
jueves (m.) *Thursday*
juez (m.) *judge*
jugador/jugadora (m./f.) *player*
jugar *to play*
jugo (m.) *juice*
julio (m.) *July*
junio (m.) *June*
junto/junta (m./f.) *together*
juzgado (m.) *court*

K

kilo (m.) *kilo, kilogram*
kilómetro (m.) *kilometer*

L

la *the (f. sg.); it (f.), her, you (f. sg. fml.)* (direct
  object pronoun)
  la de ella *hers*
  la de ellas *theirs (f. pl.)*
  la de ellos *theirs (m. pl./mixed group)*
  la de él *his*
  la de usted *yours (sg. fml.)*
  la de ustedes *yours (pl.)*
labio (m.) *lip*
lado (m.) *side*
  al lado de … *next to …*
ladrón (m./f.) *thief*
lago (m.) *lake*
lámpara (f.) *lamp*
lana (f.) *wool*
langosta (f.) *lobster*
lápiz (m.) *pencil*
largo/larga (m./f.) *long*
las *the (f. pl.); them (f.), you (f. pl.) (direct object
  pronoun)*
lástima (f.) *pity*
  Es una lástima que … *It's a pity that …*
lata (f.) *can*

lavabo (m.) *sink, wash basin*
lavadora (f.) *washing machine*
lavaplatos (m.) *dishwasher*
lavar *to wash*
  lavar a mano *to hand wash*
  lavar en seco *to dry-clean*
  lavar la ropa *to do the laundry*
  lavar los platos *to do the dishes*
lavarse *to wash oneself*
le *(to/for) him, her, it, you* (fml. sg.) (indirect object pronoun)
lección (f.) *lesson*
leche (f.) *milk*
  leche en polvo *powdered milk*
lechería (f.) *dairy store*
lechuga (f.) *lettuce*
lector (m.) *reader*
  lector de CD *CD player*
  lector de CD rom *CD-ROM drive*
  lector de DVD *DVD player*
lectura (f.) *reading*
leer *to read*
lejía (f.) *bleach*
lejos *far*
  lejos de … *far from …*
lengua (f.) *tongue, language*
lentamente *slowly*
lento/lenta (m./f.) *slow*
les *(to/for) them, you* (fml. pl.) (indirect object pronoun)
lesión (f.) *injury*
levantar *to raise, to lift*
levantarse *to get up, to rise*
  Me levanto. *I get up.*
libra (f.) *pound*
  media libra *half pound*
libre (m./f.) *free*
librería (f.) *bookstore*
libro (m.) *book*
  libro de texto *textbook*
licenciatura (f.) *bachelor's degree*
ligero/ligera (m./f.) *light, thin*
límite (m.) *limit*
limón (m.) *lemon*
limonada (f.) *lemonade*
limpio/limpia (m./f.) *clean*
línea (f.) *line*
  línea de suscriptor/abonado digital

  (DSL) *DSL*
lino (m.) *linen*
lista (f.) *list*
listo/lista (m./f.) *ready*
  ¿Listos? *Ready?*
literatura (f.) *literature*
litro (m.) *liter*
llamada (f.) *phone call*
  hacer una llamada internacional/local/ nacional *to make an international/local/ national call*
llamar *to call*
  llamar por teléfono *to make a phone call*
  llamar por teléfono a … *to call … on the phone*
  ¿Quién lo llama? *Who's calling?*
llamarse *to be called*
  ¿Cómo se llama usted? *What's your name?* (fml.)
  ¿Cómo te llamas? *What's your name?* (infml.)
  Me llamo … *My name is …*
llave (f.) *key*
llegar *to arrive*
  llegar a … *to get to …, to arrive at …*
llenar *to fill*
llevar *to wear, to carry, to take, to keep*
  llevar un diario *to keep a diary*
llorar *to cry*
llover *to rain*
  Está lloviendo. *It's raining.*
lluvia (f.) *rain*
lo *it* (m.), *him, you* (m. sg. fml.) (direct object pronoun)
  Lo siento. *I'm sorry.*
local (m./f.) *local*
  llamada (f.) local *local call*
Londres *London*
los *the* (m. pl.); *them* (m.), *you* (m. pl.) (direct object pronoun)
Los Ángeles *Los Angeles*
lotería (f.) *lottery*
luego *later, then*
  Hasta luego. *I'll see you later.*
lugar (m.) *place*
  visitar los lugares de interés *to go sightseeing*
luna (f.) *moon*
lunar (m.) *mole, beauty mark*
  de lunares *polka-dotted*

lunes (m.) *Monday*

luz (f.) *light*
  apagar las luces *to turn off the lights*
  dar a luz *to give birth*
  luz de la calle *streetlight*

M

madera (f.) *wood*
  de madera *wooden*

madrastra (f.) *stepmother*

madre (f.) *mother*

madrugada (f.) *late night, early morning (from midnight till daybreak)*
  de la madrugada *in the early morning*
  Es la una y diez de la madrugada. *It's ten after one in the morning.*

maestro/maestra (m./f.) *teacher*

mágico/mágica (m./f.) *magical*

magnífico/magnífica (m./f.) *magnificent, great*

mal *bad(ly), poorly*
  estar mal *to be not doing well*
  No está mal. *It's not bad.*

mal (m.) *illness*
  estar mal del estómago *to have an upset stomach*

maleta (f.) *suitcase*

malo/mala (m./f.) *bad*

mamá (f.) *mom*

mami (f.) *mom*

mañana (f.) *morning, tomorrow*
  a las nueve de la mañana *at nine a.m.*
  de la mañana *in the morning*
  esta mañana *this morning*
  Hasta mañana. *Until tomorrow./See you tomorrow.*

manejar *handle*

mano (f.) *hand*
  a la mano *at hand*
  a mano derecha *on the right-hand side*
  a mano izquierda *on the left-hand side*
  dar la mano *to shake hands*
  estar en buenas manos *to be in good hands*
  lavar a mano *to hand wash*

manojo (m.) *handful, bunch*

mantequilla (f.) *butter*

manzana (f.) *apple, block*

mapa (m.) *map*

mar (m.) *sea, ocean*

maravilla (f.) *wonder, miracle*

marcador (m.) *scoreboard*

marcar *to mark, to dial*
  marcar un gol *to make a goal*
  marcar un número de teléfono *to dial a phone number*

marchar *to go, to leave*

mareado/mareada (m./f.) *dizzy*

mareo (m.) *sickness*
  tener mareo *to be dizzy*

marido (m.) *husband*

marino/marina (m./f.) *marine*
  azul (m./f.) marino *navy blue*

marrón (m./f.) *brown*

martes (m.) *Tuesday*

martini (m.) *martini*

mártir (m./f.) *martyr*

marzo (m.) *March*

mas *but*

más *more, plus (+)*
  alguien más *somebody else*
  el/la/los/las (m. sg./f. sg./m. pl./f. pl.) más ... de ... *the most ... in/of ...*
  Hasta más tarde. *Until later.*
  más o menos *more or less, so-so, just okay*
  más ... que ... *more .../-er than ...*
  más tarde *later*

matemáticas (f. pl.) *mathematics*

materia (f.) *school subject*

material (m.) *material*

matrícula (f.) *registration*
  derechos (m. pl.) de matrícula *tuition*

matricularse *to register*

matrimonio (m.) *marriage*

mayo (m.) *May*

mayor (m./f.) *older, bigger*
  el/la/los/las (m. sg./f. sg./m. pl./f. pl.) mayor *the oldest, the biggest*

mazorca (f.) *corncob*

me *me* (direct object pronoun); *(to/for) me* (indirect object pronoun); *myself*
  Me aburre/aburren ... (sg./pl.) *I'm bored by ...*
  Me encanta/encantan ... (sg./pl.) *I really like ...*
  Me gusta/gustan ... (sg./pl.) *I like ...*
  Me gustaría ... *I'd like ...*
  Me interesa/interesan ... (sg./pl.) *I'm interested in ...*
  Me levanto. *I get up.*

Me llamo ... *My name is ...*

¿Me permite ... ? *May I please ... ?* (fml.)

¿Me permites ... ? *May I please ... ?* (infml.)

mecánico/mecánica (m./f.) *mechanical*

  ingeniería (f.) mecánica *mechanical engineering*

mediano/mediana (m./f.) *medium*

medianoche (f.) *midnight*

  a medianoche *at midnight*

medias (f. pl.) *stockings, socks*

medicamento (m.) *medication*

  tomar un medicamento *to take medication*

medicina (f.) *medicine*

médico/médica (m./f.) *doctor*

  consultorio (m.) del médico *doctor's office*

medida (f.) *measurement*

  hacer a la medida *to custom sew*

medio/media (m./f.) *half, midway*

  a las cinco y media *at five thirty*

  medianoche (f.) *midnight*

  medio tiempo (m.) *halftime*

  término (m.) medio *medium-rare*

mediodía (m.) *noon*

  a mediodía *at noon*

  Son las doce del mediodía. *It's twelve noon.*

medir *to measure*

mejilla (f.) *cheek*

mejor (m./f.) *better*

  el/la/los/las (m. sg./f. sg./m. pl./f. pl.) mejor *the best*

  Es mejor que ... *It's better that ...*

memoria (f.) *memory*

menor (m./f.) *younger, smaller*

  el/la/los/las (m. sg./f. sg./m. pl./f. pl.) menor *the youngest, the smallest*

menos *less, minus (-)*

  a las seis menos cuarto *at a quarter to six*

  el/la/los/las (m. sg./f. sg./m. pl./f. pl.) menos ... de ... *the least ... in/of ...*

  Es la una menos cinco. *It's five to one.* (12:55)

  más o menos *more or less, so-so, just okay*

  menos ... que ... *less ... than ...*

mensaje (m.) *message*

  dejar un mensaje después de oír la señal *to leave a message after the tone*

  mensaje instantáneo *instant message*

mente (f.) *mind*

mentir *to lie*

mercadillo (m.) *flea market*

mercado (m.) *market*

merienda (f.) *snack time*

mermelada (f.) *jam*

mes (m.) *month*

  este mes *this month*

  mes entrante *next month*

  mes pasado *last month*

  mes que viene *next month*

mesa (f.) *table*

mesera (f.) *waitress*

mesero (m.) *waiter*

metro (m.) *metro, subway*

mexicano/mexicana (m./f.) *Mexican*

México (m.) *Mexico*

mezquita (f.) *mosque*

mí *me* (after a preposition)

mi/mis (sg./pl.) *my*

microondas (m.) *microwave*

miedo (m.) *fear*

  tener miedo *to be scared/afraid*

  tener miedo de que ... *to be scared/afraid that ...*

miel (f.) *honey*

mientras *while*

  mientras tanto *meanwhile*

miércoles (m.) *Wednesday*

mil *one thousand*

  cien mil *hundred thousand*

  diez mil *ten thousand*

  veinte mil *twenty thousand*

millón *one million*

  un millón de casas *one million houses*

minuto (m.) *minute*

mío/mía/míos/mías (m. sg./f. sg./m. pl./f. pl.) *mine*

mirar *to watch, to look at*

  mirar la televisón *to watch television*

  Mire ... *Hmm .../Look ...*

mismo/misma (m./f.) *same*

  ahora mismo *right now*

mixto/mixta (m./f.) *mixed*

moda (f.) *fashion*

  de moda *in fashion, in style*

módem (m.) *modem*

moderno/moderna (m./f.) *modern*

molestarse *to be bothered*

  molestarse de que ... *to be bothered that ...*

momento (m.) *moment*
 en este momento *at this moment, right now*
 Un momento. *Hold on./One moment.*
monitor (m.) *monitor*
montaña (f.) *mountain*
montar *to ride*
monumento (m.) *monument*
morado/morada (m./f.) *purple*
moreno/morena (m./f.) *dark-haired, dark-skinned*
morir *to die*
Moscú *Moscow*
mostrador (m.) *counter*
mostrar *to show*
mover *to move*
móvil (m.) *mobile phone*
muchacha (f.) *girl*
muchacho (m.) *boy*
mucho *a lot, much, very*
mucho/mucha (m./f.) *a lot of*
 Mucho gusto. *It's a pleasure.*
muchos/muchas (m. pl./f. pl.) *many, a lot of*
 Muchas gracias. *Thanks a lot.*
muebles (m. pl.) *furniture*
muela (f.) *molar*
muerto/muerta (m./f.) *dead person, dead*
mujer (f.) *woman, wife*
 mujer de negocios *businesswoman*
 mujer policía *policewoman*
muletilla (f.) *filler word/phrase*
multa (f.) *fine*
mundial (m./f.) *worldwide, worldly*
 campeonato (m.) mundial *world championship*
mundo (m.) *world*
muñeca (f.) *wrist*
músculo (m.) *muscle*
museo (m.) *museum*
música (f.) *music*
 música clásica *classical music*
musical (m.) *musical*
músico (m./f.) *musician*
muy *very*

N

nacional (m./f.) *national*
 llamada (f.) nacional *national call*
nacionalidad (f.) *nationality*

nada *nothing*
 De nada. *You're welcome.*
 nada más *nothing else*
 No hay nada que … *There's nothing that …*
 No, para nada. *No, not at all.*
nadar *to swim*
nadie *nobody, no one*
 No hay nadie que … *There's no one who/that …*
naipes (m. pl.) *(playing) cards*
naranja (f.) *orange (fruit)*
nariz (f.) *nose*
 dar de narices *to fall flat on one's face*
natación (f.) *swimming*
natural (m./f.) *natural*
naturaleza (f.) *nature*
náusea (f.) *nausea, sickness*
 tener náusea(s) *to be nauseated, to have nausea*
navaja (f.) *pocket-knife*
 navaja de afeitar *razor*
necesario/necesaria (m./f.) *necessary*
 Es necesario que … *It's necessary that …*
necesitar *to need*
negar *to deny*
 negar que … *to deny that …*
negocio (m.) *business*
 hombre (m.) de negocios *businessman*
 mujer (f.) de negocios *businesswoman*
negro/negra (m./f.) *black*
 estar negro de la risa *to laugh very hard (lit., to turn black with laughter)*
 ver todo negro *to be a pessimist (lit., to see everything as black)*
nervio (m.) *nerve*
nevar *to snow*
 Está nevando. *It's snowing.*
nevera (f.) *refrigerator*
ni *nor*
 ni … ni *neither … nor*
niebla (f.) *fog*
 niebla tóxica/con humo *smog*
nieta (f.) *granddaughter*
nieto (m.) *grandson*
 nietos (pl.) *grandsons, grandchildren*
nieve (f.) *snow*
niña (f.) *young girl, female child*
ningún/ninguno/ninguna (before m. sg.

nouns/m. sg./f. sg.) *no, none*
No hay ningún … que … *There's no … that/ who …*
niño (m.) *young boy, male child*
no *not, no*
No, para nada. *No, not at all.*
noche (f.) *evening, night*
a las siete de la noche *at seven p.m.*
Buenas noches. *Good evening./Good night.*
de la noche *at night, in the evening*
esta noche *tonight*
medianoche *midnight*
Nochebuena *Christmas Eve*
por la noche *at night*
nombre (m.) *name*
normal (m./f.) *normal*
normalmente *normally*
norte (m.) *north*
nos *us* (direct object pronoun); *(to/for) us* (indirect object pronoun); *ourselves*
nosotras *we* (f. pl.)
nosotros *we* (m. pl./mixed group)
nota (f.) *note, grade*
sacar buenas/malas notas *to get good/bad grades*
tomar nota *to take note*
noticia (f.) *a piece of news*
noticias (pl.) *news*
novecientos/novecientas (m./f.) *nine hundred*
novela (f.) *novel*
novela rosa *romance novel*
noventa *ninety*
novia (f.) *girlfriend, fiancée*
noviembre (m.) *November*
novio (m.) *boyfriend, fiancé*
nube (f.) *cloud*
nublado/nublada (m./f.) *cloudy*
Está nublado. *It's cloudy.*
nuera (f.) *daughter-in-law*
nuestro/nuestra/nuestros/nuestras (m. sg./f. sg./m. pl./f. pl.) *our*
nuestro/nuestra/nuestros/nuestras (m. sg./f. sg./m. pl./f. pl.) *ours*
Nueva York *New York*
nuevamente *once again*
nueve *nine*
nuevo/nueva (m./f.) *new*
número (m.) *number*

número de teléfono *telephone number*
nunca *never*
casi nunca *seldom, almost never*

O

o *or*
más o menos *more or less, so-so, just okay*
o … o *either … or*
objetivo (m.) *objective, aim*
objeto (m.) *object*
obra (f.) *play (theater)*
obra dramática *drama*
obrero/obrera (m./f.) *construction worker*
occidente (m.) *west*
océano (m.) *ocean*
ochenta *eighty*
ocho *eight*
a las ocho y diez *at eight ten (8:10)*
ochocientos/ochocientas (m./f.) *eight hundred*
octubre (m.) *October*
ocupado/ocupada (m./f.) *busy*
oeste (m.) *west*
oferta (f.) *offer*
oficina (f.) *office*
oficinista (m./f.) *office worker*
ofrecer *to offer*
oír *to hear*
Ojalá que … *I hope/wish …*
ojo (m.) *eye*
ojo por ojo *an eye for an eye*
oler *to smell*
olvidar *to forget*
once *eleven*
onza (f.) *ounce*
ópera (f.) *opera*
operadora (f.) *operator*
operarse *to have an operation*
opuesto/opuesta (m./f.) *opposite*
oración (f.) *prayer*
ordenador (m.) *computer*
oreja (f.) *ear*
oriente (m.) *east*
os *all of you* (infml.) (direct object pronoun); *(to/for) you* (infml. pl.)(indirect object pronoun); *yourselves* (infml.)
oscuro/oscura (m./f.) *dark*
azul (m./f.) oscuro *dark blue*
verde (m./f.) oscuro *dark green*

otoño (m.) *fall*
otro/otra (m./f.) *another*

P

paciencia (f.) *patience*
  tener paciencia *to be patient*
padrastro (m.) *stepfather*
padre (m.) *father*
  padres (pl.) *fathers, parents*
paga (f.) *wage*
pagar *to pay*
  pagar en efectivo *to pay cash*
  pagar la cuenta *to check out, to pay the bill/
  check*
página (f.) *page*
  páginas (pl.) amarillas *yellow pages*
  página web *webpage*
pago (m.) *payment*
país (m.) *country*
palabra (f.) *word*
palacio (m.) *palace*
palmo (m.) *palm*
  conocer palmo a palmo *to know like the back
  of one's hand*
palo (m.) *stick*
pan (m.) *bread*
panadería (f.) *bakery*
panameño/panameña (m./f.) *Panamanian*
pantalla (f.) *screen*
pantalones (m. pl.) *pants*
pantis (m. pl.) *women's underwear*
pantuflas (f. pl.) *slippers*
pantymedias (f. pl.) *stockings*
papa (f.) *potato*
papá (m.) *dad*
papi (m.) *dad*
papaya (f.) *papaya*
papel (m.) *paper*
  papel higiénico *toilet paper*
paquete (m.) *package*
para *for, towards, in order to, intended for, by/
until a certain time*
  espacio (m.) para charla *chat room*
  No, para nada. *No, not at all.*
parada (f.) *stop, bus stop*
parado/parada (m./f.) *unemployed*
paraguas (m.) *umbrella*
Paraguay (m.) *Paraguay*

parar *to stop, to leave*
  pararse de cabeza *to go crazy, to go out of
  one's mind*
parcial (m./f.) *partial*
  a tiempo parcial *part-time*
pardo/parda (m./f.) *grayish brown*
parecer *to look like, to seem*
  ¿Qué te parece … ? *What do you think of … ?*
  ¿Qué te parece si … ? *How about if … ?*
pared (f.) *wall*
pariente (m./f.) *relative*
París *Paris*
parque (m.) *park*
parqueadero (m.) *parking lot*
parrilla (f.) *grill*
  a la parrilla *grilled*
parte (f.) *part, side*
  ¿De parte de quién? *Who's calling?*
  por otra parte *on the other hand*
  por una parte *on the one hand*
particular (m./f.) *particular*
partido (m.) *(sport) game*
  partido de béisbol *baseball game*
partir *to leave, to set off*
  partir de … *to start from …*
párvulo/párvula (m./f.) *young child*
pasado/pasada (m./f.) *spoiled*
pasado/pasada (m./f.) *past*
  año (m.) pasado *last year*
  mes (m.) pasado *last month*
  semana (f.) pasada *last week*
pasaje (m.) *ticket*
pasaporte (m.) *passport*
pasar *to pass, to forward, to go by, to happen, to
spend*
  Le paso. *I'm putting you through. (on the
  phone)*
  pasar el día *to spend the day*
  ¿Qué pasa? *How's it going?*
pasatiempos (m.) *hobby*
Pascua (f.) *Easter*
pastelería (f.) *bakery (for pastries, etc.)*
pastilla (f.) *pill*
patata (f.) *potato*
patio (m.) *backyard*
peaje (m.) *toll*
peatón (m.) *pedestrian*
pecho (m.) *breast, chest*

pediatra (m./f.) *pediatrician*
pediatría (f.) *pediatrics*
pedir *to order, to ask for*
  pedir que ... *to request that ...*
película (f.) *movie, film*
  películas (pl.) de aventuras *adventure films*
  películas de horror *horror films*
  películas de suspenso *suspense films*
  películas románticas *romantic films*
pelo (m.) *hair*
pelota (f.) *ball*
peluquería (f.) *hair salon*
pena (f.) *pain, pity*
  ¡Qué pena! *That's too bad!*
pendientes (m. pl.) *earrings*
penicilina (f.) *penicillin*
pensar *to think*
  no pensar que ... *not to think that ...*
pensión (f.) *pension*
peor (m./f.) *worse*
  el/la/los/las (m. sg./f. sg./m. pl./f. pl.) peor
    the worst
pepino (m.) *cucumber*
pequeño/pequeña (m./f.) *small*
pera (f.) *pear*
percibir *to perceive*
perder *to lose, to miss*
  perder la cabeza *to lose one's head*
Perdón. *Excuse me.*
perezoso/perezosa (m./f.) *lazy*
  ser perezoso *to be lazy*
perfecto/perfecta (m./f.) *perfect*
perfume (m.) *perfume*
periódico (m.) *newspaper*
periodista (m./f.) *journalist*
período (m.) *period*
  período de prueba *probationary period*
permitir *to allow*
  ¿Me permite ...? *May I please ...?* (fml.)
  ¿Me permites ...? *May I please ...?* (infml.)
pero *but*
perro (m.) *dog*
persona (f.) *person*
  persona extranjero *stranger*
personal (m.) *staff*
Perú (m.) *Peru*
peruano/peruana (m./f.) *Peruvian*
pesar *to weigh*

pescadería (f.) *fish shop, fish market*
pescado (m.) *fish*
pésimo/pésima (m./f.) *terrible*
peso (m.) *peso*
pestañas (f. pl.) *eyelashes*
piano (m.) *piano*
picante (m./f.) *spicy*
pie (m.) *foot*
  dedo (m.) del pie *toe*
  ir a pie *to walk*
  poner el pie en el freno *to hit the brakes*
  tener los pies en la tierra *to have both feet on*
    the ground
piel (f.) *skin*
pierna (f.) *leg*
pieza (f.) *piece*
  de dos piezas *two-piece*
pijama (m.) *pajamas*
pimienta (f.) *pepper (spice)*
pimiento (m.) *pepper (vegetable)*
pinta (f.) *spot, appearance*
pintor/pintora (m./f.) *painter*
pintura (f.) *painting*
piscina (f.) *swimming pool*
piso (m.) *floor, apartment*
placer (m.) *pleasure*
plan (m.) *plan*
plancha (f.) *iron*
planchar *to iron*
  tabla (f.) de planchar *ironing board*
planilla (f.) *form*
  planilla de impuestos *tax return*
plano (m.) *map*
plano/plana (m./f.) *flat*
planta (f.) *plant*
plantilla (f.) *staff*
plástico (m.) *plastic*
plátano (m.) *banana*
plateado/plateada (m./f.) *silver (color)*
plato (m.) *plate, dish*
  lavar los platos *to do the dishes*
  plato del día *special of the day*
  plato principal *main dish*
playa (f.) *beach*
plaza (f.) *plaza, square*
  plaza de mercado *outdoor market*
pluma (f.) *pen*
pobre (m./f.) *poor, poor person*

los pobres *the poor*
poco *little*
  Hablo un poco de español. *I speak a little Spanish.*
  un poco *a little*
pocos/pocas (m. pl./f. pl.) *few*
poder *can, to be able to, to have permission to*
  ¿Podría … ? *Could you … ?*
podrido/podrida (m./f.) *bad, rotten*
policía (m./f.) *police officer*
  mujer (f.) policía *policewoman*
poliéster (m.) *polyester*
pollo (m.) *chicken*
polvo (m.) *dust, powder*
  leche (f.) en polvo *powdered milk*
poner *to put, to place*
  poner el pie en el freno *to hit the brakes*
  poner en espera *to put on hold*
ponerse *to become, to turn, to put something on*
  ponerse colorado *to be embarrassed (lit., to turn red)*
por *for, by, around, at, because of, due to, in place of, in exchange for, through*
  por casualidad *by chance*
  por desgracia *unfortunately*
  ¡Por Dios! *For God's sake!*
  por eso *for this reason*
  Por favor. *Please.*
  por fin *finally, at last*
  por la noche *at night*
  por la radio *on the radio*
  por lo tanto *therefore*
  por lo visto *apparently*
  por otra parte *on the other hand*
  por qué *why*
  por supuesto *of course*
  por teléfono *on the phone*
  por una parte *on the one hand*
porque *because*
portero (m.) *goalkeeper*
portugués/portuguesa (m./f.) *Portuguese*
poseer *to own, to hold*
posible (m./f.) *possible*
  Es posible que … *It is possible that …*
  lo antes posible *as soon as possible*
postre (m.) *dessert*
practicar *to practice, to play (sports)*
precio (m.) *price*

etiqueta (f.) con el precio *price tag*
  precio económico *reasonable price*
precisamente *precisely*
preferible (m./f.) *preferable*
  Es preferible que … *It's preferable that …*
preferir *to prefer*
  preferir que … *to prefer that …*
pregunta (f.) *question*
preguntar *to ask*
premio (m.) *prize*
prenda (f.) *garment*
preocuparse *to worry*
  No se preocupe. *Don't worry.*
  preocuparse de que … *to worry that …*
preparado/preparada (m./f.) *ready, prepared*
  ¿Preparados? *Ready?*
presentación (f.) *presentation*
presentar *to introduce*
  Te presento a … *Let me introduce you to …*
presidente/presidenta (m./f.) *president*
presión (f.) *pressure*
prestigioso/prestigiosa (m./f.) *prestigious*
primavera (f.) *spring*
primer/primero/primera (before m. sg. nouns/ m./f.) *first*
primo/prima (m./f.) *cousin*
  primos (pl.) *cousins*
principal (m./f.) *main*
  plato (m.) principal *main dish*
prisa (f.) *hurry*
  aprisa *quickly*
  tener prisa *to be in a hurry*
probador (m.) *dressing room*
probar *to try, to taste*
probarse *to try on (clothes)*
problema (m.) *problem*
producir *to produce*
producto (m.) *product*
profesión (f.) *profession*
profesional (m./f.) *professional*
profesionalmente *professionally*
profesor/profesora (m./f.) *professor*
profesorado (m.) *faculty*
programa (m.) *program*
  programa de entrevistas *talk show*
  programa de televisión *television program*
prohibir *to forbid, to prohibit*
  prohibir que … *to forbid that/to …*

Glossary

prometer *to promise*
prometido/prometida (m./f.) *fiancé(e)*
pronto *soon*
propina (f.) *tip*
proteger *to protect*
provecho (m.) *benefit*
 ¡Buen provecho! *Enjoy the meal!*
próximo/próxima (m./f.) *near, next*
 próxima semana (f.) *next week*
proyecto (m.) *project*
prueba (f.) *proof, test, probation*
 período (m.) de prueba *probationary period*
pueblo (m.) *town*
puente (m.) *bridge, long weekend*
puerta (f.) *door*
 abrir la puerta *to open the door*
pues *so, since, therefore, well, then*
 Pues, aquí estamos. *Here we are.*
 Pues bien. *Fine.*
 Pues, nada. *Not much.*
puesto (m.) *(job) position, post*
pulmones (m. pl.) *lungs*
pulsera (f.) *bracelet*
punta (f.) *tip, end*
 ir de punta en blanco *to be dressed to the
 nines (lit., to go from the tip in white)*
punto (m.) *point*
 en punto *exactly*
 Son las tres en punto. *It's three o'clock sharp.*
puntual (m./f.) *punctual*
púrpura (m./f.) *purple*

Q

que *which, that* (relative pronoun, conjunction)
qué *what* (question)
 ¿A qué hora es? *At what time is it?*
 ¿De qué color es … ? *What color is … ?*
 por qué *why*
 ¡Qué … ! *How … !*
 ¡Qué bien! *How nice!*
 ¿Qué hay? *What's up?/What's going on?*
 ¿Qué hora es? *What time is it?*
 ¿Qué horas son? *What time is it?*
 ¿Qué pasa? *How's it going?*
 ¡Qué pena! *That's too bad!*
 ¿Qué quiere decir eso? *What does that mean?*
 ¿Qué tal? *What's happening?*
 ¿Qué tal si … ? *How about if … ?*

 ¿Qué te parece si … ? *How about if … ?*
 ¡Yo qué sé! *How do I know!?/How should I
 know!?*
quedar *to remain, to retain, to fit*
 quedar empatados *to be tied*
quemado/quemada (m./f.) *burnt*
querer *to want, to love*
 querer que … *to want that/to …*
 ¿Qué quiere decir eso? *What does that mean?*
 Quisiera … *I'd like …*
 Te quiero. *I love you.*
queso (m.) *cheese*
quien/quienes (sg./pl.) *who, whom* (relative
 pronoun)
quién/quiénes (sg./pl.) *who, whom* (question)
 ¿De parte de quién? *Who's calling?*
 ¿De quién … ? *Whose … ?*
 ¿Quién lo llama? *Who's calling?*
química (f.) *chemistry*
quince *fifteen*
quinientos/quinientas (m./f.) *five hundred*

R

racimo (m.) *bunch (of grapes)*
 racimo de uvas *bunch of grapes*
radio (f.) *radio*
 por la radio *on the radio*
rampa (f.) *ramp*
rápidamente *fast, quickly*
rápido *fast, quickly*
rápido/rápida (m./f.) *fast, quick*
ratón (m.) *mouse*
raya (f.) *stripe*
 a rayas *striped*
razón (f.) *reason*
 tener razón *to be right*
realismo (m.) *realism*
realista (m./f.) *realistic*
realmente *actually*
rebaja (f.) *discount*
 comprar en rebaja *to buy on sale*
rebajado/rebajada (m./f.) *reduced*
rebanada (f.) *slice*
recepción (f.) *reception desk*
recepcionista (m./f.) *receptionist*
receso (m.) *recess*
receta (f.) *recipe*
recibir *to receive*

recoger *to pick up*
recomendar *to recommend*
  recomendar que ... *to recommend that ...*
reconocer *to recognize*
recordar *to remember*
recorrido (m.) *route*
  recorrido por autobús *tour bus trip*
recreo (m.) *recreation*
recto *straight*
  Continúa recto. *Continue straight.*
redondo/redonda (m./f.) *round*
reducir *to reduce*
referencia (f.) *reference*
refresco (m.) *soft drink, soda*
regalar *to give (a gift)*
regalo (m.) *gift*
región (f.) *region*
regional (m./f.) *regional*
registrarse *to check in*
regresar *to return*
reir *to laugh*
relación (f.) *relationship*
relámpago (m.) *lightening*
relleno (m.) *stuffing, filling*
  frase (f.) de relleno *filler phrase*
reloj (m.) *watch, clock*
repetir *to repeat*
  Repita, por favor *Repeat, please.*
representante (m.) *representative*
reserva (f.) *reservation*
reservación (f.) *reservation*
resolver *to resolve*
responder *to answer*
responsable (m./f.) *responsible*
respuesta (f.) *answer*
restaurante (m.) *restaurant*
resto (m.) *rest*
resultado (m.) *result*
retransmitir *to forward*
retrasado/retrasada (m./f.) *slow, behind*
retrasar *to delay, to postpone*
retribución (f.) *repayment*
reunión (f.) *meeting*
reunir *to gather, to meet*
revista (f.) *magazine*
rico/rica (m./f.) *rich*
río (m.) *river*
risa (f.) *laughter*

estar negro de la risa *to laugh very hard (lit., to turn black with laughter)*
roca (f.) *rock*
rodilla (f.) *knee*
rojo/roja (m./f.) *red*
  estar rojo de la ira *to be very angry (lit., to be red with fury)*
romántico/romántica (m./f.) *romantic*
ropa (f.) *clothing*
  detergente (m.) de ropa *laundry detergent*
  lavar la ropa *to do the laundry*
  tienda (f.) de ropa *clothing store*
rosa (f.) *rose*
  novela (f.) rosa *romance novel*
  ver todo color de rosa *to be an optimist, to wear rose colored glasses (lit., to see everything pink)*
rosado/rosada (m./f.) *pink*
rubio/rubia (m./f.) *blonde*
rural (m./f.) *rural*
ruso (m.) *Russian (language)*

S

sábado (m.) *Saturday*
saber (intransitive verb) *to taste*
saber (transitive verb) *to know (facts, information), to learn*
  no saber ni jota de ... *to not have a clue about ...*
  ¿Quién sabe? *Who knows?*
  ¿Sabe cómo ...? *Do you know how to ...?*
  ¡Yo qué sé! *How do I know!?/How should I know!?*
saborear *to taste*
sacar *to take out, to get*
  sacar buenas notas *to get good grades*
  sacar malas notas *to get bad grades*
saco (m.) *jacket*
sal (f.) *salt*
sala (f.) *living room*
  sala de conferencias *meeting room, conference room, lecture hall*
salado/salada (m./f.) *salty*
salario (m.) *salary*
salida (f.) *exit*
salir *to leave, to go out*
  salir de viaje *to go on a trip*
salsa (f.) *sauce, salsa*

saltar *to skip*
  saltarse el semáforo *to go through a light*
saludable (m./f.) *healthy*
saludo (m.) *greeting*
  ¡Saludos! *Hello!*
sandalias (f. pl.) *sandals*
sangre (f.) *blood*
  hacerse un examen de sangre *to take a blood test*
  ser de sangre azul *to have blue blood (lit., to be of blue blood)*
se *himself, herself, itself, yourself* (fml.), *themselves, yourselves* (fml.); *(to/for) him, her, it, you* (fml. sg./pl.), *them* (indirect object pronoun, used in place of le/les when preceding lo/la/los/las); *you, people, one* (impersonal pronoun)
secadora (f.) *dryer*
sección (f.) *section*
seco/seca (m./f.) *dry*
  lavar en seco *to dry-clean*
secretaria (m./f.) *secretary*
secreto (m.) *secret*
sed (f.) *thirst*
  tener sed *to be thirsty*
seda (f.) *silk*
seguir *to follow*
  Siga derecho. *Go straight.*
  Siga por el carril de la derecha. *Stay in the right lane.*
segundo/segunda (m./f.) *second*
  segundo año *second year*
seguridad (f.) *safety, security*
  abrocharse el cinturón de seguridad *to buckle up*
seguro (m.) *insurance*
seguro/segura (m./f.) *sure, safe*
  Seguro/Segura que sí. *I'm sure.*
seis *six*
seiscientos/seiscientas (m./f.) *six hundred*
semáforo (m.) *traffic light*
  saltarse el semáforo *to go through a light*
semana (f.) *week*
  dos días a la semana *twice a week*
  esta semana *this week*
  fin (m.) de semana *weekend*
  próxima semana *next week*
  semana pasada *last week*
  semana que viene *next week*

  todas las semanas *every week*
semanal (m./f.) *weekly*
semestre (m.) *semester*
señal (f.) *signal*
  dejar un mensaje después de oír la señal *to leave a message after the tone*
senderismo (m.) *hiking*
  hacer senderismo *to go hiking*
seno (m.) *breast*
señor (m.) *Mr.*
señora (f.) *Mrs.*
sensatamente *sensibly*
sensiblemente *perceptibly*
sentar *to seat*
  estar sentado *to be seated*
sentarse *to sit down*
sentido (m.) *sense, direction*
  de sentido único *one-way*
sentir *to feel*
  Lo siento. *I'm sorry.*
  sentir que … *to regret that …*
sentirse *to feel*
septiembre (m.) *September*
ser *to be*
  Es la una. *It's one o'clock.*
  Son las tres. *It's three o'clock.*
  Son las tres en punto. *It's three o'clock sharp.*
  ser caradura *to be shameless*
serie (f.) *series*
serio/seria (m./f.) *serious*
serpiente (f.) *snake*
servicio (m.) *service*
  ¿Está incluido el servicio? *Is service included?*
servilleta (f.) *napkin*
servir *to serve*
  ¿En qué puedo servirle? *How may I help you?*
sesenta *sixty*
sesión (f.) *session*
setecientos/setecientas (m./f.) *seven hundred*
setenta *seventy*
si *if*
  ¿Qué tal si … ? *How about if … ?*
  ¿Qué te parece si … ? *How about if … ?*
sí *yes*
  ¡Claro que sí! *Of course!*
  Creo que sí. *I think so.*
  Seguro/segura que sí. *I'm sure.*

¡Yo espero que sí! *I hope so!*
sicología (f.) *psychology*
siempre *always*
siesta (f.) *nap*
siete *seven*
siglo (m.) *century*
  este siglo *this century*
significar *to mean*
silenciosamente *quietly*
silla (f.) *chair, seat*
simpático/simpática (m./f.) *friendly*
simplemente *simply, only*
sin *without*
sindicato (m.) *union*
síndrome (m.) *syndrome*
  síndrome del túnel del carpio *carpal tunnel syndrome*
síntoma (m.) *symptom*
sistema (m.) *system*
  sistema de sonido *sound system*
sitio (m.) *place*
  sitio web *website*
situación (f.) *situation*
sobre *on top of, over, above, about*
  sobre todo *especially*
sobrecocido/sobrecocida (m./f.) *overcooked*
sobremesa (f.) *after-dinner conversation*
sobrina (f.) *niece*
sobrino (m.) *nephew*
sofá (m.) *sofa, couch*
sol (m.) *sun*
  gafas (f. pl.) de sol *sunglasses*
  Hace sol. *It's sunny.*
solamente *only*
soledad (f.) *solitude*
solicitar *to apply for, to request*
solicitud (f.) *application*
sólo *merely, solely, only*
solo/sola (m./f.) *sole, only, alone*
soltero/soltera (m./f.) *single*
solución (f.) *solution*
sombrero (m.) *hat*
sonar *to sound, to ring*
soñar *to dream*
  ¡Ni lo sueñes! *Don't even dream about it!*
  soñar con … *to dream about …*
sonido (m.) *sound*
  sistema (m.) de sonido *sound system*

sonido (m.) *sound*
sonreír *to smile*
sopa (f.) *soup*
sorprenderse *to be surprised*
  sorprenderse de que … *to be surprised that …*
sorpresa (f.) *surprise*
sótano (m.) *basement*
su/sus (sg./pl.) *his, her, its, their, your* (pl./sg. fml.)
suave (m./f.) *soft*
subasta (f.) *auction*
subterráneo (m.) *subway*
suburbano/suburbana (m./f.) *suburban*
suceso (m.) *event, happening*
sucio/sucia (m./f.) *dirty*
Sudamérica *South America*
suegra (f.) *mother-in-law*
suegro (m.) *father-in-law*
sueldo (m.) *pay*
suelo (m.) *floor*
suelto/suelta (m./f.) *loose, flowing*
sueño (m.) *sleepiness, sleep*
  tener sueño *to be sleepy*
suerte (f.) *luck*
suéter (m.) *sweater*
suficiente (m./f.) *enough*
sufrir *to suffer*
sugerir *to suggest*
  sugerir que … *to suggest that …*
supermercado (m.) *supermarket*
supuesto (m.) *supposition*
  por supuesto *of course*
sur (m.) *south*
suscriptor/suscriptora (m./f.) *subscriber*
  línea (f.) de suscriptor digital (DSL) *DSL*
suspender *to fail, to suspend*
  suspender un examen *to fail a test*
suspenso (m.) *suspense*
  películas (f. pl.) de suspenso *suspense films*
suyo/suya/suyos/suyas (m. sg./f. sg./m. pl./f. pl.) *his, hers, theirs, yours*

T

tabla (f.) *table, board*
  tabla de planchar *ironing board*
tacón (m.) *heel*
tajada (f.) *slice*
tal *such*

¿Qué tal? *How's it going?*
¿Qué tal si … ? *How about if … ?*
tal vez *perhaps*
talla (f.) *size*
tamaño (m.) *size*
también *also, too*
tampoco *neither, not either*
tan *so (very)*
tan … como *as … as (comparison)*
tanto *in such a manner*
mientras tanto *meanwhile*
por lo tanto *therefore*
tanto/tanta (m./f.) *as much, as many*
tanto/tanta/tantos/tantas (m. sg./f. sg./m. pl./f. pl.) … como *as … as (comparison)*
taquilla (f.) *box office*
tarde *late*
Hasta más tarde. *Until later.*
más tarde *later*
Se me hace tarde. *I'm late.*
tarde (f.) *afternoon*
a las cuatro de la tarde *at four p.m.*
Buenas tardes. *Good afternoon.*
de la tarde *in the afternoon*
esta tarde *this afternoon*
tarea (f.) *homework*
tarjeta (f.) *card*
tarjeta de crédito *credit card*
taxi (m.) *taxi*
taxista (m./f.) *taxi driver*
taza (f.) *cup*
tazón (m.) *bowl*
te *you* (infml. sg.) *(direct object pronoun)*; *(to/for) you* (infml. sg.) *(indirect object pronoun)*; *yourself* (infml.)
Te presento a … *Let me introduce you to …*
té (m.) *tea*
teatro (m.) *theater*
techo (m.) *ceiling*
teclado (m.) *keyboard*
tecnología (f.) *technology*
tejanos (m. pl.) *jeans*
telefónico/telefónica (m./f.) *(of) telephone, telephonic*
cabina (f.) telefónica *telephone booth*
guía (f.) telefónica *phone book*
teléfono (m.) *telephone*
colgar el teléfono *to hang up the phone*

contestar el teléfono *to answer the phone*
llamar por teléfono *to make a phone call*
llamar por teléfono a … *to call … on the phone*
marcar un número de teléfono *to dial a phone number*
número (m.) de teléfono *telephone number*
televisión (f.) *television*
mirar la televisón *to watch television*
programa (m.) de televisión *television program*
televisor (m.) *television (set)*
temer *to fear, to be afraid of*
temperatura (f.) *temperature*
templo (m.) *temple*
temprano *early* (adverb)
temprano/temprana (m./f.) *early*
tendón (m.) *tendon*
tenedor (m.) *fork*
tener *to have*
Aquí tiene. *Here you are.*
¿Cuántos años tiene? *How old are you* (sg. fml.)*/is he/is she?*
Que tenga un buen día. *Have a nice day.*
tener … años *to be … years old*
tener calor *to be hot, to be warm*
tener cansancio *to be tired*
tener dolor de cabeza *to have a headache*
tener dolor de garganta *to have a sore throat*
tener fiebre *to have a fever*
tener frío *to be cold*
tener ganas de … *to feel like …*
tener hambre *to be hungry*
tener interés en … *to be interested in …*
tener la cabeza fría *to keep a cool head*
tener la tensión alta/baja *to have high/low blood pressure*
tener los pies en la tierra *to have both feet on the ground*
tener mareo *to be dizzy*
tener miedo *to be scared*
tener náusea(s) *to be nauseated, to have nausea*
tener paciencia *to be patient*
tener prisa *to be in a hurry*
tener que … *to have to …*
tener razón *to be right*
tener sed *to be thirsty*

tener sueño *to be sleepy*
tener tos *to have a cough*
tenis (m.) *tennis*
tensión (f.) *tension*
tener la tensión alta/baja *to have high/low blood pressure*
tomar la tensión *to take the blood pressure*
tercero/tercer/tercera (m. sg./m. sg. before a m. noun/f.) *third*
tercer año *third year*
terminar *to finish*
término (m.) *term, period, point*
término medio *medium-rare*
término tres cuartos *medium*
tesis (f.) *dissertation*
tetera (f.) *teakettle*
texto (m.) *text*
libro (m.) de texto *textbook*
ti *you* (infml. sg.) (after a preposition)
tía (f.) *aunt, woman*
tiempo (m.) *time, weather*
a tiempo *on time, in time*
a tiempo completo *full-time*
a tiempo parcial *part-time*
El tiempo es bueno. *The weather is good.*
¿Cómo estás de tiempo? *Do you have time?/ How are you doing for time?*
Hace muy buen tiempo. *It's beautiful.*
medio tiempo *halftime*
tienda (f.) *store, convenience store*
tienda de antigüedades *antique store*
tienda de electrodomésticos *appliances store*
tienda de ropa *clothing store*
tienda por departamentos *department store*
Tienes que … *You have to …*
tierra (f.) *land*
tener los pies en la tierra *to have both feet on the ground*
tímido/tímida (m./f.) *shy*
tinto/tinta (m./f.) *dark red*
vino (m.) tinto *red wine*
tío (m.) *uncle, man*
típico/típica (m./f.) *typical*
tipo (m.) *type*
tiquete (m.) *ticket*
título (m.) *degree, diploma*
toalla (f.) *towel*
tobillo (m.) *ankle*

tocar *to touch, to play an instrument*
tocar el piano *to play the piano*
tocar la guitarra *to play the guitar*
todavía *still, yet*
todo (m.) *everything*
sobre todo *especially*
todo/toda (m./f.) *all, every*
todas las semanas *every week*
todo el día *all day*
todos los días *every day*
tomar *to take, to have (food and drink)*
tomar la tensión *to take the blood pressure*
tomar un medicamento *to take medication*
tomate (m.) *tomato*
tono (m.) *tone, dial tone*
tormenta (f.) *storm*
torta (f.) *cake*
tos (f.) *cough*
tener tos *to have a cough*
tostada (f.) *toast*
totalmente *absolutely*
tóxico/tóxica (m./f.) *toxic*
niebla (f.) tóxica *smog*
trabajador/trabajadora (m./f.) *hardworking*
trabajar *to work*
¿En qué trabaja? *What do you do for a living?*
trabajo (m.) *job, work*
¡Buen trabajo! *Good job!*
historial (m.) de trabajo *résumé*
trabajo de investigación *research paper*
trabajo de verano *summer job*
trabajo fijo *steady job*
traducir *to translate*
traer *to bring, to get, to take*
tráfico (m.) *traffic*
traje (m.) *suit*
traje de baño *bathing suit*
tranquilo/tranquila (m./f.) *quiet, calm*
trasladar *to transfer*
tratamiento (m.) *treatment*
tratar *to treat*
¿Cómo te trata la vida? *How's life treating you?*
tratar *to try*
tratar de … *to try … (to do something)*
trece *thirteen*
treinta *thirty*
tren (m.) *train*

estación (f.) de tren   *train station*
tres *three*
trescientos/trescientas (m./f.) *three hundred*
triste (m./f.) *sad*
  Es triste que ... *It's sad that ...*
tristemente *sadly*
trotar *to jog*
trueno (m.) *thunder*
tú *you* (sg. infml.) (subject pronoun)
tu/tus (sg./pl.) *your* (sg. infml.)
túnel (m.) *tunnel*
  síndrome (m.) del túnel del carpio *carpal tunnel syndrome*
turismo (m.) *tourism*
turista (m./f.) *tourist*
tuyo/tuya/tuyos/tuyas (m. sg./f. sg./m. pl./f. pl.) *yours* (infml.)

U

último/última (m./f.) *last*
  último grito (m.) *the very latest*
un *a* (m.)
una *a* (f.), *one (o'clock)*
  Es la una. *It's one o'clock.*
It's one o'clock.
uña (f.) *nail, claw*
unas *some* (f. pl.)
único/única (m./f.) *only, unique, single*
  de sentido (m.) único *one-way*
unido/unida (m./f.) *united*
  los Estados Unidos *the United States*
universidad (f.) *university*
uno *one*
unos *some* (m. pl.)
urbano/urbana (m./f.) *urban*
urgentemente *urgently*
Uruguay (m.) *Uruguay*
uruguayo/uruguaya (m./f.) *Uruguayan*
usar *to use, to take*
usted *you* (sg. fml.) (subject pronoun)
  el de usted (m. sg.) *yours* (sg. fml.)
  la de usted (f. sg.) *yours* (sg. fml.)
ustedes *you* (pl.) (subject pronoun)
  el de ustedes (m. sg.) *yours* (pl.) (referring to a masculine singular object)
  la de ustedes (f. sg.) *yours* (pl.) (referring to a feminine singular object)
uvas (f. pl.) *grapes*

racimo (m.) de uvas *bunch of grapes*

V

vacaciones (f. pl.) *vacation*
  de vacaciones *on vacation*
vajilla (f.) *tableware*
  detergente (m.) de vajilla *dishwashing detergent*
vale (m.) *coupon, voucher*
  ¿Cuánto vale? *How much is it?*
Vamos ... *Let's go ...*
vaqueros (m. pl.) *jeans*
variedad (f.) *variety*
varios/varias (m./f.) *several*
vaso (m.) *glass*
vecino/vecina (m./f.) *neighbor*
vegetal (m.) *vegetable*
veinte *twenty*
veinticinco *twenty-five*
veinticuatro *twenty-four*
veintidós *twenty-two*
veintinueve *twenty-nine*
veintiocho *twenty-eight*
veintiséis *twenty-six*
veintisiete *twenty-seven*
veintitrés *twenty-three*
veintiuno *twenty-one*
velocidad (f.) *speed*
vendaje (m.) *bandage*
vendedor/vendedora (m./f.) *salesman/ saleswoman*
vender *to sell*
venezolano/venezolana (m./f.) *Venezuelan*
Venezuela (f.) *Venezuela*
venir *to come, to fit (somebody)*
  año (m.) que viene *next year*
  mes (m.) que viene *next month*
  Me viene bien. *It suits me fine.*
  semana (f.) que viene *next week*
venta (f.) *sale*
ventana (f.) *window*
ver *to see*
  A ver ... *Let's see ...*
  Nos vemos. *See you.* (lit., *We see each other.*)
  por lo visto *apparently*
  ver todo negro *to be a pessimist* (lit., *to see everything as black*)
verano (m.) *summer*

trabajo (m.) de verano   *summer job*
verdad (f.) *truth*
  Es verdad. *That's right.*
  No es verdad que …   *It is not true that …*
  ¿verdad? *right?*
verde (m./f.) *green*
  contar un chiste verde   *to tell a dirty joke (lit.,*
    to tell a green joke)
  verde oscuro   *dark green*
verdura (f.) *vegetable*
vertebral (m./f.) *vertebral*
  columna (f.) vertebral   *backbone, spinal*
    column
vestíbulo (m.) *hall*
vestido (m.) *dress*
  vestido de noche   *evening dress*
vestir *to dress (someone)*
vestirse *to get dressed*
veterinario/veterinaria (m./f.) *veterinarian*
vez (f.) *time*
  a veces *sometimes*
  dos veces por semana   *twice a week*
  una vez   *once*
  tal vez   *perhaps*
vía (f.) *lane*
viajar *to travel*
viaje (m.) *travel, trip*
  Buen viaje. *Have a good trip.*
  salir de viaje   *to go on a trip*
vida (f.) *life*
  ¿Cómo te trata la vida? *How's life treating*
    you?
  hoja (f.) de vida   *résumé*
viejo/vieja (m./f.) *old*
viento (m.) *wind*
  Hace viento. *It's windy.*
viento (m.) *wind*
viernes (m.) *Friday*
vincularse *to form links*
  vincularse con …   *to form links with …*
vinilo (m.) *vinyl*
  disco (m.) de vinilo   *vinyl record*
vino (m.) *wine*
  vino blanco   *white wine*
  vino tinto   *red wine*
violeta (m./f.) *violet (color)*
violín (m.) *violin*
visita guiada (f.) *guided tour*

visitante (m./f.) *visitor*
visitar *to visit*
  visitar los lugares de interés   *to go sightseeing*
vista (f.) *view*
  conocer de vista   *to know by sight*
vitorear *to cheer*
vivir *to live*
volar *to fly*
volver *to turn, to return*
vosotras *you* (f. pl. infml.) (subject pronoun)
  (used in Spain)
vosotros *you* (m. pl. infml./mixed group infml.)
  (subject pronoun) (used in Spain)
voz (f.) *voice*
  buzón (m.) de voz   *voice mail*
vuelo (m.) *flight*
vuelta (f.) *turn*
  a la vuelta de la esquina   *around the corner*
vuestro/vuestra/vuestros/vuestras (m. sg./f.
  sg./m. pl./f. pl.) *your/yours* (pl. infml.) (used in
  Spain)

W

web (f.) *web (internet)*
  página (f.) web   *webpage*
  sitio (m.) web   *website*

Y

y *and*
  a las ocho y diez   *at eight ten (8:10)*
  a las cinco y media   *at a half past five*
  treinta y uno   *thirty-one*
ya *already, now, right*
  Ya está. *That's it.*
yerno (m.) *son-in-law*
yo *I*

Z

zanahoria (f.) *carrot*
zapatería (f.) *shoe store*
zapatillas (f. pl.) *slippers*
  zapatillas deportivas   *sneakers, tennis shoes*
zapatos (m. pl.) *shoes*
zumo (m.) *juice*

English-Spanish

A

a *un/una* (m./f.)
  a lot *mucho*
  a lot of *mucho/mucha* (m./f.), *muchos/muchas*
  (m. pl./f. pl.)
abdomen *abdomen* (m.)
about *de, sobre, a eso de*
  about the (m.) *del (de + el)*
  at about nine o'clock *a eso de las nueve*
  dream about … *soñar con …*
  How about if … ? *¿Qué tal si … ?/¿Qué te*
    parece si … ?
  not have a clue about … (to) *no saber ni jota*
    de …
above *encima, sobre*
  above … *encima de …*
absolute *absoluto/absoluta* (m./f.)
absolutely *absolutamente, totalmente*
  absolutely not *en absoluto*
absurd *absurdo/absurda* (m./f.)
academic *académico/académica* (m./f.)
academy *academia* (f.)
accept (to) *aceptar*
accident *accidente* (m.)
account *cuenta* (f.)
accountant *contable* (m./f.)
across from … *enfrente de …*
actor *actor* (m.)
actress *actriz* (f.)
actually *efectivamente, realmente*
acupuncture *acupuntura* (f.)
address *dirección* (f.)
adult *adulto/adulta* (m./f.)
adventure *aventura* (f.)
  adventure films *películas* (pl.) *de aventuras*
advise (to) *aconsejar*
  advise that/to … (to) *aconsejar que …*
after … *después de …*
  after-dinner conversation *sobremesa* (f.)
  It's ten after one in the morning. *Es la una y*
    diez de la madrugada.
afternoon *tarde* (f.)
  Good afternoon. *Buenas tardes.*
  in the afternoon *de la tarde*
  this afternoon *esta tarde*

afterwards *después*
against *contra*
age *edad* (f.)
agency *agencia* (f.)
agent *agente* (m./f.)
agitated *agitado/agitada* (m./f.)
agreement *acuerdo* (m.)
aim *objetivo* (m.)
airline *aerolínea* (f.)
airplane *avión* (m.)
airport *aeropuerto* (m.)
algebra *álgebra* (f.)
all *todo/toda* (m./f.)
  all day *todo el día*
  All right. *De acuerdo.*
  No, not at all. *No, para nada.*
allergic *alérgico/alérgica* (m./f.)
allergy *alergia* (f.)
alley *callejón* (m.)
allow (to) *permitir*
almost *casi*
  almost never *casi nunca*
alone *solo/sola* (m./f.)
already *ya*
  as you already know *como ya sabes*
also *igualmente, también*
always *siempre*
a.m. *de la mañana, de la madrugada*
  at nine a.m. *a las nueve de la mañana*
American *americano/americana* (m./f.),
  estadounidense (m./f.)
amusement *diversión* (f.)
  amusement park *parque* (m.) *de diversiones*
and *y*
  and on top of that … *y encima …*
anger *ira* (f.)
ankle *tobillo* (m.)
another *otro/otra* (m./f.)
answer *respuesta* (f.)
answer (to) *responder, contestar*
  answer the phone (to) *contestar el teléfono*
answering machine *contestador* (m.)
  (automático)
antique *antigüedad* (f.)
antiques *antigüedades* (f. pl.)
  antique store *tienda* (f.) *de antigüedades*
any *cualquier*
Anything else? *¿Algo más?*

apartment *apartamento* (m.), *piso* (m.)
apology *disculpa* (f.)
apparently *por lo visto*
appeal *gracia* (f.)
appearance *pinta* (f.)
appetite *apetito* (m.)
appetizer *entrada* (f.)
apple *manzana* (f.)
application *solicitud* (f.)
apply for (to) *solicitar*
appointment *cita* (f.)
April *abril* (m.)
architect *arquitecto/arquitecta* (m./f.)
architecture *arquitectura* (f.)
area *área* (m.)
Argentina *Argentina* (f.)
Argentinian *argentino/argentina* (m./f.)
arm *brazo* (m.)
around *por, a eso de*
  around the corner *a la vuelta de la esquina*
  around town *por la ciudad*
arrive (to) *llegar*
  arrive at ... (to) *llegar a ...*
art *arte* (m.)
artist *artista* (m./f.)
as *como, cual/cuales* (sg./pl.)
  as ... as *tan ... como* (comparisons), *tanto/
  tanta/tantos/tantas* (m. sg./f. sg./m. pl./f. pl.) ...
  como (comparisons)
  as many/much *cuanto/cuanta/cuantos/
  cuantas* (m. sg./f. sg./m. pl./f. pl.), *tanto/tanta*
  (m./f.)
  as soon as possible *lo antes posible*
  as you already know *como ya sabes*
ask (to) *preguntar*
ask for (to) *pedir*
assistant *asistente* (m./f.)
astronaut *astronauta* (m./f.)
at *a, en, por*
  arrive at ... (to) *llegar a ...*
  at a quarter to six *a las seis menos cuarto*
  at about nine o'clock *a eso de las nueve*
  at dawn *al amanecer*
  at dusk *al atardecer*
  at five (o'clock) *a las cinco*
  at hand *a la mano*
  at last *por fin*
  at midnight *a medianoche*

  at night *por la noche*
  at noon *a mediodía*
  at the (m.) *al (a + el)*
  at the present time *actualmente*
  at this moment *en este momento*
  At what time is it? *¿A qué hora es?*
  look at (to) *mirar*
  No, not at all. *No, para nada.*
athlete *atleta* (m./f.)
athletic *atlético/atlética* (m./f.), *deportivo/
  deportiva* (m./f.)
attach (to) *adjuntar*
  attach a file (to) *adjuntar un documento/
  archivo*
attachment *anexo* (m.), *archivo* (m.), *documento*
  (m.) *adjunto*
attend (to) *asistir*
  attend to (to) *atender*
attention *atención* (f.)
attraction *atracción* (f.)
attractive *atractivo/atractiva* (m./f.)
auction *subasta* (f.)
August *agosto* (m.)
aunt *tía* (f.)
author *autor* (m.)
automatic *automático/automático* (m./f.)
available *disponible* (m./f.)
avenue *avenida* (f.)
avocado *aguacate* (m.)
axe *hacha* (f.)

B

baby *bebé* (m./f.)
  little baby *bebito/bebita* (m./f.)
bachelor's degree *licenciatura* (f.)
back *espalda* (f.), *atrás*
  know like the back of one's hand (to) *conocer
  palmo a palmo*
backbone *columna* (f.) *vertebral*
background *historial* (m.)
backyard *patio* (m.)
bad *malo/mala* (m./f.), *podrido/podrida* (m./f.)
  It's not bad. *No está mal.*
bad(ly) *mal*
bag *bolsa* (f.)
baggy *ancho/ancha* (m./f.)
bakery *panadería* (f.), *pastelería* (f.) (*for pastries,
  etc.*)

balcony *balcón* (m.)

bald *calvo/calva* (m./f.)

ball *balón* (m.), *pelota* (f.)

banana *plátano* (m.), *banana* (f.)

band *banda* (f.), *conjunto* (m.) *(music)*

bandage *vendaje* (m.)

bank *banco* (m.)

banker *banquero/banquera* (m./f.)

bar *bar* (m.)

barbershop *barbería* (f.)

bargain *ganga* (f.)

base *base* (f.)

baseball *béisbol* (m.)

  baseball game *partido* (m.) *de béisbol*

basement *sótano* (m.)

basketball *baloncesto* (m.)

bathe (to) *bañarse*

bathing suit *traje* (m.) *de baño*

bathing trunks *bañador* (m.)

bathroom *baño* (m.)

bathtub *bañera* (f.)

be (to) *estar, ser*

  be … years old (to) *tener … años*

  be a pessimist (to) *ver todo negro* (lit., to see everything as black)

  be able to (to) *poder*

  be afraid (to) *tener miedo*

  be afraid of (to) *temer*

  be afraid that … (to) *tener miedo de que …*

  be an optimist (to) *ver todo color de rosa* (lit., to see everything pink)

  be angry that … (to) *enfadarse de que …*

  be bored (to) *aburrirse*

  be bothered (to) *molestarse*

  be bothered that … (to) *molestarse de que …*

  be called (to) *llamarse*

  be cold (to) *tener frío*

  be dizzy (to) *tener mareo*

  be dressed to the nines (to) *ir de punta en blanco* (lit., to go from the tip in white)

  be embarrassed (to) *ponerse colorado* (lit., to turn red)

  be glad (to) *alegrarse*

  be glad that … (to) *alegrarse de que …*

  be going to (do) (to) *ir a …*

  be hot (to) *tener calor*

  be hungry (to) *tener hambre*

  be in a hurry (to) *tener prisa, tener cansancio*

be in good hands (to) *estar en buenas manos*

be interested in … (to) *tener interés en …*

be lacking (to) *faltar*

be lazy (to) *ser perezoso*

be nauseated (to) *tener náusea(s)*

be necessary (to) *faltar*

be not doing well (to) *estar mal*

be patient (to) *tener paciencia*

be present (to) *asistir*

be right (to) *tener razón*

be scared (to) *tener miedo*

be scared that … (to) *tener miedo de que …*

be seated (to) *estar sentado*

be shameless (to) *ser caradura*

be sleepy (to) *tener sueño*

be surprised (to) *sorprenderse*

be surprised that … (to) *sorprenderse de que …*

be thankful (to) *agradecer*

be thirsty (to) *tener sed*

be tied (to) *quedar empatados*

be tired (to) *tener consancio*

be very angry (to) *estar rojo de la ira* (lit., to be red with fury)

be warm (to) *tener calor*

May you be well. *Que esté bien.*

beach *playa* (f.)

bean *fríjol* (m.)

beauty mark *lunar* (m.)

because *porque*

  because of *por*

become (to) *ponerse*

bed *cama* (f.)

bedroom *dormitorio* (m.), *alcoba* (f.), *cuarto* (m.)

beef *carne* (f.)

beer *cerveza* (f.)

before *antes*

  before … *antes de …*

begin (to) *empezar, comenzar*

behind *detrás, atrás, retrasado/retrasada* (m./f.)

  behind … *detrás de …*

believe (to) *creer*

  not believe that … (to) *no creer que …*

below *bajo*

belt *cinturón* (m.)

benefit *beneficio* (m.), *provecho* (m.)

best (the) *el/la/los/las* (m. sg./f. sg./m. pl./f. pl.) *mejor*

bet *apuesta* (f.)
bet (to) *apostar*
  bet that … (to) *apuesto a que …*
better *mejor* (m./f.)
  It's better that … *Es mejor que …*
between *entre*
  between … and … *entre … y …*
bicycle *bicicleta* (f.)
big *gran/grande* (before sg. nouns/all other cases),
  gordo/gorda (m./f.)
  bigger *mayor* (m./f.)
  biggest (the) *el/la/los/las* (m. sg./f. sg./m. pl./f.
    pl.) *mayor*
biking *ciclismo* (m.)
bill *cuenta* (f.)
billboard *cartelera* (f.)
billiards *billar* (m.)
biology *biología* (f.)
bitter *amargo/amarga* (m./f.)
black *negro/negra* (m./f.)
bleach *lejía* (f.)
blender *batidora* (f.)
block *cuadra* (f.), *manzana* (f.)
  It's two blocks from here. *Está a dos cuadras
    de aquí.*
block (to) *bloquear*
blonde *rubio/rubia* (m./f.)
blood *sangre* (f.)
  have blue blood (to) *ser de sangre azul* (lit., to
    be of blue blood)
  have high/low blood pressure (to) *tener la
    tensión alta/baja*
  take a blood test (to) *hacerse un examen de
    sangre*
  take the blood pressure (to) *tomar la tensión*
blouse *blusa* (f.)
blue *azul* (m./f.)
  color light blue (the) *azul* (m.) *claro*
  dark blue *azul oscuro*
  have blue blood (to) *ser de sangre azul* (lit., to
    be of blue blood)
  light blue *azul claro*
  navy blue *azul marino*
  sky blue *celeste* (m./f.)
board *bordo* (m.), *tabla* (f.)
  ironing board *tabla de planchar*
  on board *a bordo*
  Welcome aboard. *Bienvenidos a bordo.*

body *cuerpo* (m.)
Bolivia *Bolivia* (f.)
Bolivian *boliviano/boliviana* (m./f.)
bone *hueso* (m.)
book *libro* (m.)
bookshelf *estante* (m.)
bookstore *librería* (f.)
booth *cabina* (f.)
bore (to) *aburrir*
  I'm bored by … *Me aburre/aburren …* (sg./pl.)
bored *aburrido/aburrida* (m./f.)
  be bored (to) *aburrirse*
boring *aburrido/aburrida* (m./f.)
boss *jefe/jefa* (m./f.)
bottle *botella* (f.), *frasco* (m.)
bowl *cuenco* (m.), *tazón* (m.)
box *caja* (f.)
box office *taquilla* (f.)
boy *chico* (m.), *muchacho* (m.)
boyfriend *novio* (m.)
bracelet *pulsera* (f.)
brain *cerebro* (m.)
brake (automobile) *freno* (m.)
  hit the brakes (to) *poner el pie en el freno*
Brazil *Brasil* (m.)
Brazilian *brasilero/brasilera* (m./f.) (adjective),
  brasileño/brasileña (m./f.) (noun)
bread *pan* (m.)
breakfast *desayuno* (m.)
breast *seno* (m.), *pecho* (m.)
bridge *puente* (m.)
bring (to) *traer*
brochure *folleto* (m.)
broom *escoba* (f.)
brother *hermano* (m.)
  brothers, brothers and sisters *hermanos* (pl.)
brother-in-law *cuñado* (m.)
brown *marrón* (m./f.)
  grayish brown *pardo/parda* (m./f.)
buckle up (to) *abrocharse el cinturón de
  seguridad*
building *edificio* (m.)
bunch *manojo* (m.)
  bunch of grapes *racimo* (m.) *de uvas*
burnt *quemado/quemada* (m./f.)
bus *autobús* (m.)
  tour bus *recorrido* (m.) *por autobús*
bus stop *parada* (f.)

Glossary **351**

business *negocio* (m.)
  businessman *hombre* (m.) *de negocios*
  businesswoman *mujer* (f.) *de negocios*
busy *ocupado/ocupada* (m./f.)
  The line is busy. *Está comunicando.*
but *pero, mas*
butcher shop *carnicería* (f.)
butter *mantequilla* (f.)
buy (to) *comprar*
  buy on sale (to) *comprar en rebaja*
by *por, en*
  by chance *por casualidad*
  by (a certain time) *para*
  go by (to) *pasar*
  I'm bored by … *Me aburre/aburren …* (sg./pl.)
  know by sight (to) *conocer de vista*
Bye. *Chao.*

C

cabin *cabina* (f.)
cable *cable* (m.)
café *cafetería* (f.)
cafeteria *cafetería* (f.)
cake *torta* (f.)
call (to) *llamar*
  be called (to) *llamarse*
  call … on the phone (to) *llamar por teléfono a …*
  make a phone call (to) *llamar por teléfono*
  Who's calling? *¿Quién lo llama?*
calm *tranquilo/tranquila* (m./f.)
camera *cámara* (f.)
camp *campo* (m.)
camping *cámping* (m.)
  go camping (to) *ir de cámping*
can *lata* (f.)
can *poder*
  Could you …? *¿Podría …?*
Canada *Canadá* (m.)
Canadian *canadiense* (m./f.)
cancel (to) *cancelar*
candidate *candidato/candidata* (m./f.)
capacity *capacidad* (f.)
car *auto* (m.), *automóvil* (m.), *carro* (m.), *coche* (m.)
card *tarjeta* (f.)
  playing cards *naipes* (m. pl.), *cartas* (f. pl.)
cardboard *cartón* (m.)
carefully *atentamente*

carnival *carnaval* (m.)
carpal tunnel syndrome *síndrome* (m.) *del túnel del carpio*
carpenter *carpintero/carpintera* (m./f.)
carpet *alfombra* (f.)
carpus *carpio* (m.)
carrot *zanahoria* (f.)
carry (to) *llevar*
carton *bote* (m.), *cartón* (m.)
case *caso* (m.)
cash *efectivo* (m.)
  pay cash (to) *pagar en efectivo*
cash register *caja* (f.)
casual *informal* (m./f.)
cat *gato* (m.)
catch (to) *coger*
cathedral *catedral* (f.)
CD *CD* (m.)
  CD player *lector* (m.) *de CD*
  CD-ROM *CD rom* (m.)
  CD-ROM drive *lector* (m.) *de CD rom*
ceiling *techo* (m.)
cell phone *celular* (m.)
center *centro* (m.)
century *siglo* (m.)
  this century *este siglo*
chair *silla* (f.)
champagne *champaña/champán* (f./m.)
champion *campeón/campeona* (m./f.)
championship *campeonato* (m.)
chance *casualidad* (f.)
  by chance *por casualidad*
change *cambio* (m.)
change (to) *cambiar*
channel *canal* (m.)
charm *encanto* (m.)
chat *charla* (f.)
  chat room *espacio* (m.) *para charla, chat* (m.)
cheap *barato/barata* (m./f.)
check *cheque* (m.), *cuenta* (f.)
check in (to) *registrarse*
check out (to) *pagar la cuenta*
cheek *mejilla* (f.)
cheer (to) *vitorear*
cheese *queso* (m.)
chemistry *química* (f.)
chess *ajedrez* (m.)
chest *pecho* (m.)

chicken *pollo* (m.)
child (male/female) *niño/niña* (m./f.)
  child psychology *sicología* (f.) *infantil*
  children (sons and daughters) *hijos* (pl.)
  children's *infantil* (m./f.)
  young child *párvulo/párvula* (m./f.)
Chile *Chile* (m.)
Chilean *chileno/chilena* (m./f.)
chin *barbilla* (f.)
Chinese (language) *chino* (m.)
chocolate *chocolate* (m.)
choir *coro* (m.)
choose (to) *elegir, escoger*
chop *chuleta* (f.)
  lamb chop *chuleta de cordero*
Christmas Eve *Nochebuena*
church *iglesia* (f.)
cigarette *cigarrillo* (m.)
  pack of cigarettes *cajetilla* (f.) *de cigarrillos*
circus *circo* (m.)
city *ciudad* (f.)
city hall *ayuntamiento* (m.)
class *clase* (f.)
classic *clásico/clásica* (m./f.)
  classical music *música* (f.) *clásica*
classroom *aula* (m.)
claw *uña* (f.)
clean *limpio/limpia* (m./f.)
clearly *claramente, claro*
clinic *clínica* (f.)
  clinical pharmacy *farmacia* (f.) *clínica*
clock *reloj* (m.)
close *cerca*
  close to ... *cerca de ...*
close (to) *cerrar*
closet *armario* (m.)
clothing *ropa* (f.)
  clothing store *tienda* (f.) *de ropa*
cloud *nube* (f.)
cloudy *nublado/nublada* (m./f.)
  It's cloudy. *Está nublado.*
club *club* (m.)
coach *entrenador/entrenadora* (m./f.)
coal *carbón* (m.)
coca *coca* (f.)
code *código* (m.)
coffee *café* (m.)
  coffee shop *cafetería* (f.)

coffee-colored *café* (m./f.)
coffeemaker *cafetera* (f.)
coincidence *coincidencia* (f.)
  What a coincidence! *¡Qué coincidencia!*
coincidence *casualidad* (f.)
cold *frío/fría* (m./f.)
cold temperature/sensation *frío* (m.)
  be cold (to) *tener frío*
  It's cold. *Hace frío.*
colleague *colega/colega* (m./f.)
collect (to) *coleccionar*
collection *colección* (f.)
cologne *colonia* (f.)
Colombia *Colombia* (f.)
Colombian *colombiano/colombiana* (m./f.)
color *color* (m.)
  color gray (the) *gris* (m.)
  color light blue (the) *azul* (m.) *claro*
  wear rose-colored glasses (to) *ver todo color de rosa* (lit., to see everything pink)
  What color is ... ? *¿De qué color es ... ?*
column *columna* (f.)
combine (to) *combinar*
come (to) *venir*
comedy *comedia* (f.)
comfortable *cómodo/cómoda* (m./f.)
coming *entrante* (m./f.)
comma *coma* (f.)
commercial *comercial* (m./f.)
communicate (to) *comunicar*
company *compañía* (f.)
complete (to) *completar*
completely *completamente*
computer *computadora* (f.), *ordenador* (m.)
concert *concierto* (m.)
conference *conferencia* (f.)
  conference room *sala de conferencias*
congratulate (to) *felicitar*
congratulations *enhorabuena* (f.)
  Congratulations! *¡Felicitaciones!*
connect (to) *conectar*
connection *conexión* (f.)
construction worker *obrero/obrera* (m./f.)
consult (to) *consultar*
continue (to) *continuar*
  Continue straight. *Continúa recto.*
contract *contrato* (m.)
contribution *contribución* (f.)

Glossary   **353**

convenience store *tienda* (f.)
cook (to) *cocinar*
cookie *galleta* (f.)
cooking *cocina* (f.)
copy *copia* (f.)
copy (to) *copiar*
corncob *mazorca* (f.)
corner *esquina* (f.)
  around the corner *a la vuelta de la esquina*
cost (to) *costar*
  How much does it cost? *¿Cuánto cuesta?*
cotton *algodón* (m.)
couch *sofá* (m.)
cough *tos* (f.)
  have a cough (to) *tener tos*
count (to) *contar*
counter *mostrador* (m.)
country *país* (m.)
coupon *vale* (m.)
course *curso* (m.), *asignatura* (f.)
court *juzgado* (m.)
cousin *primo/prima* (m./f.)
  cousins *primos* (pl.)
craft *artesanía* (f.)
credit *crédito* (m.)
  credit card *tarjeta* (f.) *de crédito*
creme *crema* (f.)
crime *delito* (m.)
cross (to) *cruzar*
cry *grito* (m.)
cry (to) *llorar*
cucumber *pepino* (m.)
cup *taza* (f.)
cupboard *aparador* (m.)
curriculum *currículum* (m.)
  CV *currículum vítae*
curtain *cortina* (f.)
custom sew (to) *hacer a la medida*
customer *cliente* (m./f.)
cycling *ciclismo* (m.)

D

dad *papá* (m.), *papi* (m.)
daily *diario/diaria* (m./f.)
dairy store *lechería* (f.)
dance (to) *bailar*
dancing *baile* (m.)
dark *oscuro/oscura* (m./f.)

dark blue *azul* (m./f.) *oscuro*
dark green *verde* (m./f.) *oscuro*
dark-skinned *moreno/morena* (m./f.)
date *fecha* (f.)
daughter *hija* (f.)
daughter-in-law *nuera* (f.)
dawn *amanecer* (m.)
  at dawn *al amanecer*
day *día* (m.)
  all day *todo el día*
  every day *todos los días*
  Have a nice day. *Que tenga un buen día.*
  special of the day *plato del día*
  spend the day (to) *pasar el día*
  this day *este día*
  working day *jornada* (f.)
dead person, dead *muerto/muerta* (m./f.)
decade *década* (f.)
December *diciembre* (m.)
decide (to) *decidir*
decision *decisión* (f.)
dedicate (to) *dedicar*
degree *grado* (m.), *título* (m.)
delay (to) *retrasar*
delete (to) *eliminar*
delicatessen *charcutería* (f.)
delicious *delicioso/deliciosa* (m./f.)
demand (to) *exigir*
demanding *exigente* (m./f.)
dentist *dentista* (m./f.)
deny (to) *negar*
  deny that … (to) *negar que …*
deodorant *desodorante* (m.)
department *departamento* (m.), *facultad* (f.) *(at a college/university)*
  department store *tienda* (f.) *por departamentos*
depend (to) *depender*
  depend on … (to) *depender de …*
describe (to) *describir*
description *descripción* (f.)
desert *desierto* (m.)
design *diseño* (m.)
desire *gana* (f.)
desk *escritorio* (m.)
dessert *postre* (m.)
detail *detalle* (m.)
detergent *detergente* (m.)

dishwashing detergent *detergente de vajilla*
laundry detergent *detergente de ropa*
detest (to) *detestar*
develop (to) *desarrollar*
dial (to) *marcar*
  dial a phone number (to) *marcar un número de teléfono*
dial tone *tono* (m.)
diarrhea *diarrea* (f.)
diary *diario* (m.)
  keep a diary (to) *llevar un diario*
die (to) *morir*
difference *diferencia* (f.)
different *diferente* (m./f.)
difficult *difícil* (m./f.)
  difficult situation *apuro* (m.)
digital *digital* (m./f.)
diligently *diligentemente*
diner *cafetería* (f.)
dining room *comedor* (m.)
dinner *cena* (f.), *comida* (f.)
diploma *diploma* (m.), *título* (m.)
direct (to) *dirigir*
direction *dirección* (f.), *sentido* (m.)
dirty *sucio/sucia* (m./f.)
disaster *desastre* (m.)
discount *descuento* (m.), *rebaja* (f.)
  give a discount (to) *hacer un descuento*
discuss (to) *discutir*
disease *enfermedad* (f.)
dish *plato* (m.)
  do the dishes(to) *lavar los platos*
  main dish *plato principal*
dishwasher *lavaplatos* (m.)
dishwashing detergent *detergente* (m.) *de vajilla*
disk *disco* (m.)
Disneyland *Disneylandia*
display window *escaparate* (m.)
dissertation *tesis* (f.)
diving *buceo* (m.)
divorce (someone) (to) *divorciarse de ...*
  get a divorce (to) *divorciarse*
divorced *divorciado/divorciada* (m./f.)
dizzy *mareado/mareada* (m./f.)
  be dizzy (to) *tener mareo*
do (to) *hacer*
  be not doing well (to) *estar mal*

Do me the favor of ... *Hágame el favor de ...*
  do the dishes (to) *lavar los platos*
  do the laundry (to) *lavar la ropa*
doctor *doctor/doctora* (m./f.), *médico/médica* (m./f.)
  doctor's office *consultorio* (m.) *del médico*
document *documento* (m.)
documentary *documental* (m.)
dog *perro* (m.)
dollar *dólar* (m.)
dominate (to) *dominar*
done *hecho/hecha* (m./f.)
door *puerta* (f.)
doubt (to) *dudar*
  doubt that ... (to) *dudar que ...*
download (to) *bajar*
drama *drama* (m.), *obra* (f.) *dramática*
dramatic *dramático/dramática* (m./f.)
draw (to) *empatar*
drawer *cajón* (m.)
dream (to) *soñar*
  Don't even dream about it! *¡Ni lo sueñes!*
  dream about ... *soñar con ...*
dress *vestido* (m.)
  be dressed to the nines (to) *ir de punta en blanco* (lit., to go from the tip in white)
  evening dress *vestido de noche*
dress (someone) (to) *vestir*
dressing room *probador* (m.)
drink *bebida* (f.)
drink (to) *beber*
drive (to) *conducir*
drugstore *farmacia* (f.)
drunk *borracho/borracha* (m./f.)
dry *seco/seca* (m./f.)
dry-clean (to) *lavar en seco*
dryer *secadora* (f.)
DSL *línea* (f.) *de suscriptor/abonado digital (DSL)*
due to *por*
during *durante*
dusk *atardecer* (m.)
  at dusk *al atardecer*
dust *polvo* (m.)
duty *derecho* (m.)
DVD *DVD* (m.)
  DVD player *lector* (m.) *de DVD*

E

each *cada* (m./f.)

ear *oreja* (f.)

early *temprano/temprana* (m./f.)
  early morning (from midnight till
    daybreak) *madrugada* (f.)

early (adverb) *temprano*

earn (to) *ganar*

earnings *ingreso* (m.)

earrings *pendientes* (m. pl.)

easily *fácilmente*

east *este* (m.), *oriente* (m.)

Easter *Pascua* (f.)

easy *fácil* (m./f.)

eat (to) *comer*
  eat dinner (to) *cenar*

economical *económico/económica* (m./f.)

economics *economía* (f.)

Ecuador *Ecuador* (m.)

Ecuadorian *ecuatoriano/ecuatoriana* (m./f.)

efficiently *eficientemente*

egg *huevo* (m.)

eight *ocho*
  at eight ten (8:10) *a las ocho y diez*
  eight hundred *ochocientos/ochocientas* (m./f.)
  twenty-eight *veintiocho*

eighteen *dieciocho, diez y ocho*

eighty *ochenta*

elbow *codo* (m.)

electric *eléctrico/eléctrica* (m./f.)

electrical *eléctrico/eléctrica* (m./f.)
  electrical appliance *electrodoméstico* (m.)

electrician *electricista/electricista* (m./f.)

electronic *electrónico/electrónica* (m./f.)
  electronics store *tienda* (f.) *de
    electrodomésticos*

elegant *elegante* (m./f.)

elementary school *colegio* (m.)

elephant *elefante* (m.)

eleven *once*

eliminate (to) *eliminar*

e-mail *correo* (m.) *electrónico, correo-e* (m.)
  e-mail address *dirección* (f.) *de correo
    electrónico*
  e-mail attachment *anexo* (m.) *al correo
    electrónico*

employee *empleado/empleada* (m./f.)

employment *empleo* (m.)

enchant (to) *encantar*

enclosed *adjunto/adjunta* (m./f.)

end *fin* (m.), *final* (m.), *punta* (f.)

engineer *ingeniero/ingeniera* (m./f.)

engineering *ingeniería* (f.)
  mechanical engineering *ingeniería mecánica*

England *Inglaterra* (f.)

English *inglés/inglesa* (m./f.)

English (language) *inglés* (m.)
  Do you speak English? (infml.) *¿Hablas inglés?*
  Do you speak English? (fml.) *¿Habla usted
    inglés?*

Enjoy the meal! *¡Buen provecho!*

enough *suficiente* (m./f.), *bastante*

enter (to) *entrar*

entertainment *entretenimiento* (m.)

entrance *entrada* (f.)

equal *igual* (m./f.)
  ... equals (=) ... *... es igual a ...*

erase (to) *borrar*

especially *sobre todo*

even *hasta*

evening *noche* (f.)
  evening dress *vestido* (m.) *de noche*
  Good evening. *Buenas noches.*
  in the evening *de la noche*
  this evening *esta noche* (f.)

event *suceso* (m.)

every *todo/toda* (m./f.), *cada* (m./f.)
  every day *todos los días*
  every week *todas las semanas*

everything *todo* (m.)
  How is everything going? *¿Cómo va todo?*

ex- *ex*

exact *exacto/exacta* (m./f.), *en punto*
  Exactly. *Exacto.*

exceed (to) *exceder*

excellent *excelente* (m./f.)

exception *excepción* (f.)

exchange (to) *cambiar, intercambiar*
  in exchange for *por*

exciting *emocionante* (m./f.)

excuse *disculpa* (f.)

excuse (to) *disculpar*
  Excuse me. *Disculpa./Disculpe.* (infml./fml.)/
    Perdón.

exercise *ejercicio* (m.)

exit *salida* (f.)

expense *gasto* (m.)

expensive *caro/cara* (m./f.), *costoso/costosa* (m./f.)

experience *experiencia* (f.)

explanation *explicación* (f.)

extra *extra* (m./f.)

 extra hours *horas* (f. pl.) *extras*

extraordinary *extraordinario/extraordinaria* (m./f.)

extroverted *extrovertido/extrovertida* (m./f.)

eye *ojo* (m.)

 an eye for an eye *ojo por ojo*

eyebrow *ceja* (f.)

eyeglasses *gafas* (f. pl.)

 wear rose-colored glasses (to) *ver todo color de rosa* (lit., to see everything pink)

eyelashes *pestañas* (f. pl.)

F

face *cara* (f.)

 face the circumstances (to) *dar la cara*

factory *fábrica* (f.)

faculty *profesorado* (m.)

fail (to) *suspender*

 fail a test (to) *suspender un examen*

fall *otoño* (m.)

fall (to) *caer*

 fall flat on one's face (to) *dar de narices*

fame *fama* (f.)

familiar *familiar* (m./f.)

family *familia* (f.)

 (of) family *familiar* (m./f.)

famous *famoso/famosa* (m./f.)

fan *aficionado/aficionada* (m./f.), *hincha* (m./f.)

fantastic *fantástico/fantástica* (m./f.)

far *lejos*

 far from ... *lejos de ...*

farmer *granjero/granjera* (m./f.)

fashion *moda* (f.)

 in fashion *de moda*

fast (adjective) *rápido/rápida* (m./f.)

fast (adverb) *rápidamente, rápido*

fasten (to) *abrochar*

fat *gordo/gorda* (m./f.)

father *padre* (m.)

father-in-law *suegro* (m.)

fatigue *consancio* (m.)

favor *favor* (m.)

 Do me the favor of ... *Hágame el favor de ...*

favorite *favorito/favorita* (m./f.)

fax machine *fax* (m.)

fear *miedo* (m.)

fear (to) *temer*

February *febrero* (m.)

feel (to) *sentir, sentirse*

 feel like ... (to) *tener ganas de ...*

fees *honorarios* (m. pl.)

festive *festivo/festiva* (m./f.)

fever *fiebre* (f.)

 have a fever (to) *tener fiebre*

few *pocos/pocas* (m. pl./f. pl.)

fiancé(e) *prometido/prometida* (m./f.)

field *campo* (m.)

fifteen *quince*

fifty *cincuenta*

file *archivo* (m.), *carpeta* (f.), *documento* (m.)

filing cabinet *armario* (m.)

fill (to) *llenar*

filler phrase *frase* (f.) *de relleno*

 filler word/phrase *muletilla* (f.)

filling *relleno* (m.)

film *película* (f.)

 adventure films *películas* (pl.) *de aventuras*

 horror films *películas de horror*

 romantic films *películas románticas*

 suspense films *películas de suspenso*

finally *por fin*

finance *finanzas* (f. pl.)

find (to) *encontrar*

 find (something) (to) *dar con*

fine (adjective) *estupendo/estupenda* (m./f.)

 Fine. *Pues bien.*

 I'm fine. *Estoy bien.*

fine (noun) *multa* (f.)

finger *dedo* (m.)

finish (to) *acabar, terminar*

first *primer/primero/primera* (before m. sg. nouns/m./f.)

fish *pescado* (m.)

 fish shop/market *pescadería* (f.)

fit (to) *quedar*

 fit (somebody) (to) *venir*

 It suits me fine. *Me viene bien.*

five *cinco*

 at a half past five *a las cinco y media*

 at five (o'clock) *a las cinco*

five hundred *quinientos/quinientas* (m./f.)
forty-five *cuarenta y cinco*
It's five to one. (12:55) *Es la una menos cinco.*
twenty-five *veinticinco*
fixed *fijo/fija* (m./f.)
flat *plano/plana* (m./f.)
flea market *mercadillo* (m.)
flight *vuelo* (m.)
floor *suelo* (m.), *piso* (m.)
flower *flor* (f.)
flowing *suelto/suelta* (m./f.)
fly (to) *volar*
fog *niebla* (f.)
follow (to) *seguir*
food *comida* (f.)
fool *bobo/boba* (m./f.)
foot *pie* (m.)
  have both feet on the ground (to) *tener los pies en la tierra*
football *fútbol americano*
for *por, para*
  For God's sake! *¡Por Dios!*
  for this reason *por eso*
forbid (to) *prohibir*
  forbid that/to ... (to) *prohibir que ...*
forehead *frente* (f.)
foreign *extranjero/extranjera* (m./f.)
forest *bosque* (m.)
forget (to) *olvidar*
fork *tenedor* (m.)
form *planilla* (f.)
  form links (to) *vincularse*
  form links with ... (to) *vincularse con ...*
forty *cuarenta*
  forty-five *cuarenta y cinco*
forward (to) *retransmitir, pasar*
fossil *fósil* (m.)
four *cuatro*
  at four p.m. *a las cuatro de la tarde*
  four hundred *cuatrocientos/cuatrocientas* (m./f.)
  twenty-four *veinticuatro*
fourteen *catorce*
free *gratis, libre* (m./f.)
freeway *autopista* (f.), *autovía* (f.), *carretera* (f.)
French *francés/francesa* (m./f.)
French (language) *francés* (m.)
  I speak French fluently. *Domino el francés.*

frequency *frecuencia* (f.)
frequent *frecuente* (m./f.)
frequently *frecuentemente, con frecuencia*
Friday *viernes* (m.)
fried *frito/frita* (m./f.)
friend *amigo/amiga* (m./f.)
friendly *simpático/simpática* (m./f.)
from *de, desde*
  across from ... *enfrente de ...*
  far from ... *lejos de ...*
  from the (m.) *del (de + el)*
  from ... through ... *de ... a ...*
  It's two blocks from here. *Está a dos cuadras de aquí.*
  start from ... (to) *partir de ...*
  Where are you from? *¿De dónde eres?*
fruit *fruta* (f.)
full *completo/completa* (m./f.)
  full-time *a tiempo completo*
fun *divertido/divertida* (m./f.)
  have fun (to) *divertirse*
function (to) *funcionar*
funny *gracioso/graciosa* (m./f.)
furnished *amueblado/amueblada* (m./f.)
furniture *muebles* (m. pl.)
future *futuro* (m.)

G

gallery *galería* (f.)
game *juego* (m.), *partido* (m.) (sport)
garage *garaje* (m.)
garden *jardín* (m.)
garment *prenda* (f.)
gas station *gasolinera* (f.)
gather (to) *reunir*
gel *gel* (m.)
generally *generalmente*
generous *generoso/generosa* (m./f.)
gentleman *caballero* (m.)
geography *geografía* (f.)
German *alemán/alemana* (m./f.)
German (language) *alemán* (m.)
get (to) *sacar, traer*
  get a divorce (to) *divorciarse*
  get angry (to) *enfadarse*
  get dressed (to) *vestirse*
  get good/bad grades (to) *sacar buenas/malas notas*

get married (to) *casarse*
get to … (to) *llegar a …*
get up (to) *levantarse, despertarse*
 I get up. *Me levanto.*
gift *regalo* (m.)
girl *chica* (f.), *muchacha* (f.)
girlfriend *novia* (f.)
give (to) *dar*
 give (a gift) (to) *regalar*
 give a discount (to) *hacer un descuento*
 give birth (to) *dar a luz*
 give thanks (to) *dar (las) gracias*
glass *vaso* (m.)
gloves *guantes* (m. pl.)
go (to) *ir, marchar*
 be going to (do) (to), go to (a place) (to) *ir a …*
 go by (to) *pasar*
 go camping (to) *ir de cámping*
 go crazy (to), go out of one's mind
  (to) *pararse de cabeza*
 go hiking (to) *hacer excursionismo, hacer
  senderismo*
 go on a trip (to) *salir de viaje*
 go out (to) *salir*
 go shopping (to) *ir de compras*
 go sightseeing (to) *visitar los lugares de
  interés*
 Go straight. *Siga derecho.*
 go through a light (to) *saltarse el semáforo*
 go to bed (to) *acostarse*
 go window-shopping (to) *ir de escaparates*
 go with … (to) *combinar con …*
 How's it going? *¿Qué pasa?*
 What's going on? *¿Qué hay?*
goal *gol* (m.)
 score a goal (to) *anotar/hacer/marcar un gol*
goalkeeper *portero* (m.)
God *Dios* (m.)
 For God's sake! *¡Por Dios!*
gold (color) *dorado/dorada* (m./f.)
good *buen/bueno/buena* (before m. sg. nouns/
  m./f.)
 be in good hands (to) *estar en buenas manos*
 Good afternoon. *Buenas tardes.*
 Good evening./Good night. *Buenas noches.*
 Good job! *¡Buen trabajo!*
 Good morning. *Buenos días.*
 Have a good trip. *Buen viaje.*

 It's good that … *Es bueno que …*
 The weather is good. *El tiempo es bueno.*
Good-bye. *Adiós.*
 say good-bye (to) *despedirse*
grace *gracia* (f.)
grade *nota* (f.)
 grades *calificaciones* (f. pl.)
 get good/bad grades (to) *sacar buenas/malas
  notas*
graduate (to) *graduarse*
gram *gramo* (m.)
grandchildren *nietos* (pl.)
granddaughter *nieta* (f.)
grandfather *abuelo* (m.)
grandmother *abuela* (f.)
grandparents *abuelos* (pl.)
grandson *nieto* (m.)
grapes *uvas* (f. pl.)
 bunch of grapes *racimo* (m.) *de uvas*
graphic *gráfico/gráfica* (m./f.)
grass *césped* (m.)
gray *gris* (m./f.)
 gray (the color) *gris* (m.)
great *gran/grande* (before sg. nouns/all other
  cases), *magnífico/magnífica* (m./f.)
 Great! *¡Estupendo!*
green *verde* (m./f.)
 dark green *verde oscuro*
greeting *saludo* (m.)
grill *parrilla* (f.)
 grilled *a la parrilla*
grill (to) *asar*
guava *guayaba* (f.)
guest *invitado/invitada* (m./f.)
guidebook *guía* (f.)
guided tour *visita guiada* (f.)
guitar *guitarra* (f.)
 play the guitar (to) *tocar la guitarra*
gymnasium *gimnasio* (m.)
gymnastics *gimnasia* (f.)

H

hail (to) *granizar*
 It's hailing. *Está granizando.*
hair *pelo* (m.)
hair salon *peluquería* (f.)
half *medio/media* (m./f.)
 at a half past five *a las cinco y media*

halftime *medio tiempo* (m.)
hall *vestíbulo* (m.)
ham *jamón* (m.)
hand *mano* (f.)
  at hand *a la mano*
  be in good hands (to) *estar en buenas manos*
  hand wash (to) *lavar a mano*
  know like the back of one's hand (to) *conocer palmo a palmo*
  on the left-hand side *a mano izquierda*
  on the one hand *por una parte*
  on the other hand *por otra parte*
  on the right-hand side *a mano derecha*
  shake hands (to) *dar la mano*
handbag *bolso* (m.), *cartera* (f.)
handful *manojo* (m.)
handle *manejar*
hang (to) *colgar*
  hang up the phone (to) *colgar el teléfono*
happen (to) *pasar*
  What's happening? *¿Qué tal?*
happening *suceso* (m.)
happily *felizmente*
happy *alegre* (m./f.), *contento/contenta* (m./f.), *feliz* (m./f.)
hard *duro/dura* (m./f.)
hardworking *trabajador* (m./f.)
hat *sombrero* (m.)
have (to) *tener, haber, tomar (food and drink)*
  Do you have time? *¿Cómo estás de tiempo?*
  have a cough (to) *tener tos*
  have a fever (to) *tener fiebre*
  Have a good trip. *Buen viaje.*
  have a headache (to) *tener dolor de cabeza*
  Have a nice day. *Que tenga un buen día.*
  have a sore throat (to) *tener dolor de garganta*
  have an operation (to) *operarse*
  have an upset stomach (to) *estar mal del estómago*
  have blue blood (to) *ser de sangre azul (lit., to be of blue blood)*
  have both feet on the ground (to) *tener los pies en la tierra*
  have fun (to) *divertirse*
  have high/low blood pressure (to) *tener la tensión alta/baja*
  have just ... (done something) (to) *acabar de ...*

  have lunch (to) *almorzar*
  have nausea (to) *tener náusea(s)*
  have permission to (to) *poder*
  have to ... (to) *tener que ...*
  How have you been? *¿Cómo te ha ido?*
  not have a clue about ... (to) *no saber ni jota de ...*
  What time do you have? *¿Qué hora tiene?*
  You have to ... *Tienes que ...*
he *él*
head *cabeza* (f.), *cabecera* (f.)
  have a headache (to) *tener dolor de cabeza*
  keep a cool head (to) *tener la cabeza fría*
  lose one's head (to) *perder la cabeza*
headphones *audífonos* (m. pl.)
healthy *saludable* (m./f.)
hear (to) *oír*
heart *corazón* (m.)
heat *calor* (m.)
heel *tacón* (m.)
height *alto* (m.)
Hello. *Hola.*
  Hello! *¡Saludos!*
  Hello? (on the phone) *¿Aló?/¿Dígame?*
help *ayuda* (f.)
  How may I help you? *¿En qué puedo servirle?*
  Thank you for your help. *Le agradezco su ayuda.*
help (to) *ayudar*
  Can you help me? *¿Puede ayudarme?*
her (before a noun) *su/sus* (sg./pl.)
her (direct object pronoun) *la*
  (to/for) her (indirect object pronoun) *le, se (used in place of le when preceding lo/la/los/las)*
herb *hierba* (f.)
here *aquí*
  Here is ... *Aquí está ...*
  Here you are. *Aquí tiene.*
  Here we are. *Pues, aquí estamos.*
  It's two blocks from here. *Está a dos cuadras de aquí.*
hers *suyo/suya/suyos/suyas* (m. sg./f. sg./m. pl./f. pl.), *el de ella* (m. sg.), *la de ella* (f. sg.)
herself *se*
hey (filler word) *che (Argentina), oye*
hide-and-seek *escondidas* (f. pl.)
high *alto/alta* (m./f.)
  have high blood pressure (to) *tener la tensión*

alta
highway *autopista* (f.), *autovía* (f.), *carretera* (f.)
hiking *excursionismo* (m.), *senderismo* (m.)
  go hiking (to) *hacer excursionismo, hacer senderismo*
hill *cerro* (m.), *colina* (f.)
him (direct object pronoun) *lo*
  (to/for) him (indirect object pronoun) *le, se (used in place of le when preceding lo/la/los/las)*
himself *se*
hip *cadera* (f.)
his *suyo/suya/suyos/suyas* (m. sg./f. sg./m. pl./f. pl.), *el de él* (m. sg.), *la de él* (f. sg.)
  his (before a noun) *su/sus* (sg./pl.)
history *historia* (f.)
Hmm... *Mire...*
hobby *afición* (f.), *pasatiempos* (m.)
hockey *hockey* (m.)
hold (to) *poseer*
  Hold on. *Un momento.*
  Hold on, please. *Espere, por favor.*
  put on hold (to) *poner en espera*
holiday *fiesta* (f.), *día* (m.) *festivo*
homeopathy *homeopatía* (f.)
homework *tarea* (f.)
honest *honesto/honesta* (m./f.)
honey *miel* (f.)
hope (to) *esperar*
  hope that... (to) *esperar que...*
  I hope... *Ojalá que...*
  I hope so! *¡Yo espero que sí!*
horror *horror* (m.)
  horror films *películas* (f. pl.) *de horror*
horse *caballo* (m.)
horseback riding *equitación* (f.)
hospital *hospital* (m.)
hot *caliente* (m./f.)
  be hot (to) *tener calor*
  It's hot. *Hace calor.*
hotel *hotel* (m.)
hour *hora* (f.)
  extra hours *horas* (pl.) *extras*
house *casa* (f.)
how *cómo*
  Do you know how to...? *¿Sabe cómo...?*
  How...! *¡Qué...!*
  How about if...? *¿Qué tal si...?/¿Qué te parece si...?*
How are things? *¿Cómo van las cosas?*
How are you doing for time? *¿Cómo estás de tiempo?*
How are you? *¿Cómo está usted?* (fml.)/*¿Cómo estás (tú)?* (infml.)
How do I know!?/How should I know!? *¡Yo qué sé!*
How do you say "..." in...? *¿Cómo se dice "..." en...?*
How have you been? *¿Cómo te ha ido?*
How is everything going? *¿Cómo va todo?*
how many *cuántos/cuántas* (m. pl./f. pl.)
How may I help you? *¿En qué puedo servirle?*
how much *cuánto/cuánta* (m./f.)
How much does it cost? *¿Cuánto cuesta?*
How much is it? *¿Cuánto es?/¿Cuánto vale?*
How nice! *¡Qué bien!*
How old are you* (sg. fml.)/is he/is she? *¿Cuántos años tiene?*
How's it going? *¿Qué pasa?*
How's life treating you? *¿Cómo te trata la vida?*
learn how to... (to) *aprender a...*
huge *enorme* (m./f.)
human *humano/humana* (m./f.)
  human body *cuerpo* (m.) *humano*
hundred *cien/ciento* (before a noun/before a number except mil)
  eight hundred *ochocientos/ochocientas* (m./f.)
  five hundred *quinientos/quinientas* (m./f.)
  four hundred *cuatrocientos/cuatrocientas* (m./f.)
  hundred thousand *cien mil*
  nine hundred *novecientos/novecientas* (m./f.)
  one hundred and three dollars *ciento tres dólares*
  one hundred people *cien personas*
  one hundred percent *cien por ciento*
  seven hundred *setecientos/setecientas* (m./f.)
  six hundred *seiscientos/seiscientas* (m./f.)
  three hundred *trescientos/trescientas* (m./f.)
  two hundred *doscientos/doscientas* (m./f.)
hunger *hambre* (f.)
hunting *caza* (f.)
hurricane *huracán* (m.)
hurry *prisa* (f.)
  be in a hurry (to) *tener prisa*

husband *esposo* (m.), *marido* (m.)
hygienic *higiénico/higiénica* (m./f.)

I
_____

I *yo*
ice *hielo* (m.)
ice cream *helado* (m.)
  ice cream parlor *heladería* (f.)
idea *idea* (f.)
ideal *ideal* (m./f.)
idiot *bobo/boba* (m./f.)
if *si*
  How about if …? *¿Qué tal si … ?/¿Qué te parece si … ?*
illness *enfermedad* (f.), *mal* (m.)
imagine (to) *imaginar*
immediate *inmediato/inmediata* (m./f.)
immediately *inmediatamente, de inmediato*
important *importante* (m./f.)
impossible *imposible* (m./f.)
  It is impossible that … *Es imposible que …*
impressive *impresionante* (m./f.)
in *en*
  be in a hurry (to) *tener prisa*
  be in good hands (to) *estar en buenas manos*
  be interested in … (to) *tener interés en …*
  check in (to) *registrarse*
  in exchange for *por*
  in fashion *de moda*
  in front *delante*
  in front of … *delante de …/enfrente de …*
  in love *enamorado/enamorada* (m./f.)
  in order to *para*
  in place of *por*
  in style *de moda*
  in the afternoon *de la tarde*
  in the early morning *de la madrugada*
  in the evening *de la noche*
  in the morning *de la mañana*
incentive *incentivo* (m.)
include (to) *incluir*
  Is service included? *¿Está incluido el servicio?*
information *información* (f.)
  information center *centro* (m.) *de información*
ingredient *ingrediente* (m.)
inherit (to) *heredar*
injury *lesión* (f.)

inside *dentro*
  inside of … *dentro de …*
insist (to) *insistir*
  insist that … (to) *insistir en que …*
instantaneous *instantáneo/instantánea* (m./f.)
instant message *mensaje* (m.) *instantáneo*
insurance *seguro* (m.)
intelligent *inteligente* (m./f.)
intended for *para*
interest *interés* (m.)
interest (to) *interesar*
  be interested in … (to) *tener interés en …*
  I'm interested in … (to) *Me interesa/interesan …* (sg./pl.)
interesting *interesante* (m./f.)
intermediate *intermedio/intermedia* (m./f.)
international *internacional* (m./f.)
  international call *llamada* (f.) *internacional*
internet *Internet*
intersection *cruce* (m.), *intersección* (f.)
interview *entrevista* (f.)
interview (to) *entrevistar*
introduce (to) *presentar*
  Let me introduce you to … *Te presento a …*
investigation *investigación* (f.)
invitation *invitación* (f.)
invite (to) *invitar*
iron *plancha* (f.)
iron (to) *planchar*
  ironing board *tabla* (f.) *de planchar*
it (direct object pronoun) *lo/la* (m./f.)
  (to/for) it (indirect object pronoun) *le, se (used in place of le when preceding lo/la/los/las)*
  That's it. *Ya está.*
It is … *Es …/Está …*
  It's a pity that … *Es una lástima que …*
  It's a pleasure. *Mucho gusto.*
  It's beautiful. (weather) *Hace muy buen tiempo.*
  It's better that … *Es mejor que …*
  It's cloudy. *Está nublado.*
  It's cold. *Hace frío.*
  It's five to one. (12:55) *Es la una menos cinco.*
  It's good that … *Es bueno que …*
  It's hailing. *Está granizando.*
  It's hot. *Hace calor.*
  It's impossible that … *Es imposible que …*
  It's necessary that … *Es necesario que …*

It's necessary to … *Hay que …*
It's not bad. *No está mal.*
It's not true that … *No es cierto que …*
It's one o'clock. *Es la una.*
It's possible that … *Es posible que …*
It's preferable that … *Es preferible que …*
It's raining. *Está lloviendo.*
It's sad that … *Es triste que …*
It's snowing. *Está nevando.*
It's sunny. *Hace sol.*
It's ten after one in the morning. *Es la una y diez de la madrugada.*
It's three o'clock sharp. *Son las tres en punto.*
It's three o'clock. *Son las tres.*
It's twelve noon. *Son las doce del mediodía.*
It's two blocks from here. *Está a dos cuadras de aquí.*
It's windy. *Hace viento.*
Italian *italiano/italiana* (m./f.)
Italian (language) *italiano* (m.)
its *su/sus* (sg./pl.)
itself *se*

J

jacket *americana* (f.), *chaqueta* (f.), *saco* (m.)
jam *mermelada* (f.)
January *enero* (m.)
jar *frasco* (m.)
jazz *jazz* (m.)
jealous *celoso/celosa* (m./f.)
jeans *jeans* (m. pl.), *tejanos* (m. pl.), *vaqueros* (m. pl.)
job *trabajo* (m.), *empleo* (m.)
 Good job! *¡Buen trabajo!*
 summer job *trabajo de verano*
 steady job *trabajo fijo*
jog (to) *trotar*
joke *chiste* (m.)
 tell a dirty joke (to) (lit., to tell a green joke) *contar un chiste verde*
journalist *periodista* (m./f.)
judge *juez* (m.)
juice *jugo* (m.), *zumo* (m.)
July *julio* (m.)
June *junio* (m.)

K

keep (to) *llevar, guardar*
 keep a cool head (to) *tener la cabeza fría*

keep a diary (to) *llevar un diario*
key *llave* (f.)
keyboard *teclado* (m.)
kid *crío/cría* (m./f.)
kilo, kilogram *kilo* (m.)
kilometer *kilómetro* (m.)
kind *clase* (f.)
 all kinds *toda clase*
kiss (to) *besar*
kitchen *cocina* (f.)
knee *rodilla* (f.)
knife *cuchillo* (m.)
know (to) *saber (facts, information), conocer (people, places)*
 as you already know *como ya sabes*
 Do you know how to … ? *¿Sabe cómo … ?*
 How do I know!?/How should I know!? *¡Yo qué sé!*
 know by sight (to) *conocer de vista*
 know like the back of one's hand (to) *conocer palmo a palmo*
 make known (to) *dar a conocer*
 not have a clue about … (to) *no saber ni jota de …*
 not know (to) *desconocer*
 Who knows? *¿Quién sabe?*

L

label *etiqueta* (f.)
lake *lago* (m.)
lamb *cordero/cordera* (m./f.)
 lamb chop *chuleta* (f.) *de cordero*
lamp *lámpara* (f.)
lamppost *farola* (f.)
land *tierra* (f.)
lane *carril* (m.), *vía* (f.)
 Stay in the right lane. *Siga por el carril de la derecha.*
language *idioma* (m.), *lengua* (f.)
large *gran/grande* (before sg. nouns/all other cases)
last *último/última* (m./f.)
 at last *por fin*
 last month *mes* (m.) *pasado*
 last night *anoche*
 last week *semana* (f.) *pasada*
 last year *año* (m.) *pasado*
late *tarde*

I'll see you later. *Hasta luego.*
I'm late. *Se me hace tarde.*
late night (from midnight) *madrugada* (f.)
later *más tarde, luego*
Until later. *Hasta más tarde.*
very latest (the) *último grito* (m.)
laugh (to) *reír*
  laugh very hard (to) (lit., to turn black with laughter) *estar negro de la risa*
laughter *risa* (f.)
laundry detergent *detergente* (m.) *de ropa*
law *derecho* (m.)
lawn *césped* (m.)
lawyer *abogado/abogada* (m./f.)
lazy *perezoso/perezosa* (m./f.)
  be lazy (to) *ser perezoso*
learn (to) *aprender, saber*
  I'm learning Spanish. *Estoy aprendiendo español.*
least ... in/of ... (the) *el/la/los/las* (m. sg./f. sg./m. pl./f. pl.) *menos ... de ...*
leather *cuero* (m.)
leave (to) *dejar, marchar, parar, partir, salir*
  leave a message after the tone (to) *dejar un mensaje después de oír la señal*
lecture *conferencia* (f.)
  lecture hall *sala* (f.) *de conferencias*
left side *izquierda* (f.)
  on the left *a la izquierda*
  Turn left. *Gira a la izquierda.*
left-hand *izquierdo/izquierda* (m./f.)
  on the left-hand side *a mano izquierda*
leg *pierna* (f.)
lemon *limón* (m.)
lemonade *limonada* (f.)
less *menos*
  least ... in/of ... (the) *el/la/los/las* (m. sg./f. sg./m. pl./f. pl.) *menos ... de ...*
  less ... than ... *menos ... que ...*
  more or less *más o menos*
lesson *lección* (f.)
Let's go ... *Vamos ...*
Let's see ... *A ver ...*
letter *cartas* (f. pl.)
lettuce *lechuga* (f.)
library *biblioteca* (f.)
lie (to) *mentir*

life *vida* (f.)
  How's life treating you? *¿Cómo te trata la vida?*
lift (to) *levantar*
light *luz* (f.)
  turn off the lights (to) *apagar las luces*
light *claro/clara* (m./f.), *ligero/ligera* (m./f.)
  light blue *azul* (m./f.) *claro*
lightening *relámpago* (m.)
like *como*
like (to) *(se) gustar*
  I like ... *Me gusta/gustan ...* (sg./pl.)
  I really like ... *Me encanta/encantan ...* (sg./pl.)
  I'd like ... *Me gustaría ...*
  like (it) that ... (to) *gustar que ...*
  What would you like? *¿Qué desea?*
likewise *igualmente*
limit *límite* (m.)
line *cola* (f.), *fila* (f.), *línea* (f.)
  stand in line (to) *hacer una cola/fila*
  The line is busy. *Está comunicando.*
linen *lino* (m.)
lip *labio* (m.)
list *lista* (f.)
  list of plays *cartelera* (f.)
listen to (to) *escuchar*
liter *litro* (m.)
literature *literatura* (f.)
little *poco*
  a little *un poco*
  I speak a little Spanish. *Hablo un poco de español.*
live (to) *vivir*
  What do you do for a living? *¿En qué trabaja?*
living room *sala* (f.)
loan *crédito* (m.), *préstamo* (m.)
lobster *langosta* (f.)
local *local* (m./f.)
  local call *llamada* (f.) *local*
London *Londres*
long *largo/larga* (m./f.)
  long weekend *puente* (m.)
look at (to) *mirar*
look for (to) *buscar*
look like (to) *parecer*
look up (to) *consultar*
loose *suelto/suelta* (m./f.)
Los Angeles *Los Ángeles*

lose (to) *perder*
  lose one's head (to) *perder la cabeza*
lottery *lotería* (f.)
love (to) *querer, amar*
  I love you. *Te quiero.*
  I'd love to! *¡Me encantaría!*
  in love *enamorado/enamorada* (m./f.)
low-cost *económico/económica* (m./f.)
low-cut *escotado/escotada* (m./f.)
lower (to) *bajar*
LP *disco de vinilo* (m.)
luck *suerte* (f.)
lunch *almuerzo* (m.)
  have lunch (to) *almorzar*
lungs *pulmones* (m. pl.)

M

made *hecho/hecha* (m./f.)
magazine *revista* (f.)
magical *mágico/mágica* (m./f.)
magnificent *magnífico/magnífica* (m./f.)
mailbox *buzón* (m.)
main *principal* (m./f.)
  main dish *plato* (m.) *principal*
major *carrera* (f.), *especialidad* (f.)
major in … (to) *especializarse en …*
  make (to) *hacer*
  make an international/local/national call
    (to) *hacer una llamada internacional/local/*
    nacional
  make known (to) *dar a conocer*
man *hombre* (m.), *tío* (m., colloquial)
manager *gerente* (m.)
manner *forma* (f.)
many *muchos/muchas* (m. pl./f. pl.)
  how many *cuántos/cuántas* (m. pl./f. pl.)
map *mapa* (m.), *plano* (m.)
March *marzo* (m.)
marine *marino/marina* (m./f.)
mark (to) *marcar*
market *mercado* (m.)
  flea market *mercadillo*
marriage *matrimonio* (m.)
married *casado/casada* (m./f.)
marry (someone) (to) *casarse con*
  get married (to) *casarse*
martini *martini* (m.)
martyr *mártir* (m./f.)

marvelous *estupendo/estupenda* (m./f.)
master (to) *dominar*
master's degree *maestría* (f.), *especialización* (f.)
match (to) *combinar*
material *material* (m.)
mathematics *matemáticas* (f. pl.)
matter (to) *importar*
  It doesn't matter. *No importa.*
May *mayo* (m.)
May I please … ? (fml.) *¿Me permite … ?*
  (fml.)/*¿Me permites … ?* (infml.)
  May you be well. *Que esté bien.*
mayor *alcalde* (m.)
me (after a proposition) *mí*
  me (direct object pronoun) *me*
  (to/for) me (indirect object pronoun) *me*
mean (to) *significar*
  What does that mean? *¿Qué quiere decir eso?*
meanwhile *mientras tanto*
measure (to) *medir*
measurement *medida* (f.)
meat *carne* (f.)
mechanical *mecánico/mecánica* (m./f.)
  mechanical engineering *ingeniería* (f.)
    mecánica
medication *medicamento* (m.)
  take medication (to) *tomar un medicamento*
medicine *medicina* (f.)
  medicine cabinet *botiquín* (m.)
medium *mediano/mediana* (m./f.), *término* (m.)
  tres cuartos (cooked meat)
  medium-rare *término* (m.) *medio*
meet (to) *conocer, reunirse*
  meet (somebody) (to) *conocer (a alguien),*
    encontrarse con
  meet up with (to) *encontrar*
  Pleased to meet you. *Gusto en conocerlo/la.*
meeting *reunión* (f.), *conferencia* (f.)
  meeting room *sala* (f.) *de conferencias*
memory *memoria* (f.)
menu *carta* (f.)
merely *sólo*
message *mensaje* (m.)
  instant message *mensaje instantáneo*
  leave a message after the tone (to) *dejar un*
    mensaje después de oír la señal
metro *metro* (m.)
Mexican *mexicano/mexicana* (m./f.)

Mexico *México* (m.)

microwave *microondas* (m.)

midnight *medianoche* (f.), *media noche* (f.)

at midnight *a medianoche*

midway *medio/media* (m./f.)

milk *leche* (f.)

powdered milk *leche en polvo*

skim milk *leche descremada*

million *millón*

one million houses *un millón de casas*

mind *mente* (f.)

go out of one's mind (to) *pararse de cabeza*

mine *mío/mía/míos/mías* (m. sg./f. sg./m. pl./f. pl.)

minus (-) *menos*

minute *minuto* (m.)

miracle *maravilla* (f.)

mirror *espejo* (m.)

misfortune *desgracia* (f.)

miss (to) *perder, faltar*

mixed *mixto/mixta* (m./f.)

mobile phone *móvil* (m.)

modem *módem* (m.)

modern *moderno/moderna* (m./f.)

molar *muela* (f.)

mole *lunar* (m.)

mom *mamá* (f.), *mami* (f.)

moment *momento* (m.)

at this moment *en este momento*

One moment. *Un momento.*

Monday *lunes* (m.)

money *dinero* (m.)

monitor *monitor* (m.)

month *mes* (m.)

last month *mes pasado*

next month *mes entrante, mes que viene*

this month *este mes*

monument *monumento* (m.)

moon *luna* (f.)

more *más*

more or less *más o menos*

more .../-er than ... *más ... que ...*

moreover *además*

morning *mañana* (f.)

early morning (from midnight till daybreak) *madrugada* (f.)

Good morning. *Buenos días.*

in the early morning *de la madrugada*

in the morning *de la mañana*

It's ten after one in the morning. *Es la una y diez de la madrugada.*

this morning *esta mañana*

Moscow *Moscú*

mosque *mezquita* (f.)

most ... in/of ... (the) *el/la/los/las* (m. sg./f. sg./m. pl./f. pl.) *más ... de ...*

mother *madre* (f.)

mother-in-law *suegra* (f.)

mountain *montaña* (f.)

mouse *ratón* (m.)

mouth *boca* (f.)

move (to) *mover*

movie *película* (f.)

movie listing *cartelera de cine*

movie theater *cine* (m.)

Mr. *señor* (m.), *don* (m.)

Mrs. *señora* (f.), *doña* (f.)

much *mucho*

how much *cuánto/cuánta* (m./f.)

municipal building *ayuntamiento* (m.), *alcaldía* (f.)

muscle *músculo* (m.)

museum *museo* (m.)

music *música* (f.)

classical music *música clásica*

musical *musical* (m.)

musician *músico* (m.)

must *deber*

my *mi/mis* (sg./pl.)

myself *me*

N

nail *uña* (f.)

name *nombre* (m.)

My name is ... *Me llamo ...*

What's your name? *¿Cómo se llama usted?* (fml.)/*¿Cómo te llamas?* (infml.)

nap *siesta* (f.)

napkin *servilleta* (f.)

narrow *angosto/angosta* (m./f.), *estrecho/estrecha* (m./f.)

national *nacional* (m./f.)

national call *llamada* (f.) *nacional*

nationality *nacionalidad* (f.)

natural *natural* (m./f.)

nature *naturaleza* (f.)

nausea *náusea* (f.)

be nauseated/have nausea (to) *tener
náusea(s)*

navy blue *azul* (m./f.) *marino*

near *cerca, próximo/próxima* (m./f.)
near ... *cerca de ...*

necessary *necesario/necesaria* (m./f.)
be necessary (to) *faltar*
It's necessary that ... *Es necesario que ...*
It's necessary to ... *Hay que ...*

neck *cuello* (m.)

necklace *collar* (m.)

need (to) *necesitar*

needle *aguja* (f.)

neighbor *vecino/vecina* (m./f.)

neighborhood *barrio* (m.)

neither *tampoco*
neither ... nor *ni ... ni*

nephew *sobrino* (m.)

nerve *nervio* (m.)

never *nunca*
almost never *casi nunca*

new *nuevo/nueva* (m./f.)

news *noticias* (pl.)
a piece of news *noticia* (f.)

newspaper *periódico* (m.)

New York *Nueva York*

next *próximo/próxima* (m./f.)
next month *mes* (m.) *que viene*
next to ... *al lado de ...*
next week *próxima semana* (f.), *semana* (f.)
que viene
next year *año* (m.) *que viene*

nice *bonito/bonita* (m./f.)
Have a nice day. *Que tenga un buen día.*
How nice! *¡Qué bien!*

niece *sobrina* (f.)

night *noche* (f.)
at night *de la noche*
Good night. *Buenas noches.*
last night *anoche*
late night (from midnight) *madrugada* (f.)

nine *nueve*
at about nine o'clock *a eso de las nueve*
at nine a.m. *a las nueve de la mañana*
be dressed to the nines (to) *ir de punta en
blanco* (lit., to go from the tip in white)
nine hundred *novecientos/novecientas* (m./f.)
twenty-nine *veintinueve*

nineteen *diecinueve, diez y nueve*

ninety *noventa*

no *no, ningún/ninguno/ninguna* (before m. sg.
nouns/m. sg./f. sg.)
no one *nadie*
No, not at all. *No, para nada.*
There's no ... that/who ... *No hay ningún ...
que ...*
There's no one who/that ... *No hay nadie
que ...*

nobody *nadie*
There's no one who/that ... *No hay nadie
que ...*

none *ningún/ninguno/ninguna* (before m. sg.
nouns/m. sg./f. sg.)

noon *mediodía* (m.)
at noon *a mediodía*
It's twelve noon. *Son las doce del mediodía.*

nor *ni*
neither ... nor *ni ... ni*

normal *normal* (m./f.)

normally *normalmente*

north *norte* (m.)

nose *nariz* (f.)

not *no*
absolutely not *en absoluto*
be not doing well (to) *estar mal*
It's not bad. *No está mal.*
No, not at all. *No, para nada.*
not either *tampoco*

note *nota* (f.)
take note (to) *tomar nota*

notebook *cuaderno* (m.)

nothing *nada*
nothing else *nada más*
There's nothing that ... *No hay nada que ...*

novel *novela* (f.)
romance novel *novela rosa*

November *noviembre* (m.)

now *ahora, ya*
right now *ahora mismo*

nowadays *hoy en día*

number *número* (m.)
telephone number *número de teléfono*

O

object *objeto* (m.)

objective *objetivo* (m.)

ocean *océano* (m.), *mar* (m.)

October *octubre* (m.)

of *de*

~~because of~~ *por*

in place of *por*

of course *por supuesto*

Of course! *¡Claro que sí!*

of the (m.) *del (de + el)*

of which (relative pronoun) *cuyo/cuya/cuyos/cuyas* (m. sg./f. sg./m. pl./f. pl.)

on top of *sobre*

outside of ... *fuera de ...*

Yes, of course. *Sí, claro.*

offer *oferta* (f.)

offer (to) *ofrecer*

office *oficina* (f.), *despacho* (m.), *estudio* (m.), *consultorio* (m.)

doctor's office *consultorio del médico*

office worker *oficinista* (m./f.)

often *con frecuencia*

oil *aceite* (m.)

(just) okay *más o menos*

old *viejo/vieja* (m./f.), *antiguo/antigua* (m./f.)

be ... years old (to) *tener ... años*

How old are you (sg. fml.)/is he/is she? *¿Cuántos años tiene?*

older *mayor* (m./f.)

oldest (the) *el/la/los/las* (m. sg./f. sg./m. pl./f. pl.) *mayor*

on *en*

buy on sale (to) *comprar en rebaja*

depend on ... (to) *depender de ...*

go on a trip (to) *salir de viaje*

Hold on, please. *Espere, por favor.*

Hold on. *Un momento.*

on board *a bordo*

on the left *a la izquierda*

on the left-hand side *a mano izquierda*

on the one hand *por una parte*

on the other hand *por otra parte*

on the phone *por teléfono*

on the radio *por la radio*

on the right *a la derecha*

on the right-hand side *a mano derecha*

on the sidewalk *por el andén*

on time *a tiempo*

on top of *sobre*

on vacation *de vacaciones*

put on hold (to) *poner en espera*

put something on (to) *ponerse*

try on (clothes) (to) *probarse*

once again *nuevamente*

one *uno*

It's five to one. (12:55) *Es la una menos cinco.*

It's one o'clock. *Es la una.*

no one *nadie*

on the one hand *por una parte*

one (o'clock) *una*

One moment. *Un momento.*

once *una vez*

once again *nuevamente*

one-piece *enterizo/enteriza* (m./f.)

one-way *de sentido* (m.) *único*

thirty-one *treinta y uno*

twenty-one *veintiuno*

one (impersonal pronoun) *se*

onion *cebolla* (f.)

online *por Internet, en línea*

only (adjective) *único/única* (m./f.), *solo/sola* (m./f.)

only (adverb) *solamente, sólo, simplemente*

open (to) *abrir*

open the door (to) *abrir la puerta*

opera *ópera* (f.)

operator *operadora* (f.)

opposite *opuesto/opuesta* (m./f.)

or *o*

either ... or *o ... o*

more or less *más o menos*

orange (color) *anaranjado/anaranjada* (m./f.)

orange (fruit) *naranja* (f.)

order (to) *pedir*

in order to *para*

ounce *onza* (f.)

our *nuestro/nuestra/nuestros/nuestras* (m. sg./f. sg./m. pl./f. pl.)

ours *nuestro/nuestra/nuestros/nuestras* (m. sg./f. sg./m. pl./f. pl.)

ourselves *nos*

outbound journey *ida* (f.)

outdoor market *plaza de mercado*

outside (adverb) *afuera, fuera*

outside of ... *fuera de ...*

outside (noun) *exterior* (m.)

outskirts *afueras* (f. pl.)

oven *horno* (m.)

over *sobre*
overcoat *abrigo* (m.)
overcooked *sobrecocido/sobrecocida* (m./f.)
overtime *horas* (f. pl.) *extras*
owe (to) *deber*
own (to) *poseer*

P

package *paquete* (m.)
packet *cajetilla* (f.)
  pack of cigarettes *cajetilla de cigarrillos*
page *página* (f.)
  yellow pages *páginas* (pl.) *amarillas*
  webpage *página web*
pain *dolor* (m.), *pena* (f.)
painter *pintor/pintora* (m./f.)
painting *pintura* (f.), *cuadro* (m.)
pajamas *pijama* (m.)
palace *palacio* (m.)
palm *palmo* (m.)
Panamanian *panameña/panameño* (m./f.)
pants *pantalones* (m. pl.)
papaya *papaya* (f.)
paper *papel* (m.)
  research paper *trabajo* (m.) *de investigación*
Paraguay *Paraguay* (m.)
Pardon me? *¿Cómo?*
parents *padres* (pl.)
Paris *París*
park *parque* (m.)
parking lot *parqueadero* (m.)
part *parte* (f.)
partial *parcial* (m./f.)
particular *particular* (m./f.)
part-time *a tiempo parcial*
party *fiesta* (f.)
pass (to) *aprobar, pasar*
  pass a course (to) *aprobar un curso*
  pass a test (to) *aprobar un examen*
passport *pasaporte* (m.)
past *pasado/pasada* (m./f.)
  at a half past five *a las cinco y media*
  at a quarter past six *a las seis y cuarto*
pastry *dulce* (m.)
path *camino* (m.)
patience *paciencia* (f.)
  be patient (to) *tener paciencia*
patterned, with a pattern *estampado/*

  estampada (m./f.)
pay *sueldo* (m.)
pay (to) *pagar*
  pay cash (to) *pagar en efectivo*
payment *pago* (m.)
pear *pera* (f.)
pedestrian *peatón* (m.)
pediatrician *pediatra* (m./f.)
  regular pediatrician *pediatra* (m./f.) *de*
    cabecera
pediatrics *pediatría* (f.)
pen *bolígrafo* (m.), *pluma* (f.)
pencil *lápiz* (m.)
penicillin *penicilina* (f.)
pension *pensión* (f.)
people *gente* (f.)
people (impersonal pronoun) *se*
pepper *pimienta* (f.) (*spice*), *pimiento* (m.)
  (*vegetable*)
perceive (to) *percibir*
percent *por ciento*
perceptibly *sensiblemente*
perfect *perfecto/perfecta* (m./f.)
perfume *perfume* (m.)
perhaps *tal vez*
period *período* (m.)
period *término* (m.)
permanent *fijo/fija* (m./f.)
person *persona* (f.)
Peru *Perú* (m.)
Peruvian *peruano/peruana* (m./f.)
peso *peso* (m.)
pharmacist *farmacéutico/farmacéutico* (m./f.)
pharmacy *farmacia* (f.)
philosophy *filosofía* (f.)
phone book *guía* (f.) *telefónica*
phone call *llamada* (f.)
  make an international/local/national call
    (to) *hacer una llamada internacional/local/*
    nacional
photograph *foto* (f.)
photography *fotografía* (f.)
phrase *frase* (f.)
physics *física* (f.)
piano *piano* (m.)
pick up (to) *recoger, coger, buscar*
picture *foto* (f.), *cuadro* (m.)
  take a picture (to) *hacer una foto*

piece   *pieza* (f.)
  one-piece   *enterizo/enteriza* (m./f.)
  two-piece   *de dos piezas*
pig   *cerdo/cerda* (m./f.)
piglet   *chanchito/chanchita* (m./f.)
pill   *pastilla* (f.)
pink   *rosado/rosada* (m./f.)
pity   *lástima* (f.), *pena* (f.)
  It's a pity that . . .   *Es una lástima que . . .*
place   *lugar* (m.), *sitio* (m.)
  in place of   *por*
place (to)   *poner*
plaid   *a cuadros*
plan   *plan* (m.)
plant   *planta* (f.)
plastic   *plástico* (m.)
plate   *plato* (m.)
play (to)   *jugar, practicar (sports), tocar*
  (instrument)
  play sports (to)   *hacer deporte*
  play the piano (to)   *tocar el piano*
  play the guitar (to)   *tocar la guitarra*
play (theater)   *obra* (f.)
player   *jugador/jugadora* (m./f.)
plaza   *plaza* (f.)
pleasant   *agradable* (m./f.)
please (to)   *gustar*
  Pleased to meet you.   *Encantado./Encantada.*
   (said by a man/said by a woman)/*Gusto en*
   conocerlo/la.
Please.   *Por favor.*
pleasure   *placer* (m.), *gusto* (m.)
  It's a pleasure.   *Mucho gusto.*
plumber   *fontanero/fontanera* (m./f.)
plus (+)   *más*
p.m.   *de la tarde, de la noche*
  at four p.m.   *a las cuatro de la tarde*
  at seven p.m.   *a las siete de la noche*
pocket-knife   *navaja* (f.)
point   *punto* (m.), *término* (m.)
police officer   *policía* (m./f.)
  policewoman   *mujer* (f.) *policía*
polka-dot   *de lunares*
polyester   *poliéster* (m.)
pond   *estanque* (m.)
pool   *piscina* (f.)
poor, poor person   *pobre* (m./f.)
  poor (the)   *los pobres*

poorly   *mal*
pork   *cerdo* (m.), *carne* (f.) *de cerdo*
Portuguese   *portugués/portuguesa* (m./f.)
position (job)   *puesto* (m.)
possible   *posible* (m./f.)
  as soon as possible   *lo antes posible*
  It is possible that . . .   *Es posible que . . .*
post (job)   *puesto* (m.)
postage stamp   *estampilla* (f.)
post office   *correo* (m.)
postpone (to)   *retrasar*
potato   *papa* (f.), *patata* (f.)
pound   *libra* (f.)
  half pound   *media libra*
powder   *polvo* (m.)
  powdered milk   *leche* (f.) *en polvo*
practice (to)   *practicar*
prayer   *oración* (f.)
precisely   *precisamente*
prefer (to)   *preferir*
  prefer that . . . (to)   *preferir que . . .*
preferable   *preferible* (m./f.)
  It's preferable that . . .   *Es preferible que . . .*
pregnant   *embarazada* (f.)
prepared   *preparado/preparada* (m./f.)
presentation   *presentación* (f.)
president   *presidente/presidenta* (m./f.)
pressure   *presión* (f.)
  have high/low blood pressure (to)   *tener la*
   tensión alta/baja
prestigious   *prestigioso/prestigiosa* (m./f.)
pretty   *bonito/bonita* (m./f.)
prevent (to)   *impedir*
price   *precio* (m.)
  price tag   *etiqueta* (f.) *con el precio*
  reasonable price   *precio económico*
printer   *impresora* (f.)
prison   *cárcel* (f.)
prize   *premio* (m.)
probation   *prueba* (f.)
  probationary period   *período* (m.) *de prueba*
problem   *problema* (m.)
produce (to)   *producir*
product   *producto* (m.)
profession   *profesión* (f.)
professional   *profesional* (m./f.)
professionally   *profesionalmente*
professor   *profesor/profesora* (m./f.)

program *programa* (m.)
  television program *programa de televisión*
prohibit (to) *prohibir*
project *proyecto* (m.)
promise (to) *prometer*
proof *prueba* (f.)
protect (to) *proteger*
psychology *sicología* (f.)
punctual *puntual* (m./f.)
purchase *compra* (f.)
purple *morado/morada* (m./f.), *púrpura* (m./f.)
put (to) *poner*
  I'm putting you through. (on the phone) *Lo paso.*
  put on hold (to) *poner en espera*
  put something on (to) *ponerse*

Q

qualification *cualificación* (f.)
qualified *cualificado/cualificada* (m./f.)
quarter *cuarto* (m.)
  at a quarter past six *a las seis y cuarto*
  at a quarter to six *a las seis menos cuarto*
question *pregunta* (f.)
questionnaire *cuestionario* (m.)
quick *rápido/rápida* (m./f.)
quickly *rápidamente, rápido, aprisa*
quiet *tranquilo/tranquila* (m./f.)
quietly *silenciosamente*
quite, quite a lot *bastante*

R

radio *radio* (f.)
  on the radio *por la radio*
railroad *ferrocarril* (m.)
rain *lluvia* (f.)
rain (to) *llover*
  It's raining. *Está lloviendo.*
raincoat *gabardina* (f.)
raise (to) *levantar*
ramp *rampa* (f.)
rash *brote* (m.)
razor *navaja* (f.) *de afeitar*
read (to) *leer*
reader *lector* (m.)
reading *lectura* (f.)
ready *listo/lista* (m./f.), *preparado/preparada* (m./f.)

Ready? *¿Listos?/¿Preparados?*
realism *realismo* (m.)
realistic *realista* (m./f.)
Really? *No me digas.*
reason *razón* (f.)
reasonable price *precio* (m.) *económico*
receive (to) *recibir*
reception desk *recepción* (f.)
receptionist *recepcionista* (m./f.)
recess *receso* (m.)
recipe *receta* (f.)
recognize (to) *reconocer*
recommend (to) *recomendar*
  recommend that … (to) *recomendar que …*
record *registro* (m.), *historial* (m.), *disco* (m.)
record (to) *anotar*
recreation *recreo* (m.)
red *rojo/roja* (m./f.), *colorado/colorada* (m./f.)
  red wine *vino* (m.) *tinto*
reduce (to) *reducir*
reduced *rebajado/rebajada* (m./f.)
reference *referencia* (f.)
refrigerator *nevera* (f.)
regain strength (to) *coger fuerzas* (f. pl.)
regarding … *en cuanto a …*
region *región* (f.)
regional *regional* (m./f.)
register (to) *matricularse*
registration *matrícula* (f.)
regret that … (to) *sentir que …*
relationship *relación* (f.)
relative *pariente* (m./f.)
remain (to) *quedar*
remember (to) *recordar*
rent (to) *alquilar*
repayment *retribución* (f.)
repeat (to) *repetir*
  Repeat, please. *Repita, por favor*
reply to (to) *contestar*
report *informe* (m.)
  report card *calificaciones* (f. pl.)
representative *representante* (m.)
request (to) *solicitar*
  request that … (to) *pedir que …*
research *investigación* (f.)
  research paper *trabajo* (m.) *de investigación*
reservation *reserva* (f.), *reservación* (f.)
resolve (to) *resolver*

Glossary

responsible *responsable* (m./f.)
rest *resto* (m.)
rest (to) *descansar*
restaurant *restaurante* (m.)
result *resultado* (m.)
résumé *historial* (m.) *de trabajo, currículum vítae, hoja* (f.) *de vida*
retain (to) *quedar*
retired, retired person *jubilado/jubilada* (m./f.)
return (to) *regresar, volver*
rice *arroz* (m.)
rich *rico/rica* (m./f.)
ride (to) *montar*
right *derecho* (m.), *ya*
  be right (to) *tener razón*
  right? *¿verdad?*
  on the right *a la derecha*
  on the right-hand side *a mano derecha*
  right now *en este momento, ahora mismo*
  right side *derecha* (f.)
  right-side *derecho/derecha* (m./f.)
  That's right. *Es verdad./Así es.*
  Turn right. *Gira a la derecha.*
ring *anillo* (m.)
ring (to) *sonar*
rise (to) *levantarse*
river *río* (m.)
robe *albornoz* (m.), *bata* (f.), *deshabillé* (m.)
rock *roca* (f.)
romance novel *novela* (f.) *rosa*
romantic *romántico/romántica* (m./f.)
  romantic films *películas* (f. pl.) *románticas*
room *alcoba* (f.), *cuarto* (m.), *habitación* (f.)
rose *rosa* (f.)
  wear rose-colored glasses (to) *ver todo color de rosa* (lit., to see everything pink)
rotten *podrido/podrida* (m./f.)
rough *agitado/agitada* (m./f.)
round *redondo/redonda* (m./f.)
route *recorrido* (m.)
run (to) *correr*
rural *rural* (m./f.)
Russian (language) *ruso* (m.)

S

sack *bolsa* (f.)
sad *triste* (m./f.)
  It's sad that … *Es triste que …*

sadly *tristemente*
safe *seguro/segura* (m./f.)
safety *seguridad* (f.)
salad *ensalada* (f.)
salary *salario* (m.)
sale *venta* (f.)
  buy on sale (to) *comprar en rebaja*
salesman/saleswoman *vendedor/vendedora* (m./f.)
salsa *salsa* (f.)
salt *sal* (f.)
salty *salado/salada* (m./f.)
same *mismo/misma* (m./f.)
  The same to you. *Igualmente.*
sand *arena* (f.)
sandals *sandalias* (f. pl.)
Saturday *sábado* (m.)
sauce *salsa* (f.)
save (to) *ahorrar, guardar*
say (to) *decir*
  How do you say " … " in … ? *¿Cómo se dice " … " en … ?*
  say good-bye (to) *despedirse*
scarf *bufanda* (f.)
scary *espantoso/espantosa* (m./f.)
schedule *horario* (m.)
scholarship *beca* (f.)
school *escuela* (f.), *academia* (f.)
  school subject *materia* (f.)
science *ciencia* (f.)
scoreboard *marcador* (m.)
scream *grito* (m.)
scream (to) *gritar*
screen *pantalla* (f.)
sculpture *escultura* (f.)
sea *mar* (m.)
season *estación* (f.)
seat *silla* (f.)
seat (to) *sentar*
  be seated (to) *estar sentado*
second *segundo/segunda* (m./f.)
  second year *segundo año*
secondary school *colegio* (m.)
secret *secreto* (m.)
secretary *secretaria* (m./f.)
section *sección* (f.)
security *seguridad* (f.)
see (to) *ver*

I'll see you later. *Hasta luego.*
Let's see … *Vamos … /A ver …*
See you. *Nos vemos. (lit., We see each other.)*
See you soon. *Hasta pronto.*
See you tomorrow. *Hasta mañana.*
seem (to) *parecer*
seldom *casi nunca*
sell (to) *vender*
semester *semestre* (m.)
send (to) *enviar*
sense *sentido* (m.)
sensibly *sensatamente*
September *septiembre* (m.)
series *serie* (f.)
serious *grave* (m./f.), *serio/seria* (m./f.)
serve (to) *servir, atender*
service *servicio* (m.)
  Is service included? *¿Está incluido el servicio?*
session *sesión* (f.)
set off (to) *partir*
seven *siete*
  at seven p.m. *a las siete de la noche*
  seven hundred *setecientos/setecientas* (m./f.)
  twenty-seven *veintisiete*
seventeen *diecisiete, diez y siete*
seventy *setenta*
several *varios/varias* (m./f.)
sewing *costura* (f.)
shake hands (to) *dar la mano*
shampoo *champú* (m.)
shave (to) *afeitar*
  shave (oneself) (to) *afeitarse*
shaving cream *crema de afeitar*
she *ella*
sheet (of paper) *hoja* (f.)
shelf *estante* (m.)
shirt *camisa* (f.)
shoes *zapatos* (m. pl.)
  shoe store *zapatería* (f.)
  tennis shoes *zapatillas* (f. pl.) *deportivas*
  What shoe size do you wear? *¿Qué número calza?*
shop (to) *comprar*
shopping mall *centro* (m.) *comercial*
short *bajo/baja* (m./f.), *corto/corta* (m./f.)
shoulder *hombro* (m.)
shout (to) *gritar*
show (to) *mostrar, dar*

shower *ducha* (f.)
shrimp *camarón* (m.), *gamba* (f.)
shy *tímido/tímida* (m./f.)
siblings *hermanos* (pl.)
sick *enfermo/enferma* (m./f.)
sickness *mareo* (m.), *náusea* (f.)
side *lado* (m.), *parte* (f.)
  on the left-hand side *a mano izquierda*
  on the right-hand side *a mano derecha*
sidewalk *andén* (m.), *acera* (f.)
  on the sidewalk *por el andén/la acera*
signal *señal* (f.)
signature *firma* (f.)
silk *seda* (f.)
silver (color) *plateado/plateada* (m./f.)
simply *simplemente*
since *desde, pues*
sing (to) *cantar*
singer *cantante* (m./f.)
single *único/única* (m./f.), *soltero/soltera* (m./f.)
sink *lavabo* (m.), *fregadero* (m.) *(kitchen)*
sister *hermana* (f.)
sister-in-law *cuñada* (f.)
sit down (to) *sentarse*
situation *situación* (f.)
six *seis*
  at a quarter past six *a las seis y cuarto*
  at a quarter to six *a las seis menos cuarto*
  six hundred *seiscientos/seiscientas* (m./f.)
  twenty-six *veintiséis*
sixteen *dieciséis, diez y seis*
sixty *sesenta*
size *talla* (f.), *tamaño* (m.)
  What shoe size do you wear? *¿Qué número calza?*
ski (to) *esquiar*
skill *destreza* (f.), *cualificación* (f.)
skimmed *descremado/descremada* (m./f.)
skim milk *leche* (f.) *descremada*
skin *piel* (f.)
skip (to) *saltar*
skirt *falda* (f.)
sky *cielo* (m.)
  sky blue *celeste* (m./f.)
sleep *sueño* (m.)
  be sleepy (to) *tener sueño*
sleep (to) *dormir*
sleepiness *sueño* (m.)

slice   *rebanada* (f.), *tajada* (f.)

slippers   *chinelas* (f. pl.), *pantuflas* (f. pl.), *zapatillas* (f. pl.)

slow   *lento/lenta* (m./f.), *retrasado/retrasada* (m./f.)

slowly   *despacio, lentamente*
  Speak more slowly, please.   *Hable más despacio, por favor.*

small   *pequeño/pequeña* (m./f.)
  smaller   *menor* (m./f.)
  smallest (the)   *el/la/los/las* (m. sg./f. sg./m. pl./f. pl.) *menor*

smart   *inteligente* (m./f.)

smell (to)   *oler*

smile (to)   *sonreír*

smog   *niebla* (f.) *tóxica/con humo*

smoke (to)   *fumar*

smoked   *ahumado/ahumada* (m./f.)

snack time   *merienda* (f.)

snake   *serpiente* (f.)

sneakers   *zapatillas* (f. pl.) *deportivas*

snow   *nieve* (f.)

snow (to)   *nevar*
  It's snowing.   *Está nevando.*

so   *así, pues*
  I hope so!   *¡Yo espero que sí!*
  I think so.   *Creo que sí.*
  so-so   *más o menos*
  So ...   *Así que ...*
  so to speak   *por así decir*

so (very)   *tan*

soap   *jabón* (m.)

soccer   *fútbol* (m.)

socks   *calcetines* (m. pl.), *medias* (f. pl.)

soda   *refresco* (m.)

sofa   *sofá* (m.)

soft   *suave* (m./f.)

soft drink   *refresco* (m.)

sole   *solo/sola* (m./f.)

solely   *sólo*

solitude   *soledad* (f.)

solution   *solución* (f.)

some   *unos/unas* (m. pl./f. pl.), *algún/alguno/alguna* (before m. sg. nouns/m. sg./f. sg.), *algunos/algunas* (m. pl./f. pl.)

somebody, someone   *alguien*
  somebody else   *alguien más*

something   *algo, algún/alguno/alguna* (before m. sg. nouns/m. sg./f. sg.), *algunos/algunas* (m. pl./f. pl.)

sometimes   *a veces*

somewhat   *algo*

son   *hijo* (m.)

song   *canción* (f.)

son-in-law   *yerno* (m.)

soon   *pronto*
  as soon as possible   *lo antes posible*
  See you soon.   *Hasta pronto.*

(I'm) sorry.   *Lo siento.*

sound   *sonido* (m.)
  sound system   *sistema* (m.) *de sonido*

sound (to)   *sonar*

soup   *sopa* (f.)

sour   *agrio/agria* (m./f.), *cortado/cortada* (m./f.), *amargo/amarga* (m./f.)

south   *sur* (m.)

South America   *Sudamérica*

space   *espacio* (m.)

Spain   *España* (f.)

Spanish   *español/española* (m./f.)

Spanish (language)   *español* (m.)
  I'm learning Spanish.   *Estoy aprendiendo español.*
  I speak a little Spanish.   *Hablo un poco de español.*

speak (to)   *hablar*
  Do you speak English? (fml.)   *¿Habla usted inglés?*
  Do you speak English? (infml.)   *¿Hablas inglés?*
  I speak a little Spanish.   *Hablo un poco de español.*
  I speak French fluently.   *Domino el francés.*
  so to speak   *por así decir*
  Speak more slowly, please.   *Hable más despacio, por favor.*
  speak to ... (to)   *hablar con ....*

specialization   *especialización* (f.)

specialize (to)   *especializarse*

special of the day   *plato del día*

specialty   *especialidad* (f.)

spectator   *espectador/espectadora* (m./f.)

speed   *velocidad* (f.)

spend (to)   *pasar*
  spend the day (to)   *pasar el día*

spicy   *condimentado/condimentada* (m./f.), *picante* (m./f.)

spinal column *columna* (f.) *vertebral*
spoiled *pasado/pasada* (m./f.)
spoon *cuchara* (f.)
sport *deporte* (m.)
  person who plays sports *deportista* (m./f.)
spot *pinta* (f.)
spring *primavera* (f.)
spy *espía* (m./f.)
square *cuadro* (m.), *plaza* (f.)
stadium *estadio* (m.)
staff *personal* (m.), *plantilla* (f.)
stairs *escaleras* (f. pl.)
stamp collecting *filatelia* (f.)
stand in line (to) *hacer una cola/fila*
star *estrella* (f.)
start (to) *comenzar*
  start ... (doing something) (to) *comenzar a ...*
  start from ... (to) *partir de ...*
state *estado* (m.)
station *estación* (f.)
  train station *estación de tren, estación de ferrocarril*
Stay in the right lane. *Siga por el carril de la derecha.*
steady job *trabajo* (m.) *fijo*
stepdaughter *hijastra* (f.)
stepfather *padrastro* (m.)
stepmother *madrastra* (f.)
stepson *hijastro* (m.)
stick *palo* (m.)
still *todavía*
stockings *pantymedias* (f. pl.), *medias* (f. pl.)
stomach *estómago* (m.)
  have an upset stomach (to) *tener mal de estómago*
stop *alto* (m.), *parada* (f.)
  Stop! *¡Alto!*
stop (to) *parar, cesar*
  stop ... (doing something) (to) *cesar de ...*
store *tienda* (f.)
  antique store *tienda de antigüedades*
  clothing store *tienda de ropa*
  convenience store *tienda* (f.)
  department store *tienda por departamentos*
  electronics store *tienda de electrodomésticos*
  store clerk *dependiente/dependienta* (m./f.)
storm *tormenta* (f.)

stove *cocina* (f.)
straight *recto, derecho*
  Continue straight. *Continúa recto.*
  Go straight. *Siga derecho.*
strange *extraño/extraña* (m./f.)
stranger *extranjero/extranjera* (m.)
street *calle* (f.)
streetlight *luz* (f.) *de la calle*
strength *fuerza* (f.)
  regain strength (to) *coger fuerzas* (f. pl.)
stressing, stressful *estresante* (m./f.)
stripe *raya* (f.)
striped *a rayas*
strong *fuerte* (m./f.)
student *estudiante/estudiante* (m./f.), *alumno/ alumna* (m./f.)
study *estudio* (m.)
  studies *estudios* (pl.)
study (to) *estudiar*
stuffing *relleno* (m.)
style *estilo* (m.)
  in style *de moda*
subject *asignatura* (f.)
submit (to) *entregar*
subscriber *abonado/abonada* (m./f.)
suburban *suburbano/suburbana* (m./f.)
subway *subterráneo* (m.), *metro* (m.)
success *éxito* (m.)
such *tal*
suede *gamuza* (f.)
suffer (to) *sufrir*
sugar *azúcar* (m.)
suggest (to) *sugerir*
  suggest that ... (to) *sugerir que ...*
suit *traje* (m.)
suitcase *maleta* (f.)
summer *verano* (m.)
  summer job *trabajo* (m.) *de verano*
sun *sol* (m.)
  It's sunny. *Hace sol.*
Sunday *domingo* (m.)
sunglasses *gafas* (f. pl.) *de sol*
supermarket *supermercado* (m.)
supporter *hincha* (m./f.)
supposition *supuesto* (m.)
sure *seguro/segura* (m./f.)
  I'm sure. *Seguro/segura que sí.*
surprise *sorpresa* (f.)

be surprised (to) *sorprenderse*
be surprised that ... (to) *sorprenderse de que ...*
suspend (to) *suspender*
suspense *suspenso* (m.)
  suspense films *películas* (f. pl.) *de suspenso*
sweater *suéter* (m.), *jersey* (m.)
sweet (adjective) *dulce* (m./f.)
sweet (noun) *dulce* (m.)
swell (to) *hincharse*
swim (to) *nadar*
swimming *natación* (f.)
  swimming pool *piscina* (f.)
switchboard *centralita* (f.)
symptom *síntoma* (m.)
syndrome *síndrome* (m.)
  carpal tunnel syndrome *síndrome del túnel del carpio*
system *sistema* (m.)
  sound system *sistema de sonido*

T

table *mesa* (f.), *tabla* (f.)
tableware *vajilla* (f.)
tag *etiqueta* (f.)
  price tag *etiqueta con el precio*
tail *cola* (f.)
take (to) *tomar, traer, coger, usar, llevar*
  take a bath (to) *bañarse*
  take a blood test (to) *hacerse un examen de sangre*
  take a picture (to) *hacer una foto*
  take a shower (to) *ducharse*
  take a test (to) *hacer un examen, presentarse a un examen*
  Take care. *Que estés bien.*
  take care of (to) *atender*
  take into acount (to) *tener en cuenta*
  take medication (to) *tomar un medicamento*
  take out (to) *sacar*
  take the blood pressure (to) *tomar la tensión*
talented *dotado/dotada* (m./f.)
talk (to) *hablar*
talk show *programa* (m.) *de entrevistas*
tall *alto/alta* (m./f.)
taste *gusto* (m.)
taste (to) *saborear, probar, saber*
tax *impuesto* (m.)

tax return *planilla* (f.) *de impuestos*
taxi *taxi* (m.)
  taxi driver *taxista* (m./f.)
tea *té* (m.)
teacher *maestro/maestra* (m./f.)
teakettle *tetera* (f.)
team *equipo* (m.)
technology *tecnología* (f.)
teenager *adolescente* (m.)
telephone *teléfono* (m.)
  answer the phone (to) *contestar el teléfono*
  call ... on the phone (to) *llamar por teléfono a ...*
  dial a phone number (to) *marcar un número de teléfono*
  hang up the phone (to) *colgar el teléfono*
  make a phone call (to) *llamar por teléfono*
  on the phone *por teléfono*
  telephone booth *cabina* (f.) *telefónica*
  telephone number *número* (m.) *de teléfono*
telephonic *telefónico/telefónica* (m./f.)
television *televisión* (f.)
  television program *programa* (m.) *de televisión*
  television set *televisor* (m.)
  watch television (to) *mirar la televisón*
tell (to) *contar, decir*
  tell a dirty joke (to) *contar un chiste verde (lit., to tell a green joke)*
  tell time (to) *dar la hora*
temperature *temperatura* (f.)
temple *templo* (m.)
ten *diez*
  at eight ten (8:10) *a las ocho y diez*
  It's ten after one in the morning. *Es la una y diez de la madrugada.*
  ten thousand *diez mil*
tendon *tendón* (m.)
tennis *tenis* (m.)
  tennis shoes *zapatillas* (f. pl.) *deportivas*
tension *tensión* (f.)
term *término* (m.)
terrible *pésimo/pésima* (m./f.)
test *examen* (m.), *prueba* (f.)
  fail a test (to) *suspender un examen*
  pass a test (to) *aprobar un examen*
  take a blood test (to) *hacerse un examen de sangre*

take a test (to) *hacer un examen, presentarse a un examen*

text *texto* (m.)

textbook *libro* (m.) *de texto*

than *que*

less ... than ... *menos ... que ...*

more ... /-er than ... *más ... que ...*

thanks *gracias* (pl.)

be thankful (to) *agradecer*

give thanks (to) *dar (las) gracias*

Thanks a lot. *Muchas gracias.*

Thank you. *Gracias.*

Thank you for your help. *Le agradezco su ayuda.*

that (demonstrative) *ese/esa* (m. sg./f. sg.) (*near the listener*), *aquel/aquella* (m. sg./f. sg.) (*far from the speaker and the listener*)

that (one) *ése/ésa* (m. sg./f. sg.) (*near the listener*)

that (one) over there *aquél/aquélla* (m. sg./f. sg.) (*far from the speaker and the listener*)

that (one, thing) (neuter) *eso* (m.) (*near the listener*)

that (one, thing) over there (neuter) *aquello* (m.) (*far from the speaker and the listener*)

That's it. *Ya está.*

That's right. *Es verdad./Así es.*

That's too bad! *¡Qué pena!*

that (conjunction, relative pronoun) *que*

the *el/la/los/las* (m. sg./f. sg./m. pl./f. pl.)

of the (m.)/from the (m.)/about the (m.) *del (de + el)*

to the (m.)/at the (m.) *al (a + el)*

theater *teatro* (m.)

their *su/sus* (sg./pl.)

theirs (m./f.) *suyo/suya/suyos/suyas* (m. sg./f. sg./m. pl./f. pl.)

theirs (f. pl.) *el de ellas* (m. sg.), *la de ellas* (f. sg.)

theirs (m. pl./mixed group) *el de ellos* (m. sg.), *la de ellos* (f. sg.)

them (direct object pronoun) *los/las* (m./f.)

(to/for) them (indirect object pronoun) *les, se* (used in place of les when preceding lo/la/los/las)

themselves *se*

then *entonces, luego, pues*

Until then. *Hasta entonces.*

there *ahí, allí*

There is ... /There are ... *Hay ...*

There's no ... that/who ... *No hay ningún ... que ...*

There's no one who/that ... *No hay nadie que ...*

There's nothing that ... *No hay nada que ...*

therefore *por lo tanto, pues*

these *estos/estas* (m. pl./f. pl.)

these (ones) *éstos/éstas* (m. pl./f. pl.)

they *ellos/ellas* (m. pl. & mixed group/f. pl.)

thick *espeso/espesa* (m./f.)

thief *ladrón* (m./f.)

thin *delgado/delgada* (m./f.), *ligero/ligera* (m./f.)

thing *cosa* (f.)

How are things? *¿Cómo van las cosas?*

think (to) *creer, pensar*

Don't you think? *¿No crees?*

I think so. *Creo que sí.*

not think that ... (to) *no pensar que ...*

What do you think of ... ? *¿Qué te parece ... ?*

third *tercero/tercer/tercera* (m. sg./m. sg. before a noun/f. sg.)

third year *tercer año*

thirst *sed* (f.)

be thirsty (to) *tener sed*

thirteen *trece*

thirty *treinta*

thirty-one *treinta y uno*

thirty percent off *treinta por ciento de descuento*

this *este/esta* (m. sg./f. sg.)

this (one) *éste/ésta* (m. sg./f. sg.)

this (one, thing)(neuter) *esto* (m.)

this afternoon *esta tarde*

this day *este día*

this evening *esta noche* (f.)

those *aquellos/aquellas* (m. pl./f. pl.) (*far from the speaker and the listener*)

those (ones) over there *aquéllos/aquéllas* (m. pl./f. pl.) (*far from the speaker and the listener*)

thousand *mil*

hundred thousand *cien mil*

ten thousand *diez mil*

twenty thousand *veinte mil*

three *tres*

It's three o'clock. *Son las tres.*

It's three o'clock sharp. *Son las tres en punto.*

one hundred and three dollars *ciento tres dólares*

three hundred *trescientos/trescientas* (m./f.)
twenty-three *veintitrés*
throat *garganta* (f.)
  have a sore throat (to) *tener dolor de garganta*
through *por*
  from ... through ... *de ... a ...*
  go through a light (to) *saltarse el semáforo*
  I'm putting you through. (on the phone) *Lo paso.*
thunder *trueno* (m.)
Thursday *jueves* (m.)
ticket *billete* (m.), *boleto* (m.), *pasaje* (m.), *tiquete* (m.), *entrada* (f.)
tie *corbata* (f.)
tie (to) *empatar*
tied *empatado/empatada* (m./f.)
  be tied (to) *quedar empatados*
tight *ajustado/ajustada* (m./f.)
time *hora* (f.), *tiempo* (m.), *vez* (f.)
  at the present time *actualmente*
  At what time is it? *¿A qué hora es?*
  Do you have time?/How are you doing for time? *¿Cómo estás de tiempo?*
  full-time *a tiempo completo*
  on time, in time *a tiempo*
  overtime *horas* (f. pl.) *extras*
  part-time *a tiempo parcial*
  tell time (to) *dar la hora*
  What time is it? *¿Qué hora es?/¿Qué horas son?*
  What time do you have? *¿Qué hora tiene?*
tingling feeling *cosquilleo* (m.)
tip *propina* (f.), *punta* (f.)
tired *cansado/cansada* (m./f.)
  be tired (to) *tener cansancio*
to *a, con*
  in order to *para*
  It's five to one. (12:55) *Es la una menos cinco.*
  to the (m.) *al (a + el)*
toast *tostada* (f.)
today *hoy*
toe *dedo del pie*
together *junto/junta* (m./f.)
toilet *inodoro* (m.)
  toilet paper *papel* (m.) *higiénico*
toll *peaje* (m.)
tomato *tomate* (m.)
tomorrow *mañana* (f.)

Until tomorrow./See you tomorrow. *Hasta mañana.*
tone *tono* (m.), *señal* (f.)
  leave a message after the tone (to) *dejar un mensaje después de oír la señal*
tongue *lengua* (f.)
tonight *esta noche*
too *también*
  too much, too many *demasiado/demasiada* (m./f.)
tooth *diente* (m.)
touch (to) *tocar*
tour bus trip *recorrido por autobús*
tourism *turismo* (m.)
tourist *turista* (m./f.)
toward(s) *hacia, para*
towel *toalla* (f.)
town *ciudad* (f.), *pueblo* (m.)
  around town *por la ciudad*
toxic *tóxico/tóxica* (m./f.)
traffic *tráfico* (m.)
  go through a traffic light (to) *saltarse el semáforo*
  traffic jam *embotellamiento* (m.)
  traffic light *semáforo* (m.)
train *tren* (m.), *ferrocarril* (m.)
  train station *estación* (f.) *de tren, estación* (f.) *de ferrocarril*
transfer (to) *trasladar*
translate (to) *traducir*
travel *viaje* (m.)
travel (to) *viajar*
treat (to) *tratar*
  How's life treating you? *¿Cómo te trata la vida?*
treatment *tratamiento* (m.)
tree *árbol* (m.)
trip *viaje* (m.)
  go on a trip (to) *salir de viaje*
  Have a good trip. *Buen viaje.*
true *cierto/cierta* (m./f.)
  It is not true that ... *No es cierto que ...*
truth *verdad* (f.)
try (to) *tratar, probar*
  try ... (to do something) (to) *tratar de ...*
  try on (clothes) (to) *probarse*
T-shirt *camiseta* (f.)
Tuesday *martes* (m.)

tuition *derechos* (m. pl.) *de matrícula*
tuna *atún* (m.)
tunnel *túnel* (m.)
turn *vuelta* (f.)
turn (to) *doblar, girar, volver, ponerse*
  turn around (to) *dar la vuelta*
  Turn left. *Gira a la izquierda.*
  turn off (to) *apagar*
  turn off the lights (to) *apagar las luces*
  Turn right. *Gira a la derecha.*
twelve *doce*
  It's twelve noon. *Son las doce del mediodía.*
twenty *veinte*
  twenty-eight *veintiocho*
  twenty-five *veinticinco*
  twenty-four *veinticuatro*
  twenty-nine *veintinueve*
  twenty-one *veintiuno*
  twenty-seven *veintisiete*
  twenty-six *veintiséis*
  twenty-three *veintitrés*
  twenty-two *veintidós*
two *dos*
  twenty-two *veintidós*
  twice a week *dos veces por semana*
  two hundred *doscientos/doscientas* (m./f.)
  two-piece *de dos piezas*
type *tipo* (m.)
typical *típico/típica* (m./f.)

U

ugly *feo/fea* (m./f.)
umbrella *paraguas* (m.)
uncle *tío* (m.)
uncomfortable *incómodo/incómoda* (m./f.)
under *bajo*
undergarments (men's) *calzones* (m. pl.)
underneath *debajo*
  underneath … *debajo de …*
underpants (men's) *calzoncillos* (m. pl.)
undershirt *camisilla* (f.), *camiseta* (f.)
understand (to) *comprender, entender*
underwear (women's) *bombachas* (f. pl.), *bragas* (f. pl.), *calzoncitos* (m. pl.), *pantis* (m. pl.)
unemployed *parado/parada* (m./f.)
unfortunately *desafortunadamente, por desgracia*
unfriendly *antipático/antipática* (m./f.)

union *sindicato* (m.)
unique *único/única* (m./f.)
united *unido/unida* (m./f.)
United States (the) *los Estados Unidos*
university *universidad* (f.)
  university course *carrera* (f.)
unpleasant *desagradable* (m./f.)
until *hasta, para*
  Till then. *Hasta entonces.*
  Until later. *Hasta más tarde.*
  Until then. *Hasta entonces.*
  Until tomorrow. *Hasta mañana.*
urban *urbano/urbana* (m./f.)
urgently *urgentemente*
Uruguay *Uruguay* (m.)
Uruguayan *uruguayo/uruguaya* (m./f.)
us (direct object pronoun); (to/for) us (indirect object pronoun) *nos*
use (to) *usar*
  use for the first time (to) *estrenar*

V

vacation *vacaciones* (f. pl.)
  on vacation *de vacaciones*
variety *variedad* (f.)
vegetable *vegetal* (m.), *verdura* (f.)
Venezuela *Venezuela* (f.)
Venezuelan *venezolano/venezolana* (m./f.)
vertebral *vertebral* (m./f.)
very *muy, mucho*
veterinarian *veterinario/veterinaria* (m./f.)
view *vista* (f.)
village *aldea* (f.)
vinyl *vinilo* (m.)
  vinyl record *disco* (m.) *de vinilo*
violet (color) *violeta* (m./f.)
violin *violín* (m.)
visit (to) *visitar*
visitor *visitante* (m./f.)
voice *voz* (f.)
  voice mail *buzón* (m.) *de voz*
voucher *vale* (m.)

W

wage *paga* (f.), *jornal* (m.)
wait *espera* (f.)
wait (to) *esperar*
waiter *camarero* (m.), *mesero* (m.)

waitress *camarera* (f.), *mesera* (f.)

wake up (to) *despertarse*

walk (to) *andar, caminar, ir a pie/caminar*

wall *pared* (f.)

wallet *cartera* (f.)

want (to) *querer, desear*

  want that/to … (to) *querer que …*

wish (to) *desear*

  I wish … *Ojalá que …*

  wish that … (to) *desear que …*

wash (to) *lavar*

  hand wash (to) *lavar a mano*

  wash oneself (to) *lavarse*

wash basin *lavabo* (m.)

washing machine *lavadora* (f.)

watch *reloj* (m.)

watch (to) *mirar*

  watch television (to) *mirar la televisón*

water *agua* (f.)

  mineral water *agua mineral*

  water (the) *el agua*

  waters (the) *las aguas*

way *camino* (m.), *forma* (f.)

  one-way *de sentido* (m.) *único*

we *nosotros* (m. pl./mixed group), *nosotras* (f. pl.)

weak *débil* (m./f.)

wear (to) *llevar, calzar (shoes)*

  wear rose-colored glasses (to) *ver todo color de rosa (lit., to see everything pink)*

  What shoe size do you wear? *¿Qué número calza?*

weather *tiempo* (m.)

  The weather is good. *El tiempo es bueno.*

web (on the computer) *web* (f.)

  webpage *página* (f.) *web*

  website *sitio* (m.) *web*

Wednesday *miércoles* (m.)

week *semana* (f.)

  every week *todas las semanas*

  last week *semana pasada*

  next week *próxima semana, semana que viene*

  this week *esta semana*

  twice a week *dos días a la semana*

weekend *fin* (m.) *de semana*

  long weekend *puente* (m.)

weekly *semanal* (m./f.)

weigh (to) *pesar*

Welcome. *Bienvenido./Bienvenida.* (m./f.) (to a man/to a woman)

  You're welcome. *De nada.*

well *bien, pues*

  be not doing well (to) *estar mal*

  May you be well. *Que esté bien.*

  well-done *bien asada*

west *oeste* (m.), *occidente* (m.)

what *qué, cuál/cuáles* (sg./pl.)

  At what time is it? *¿A qué hora es?*

  What a coincidence! *¡Qué coincidencia!*

  What color is … ? *¿De qué color es … ?*

  What do you do for a living? *¿En qué trabaja?*

  What do you think of … ? *¿Qué te parece … ?*

  What does that mean? *¿Qué quiere decir eso?*

  What shoe size do you wear? *¿Qué número calza?*

  What time do you have? *¿Qué hora tiene?*

  What time is it? *¿Qué hora es?/¿Qué horas son?*

  What would you like? *¿Qué desea?*

  What?/Pardon me? *¿Cómo?*

  What's going on? *¿Qué hay?*

  What's happening? *¿Qué tal?*

  What's up?/What's going on? *¿Qué hay?*

  What's your name? *¿Cómo se llama usted?* (fml.)*/¿Cómo te llamas?* (infml.)

when *cuándo* (question), *cuando* (relative adverb)

where *dónde* (question), *donde* (relative adverb)

  Where are you from? *¿De dónde eres?*

which *cuál/cuáles* (sg./pl.) (question), *cual/cuales* (sg./pl.) (relative pronoun)

  of which (relative pronoun) *cuyo/cuya/cuyos/cuyas* (m. sg./f. sg./m. pl./f. pl.)

while *mientras*

white *blanco/blanca* (m./f.)

  white wine *vino* (m.) *blanco*

who *quién/quiénes* (sg./pl.) (question), *quien/quienes* (sg./pl.) (relative pronoun)

  Who knows? *¿Quién sabe?*

  Who's calling? *¿De parte de quién?/¿Quién lo llama?*

whole *entero/entera* (m./f.)

  whole milk *leche* (f.) *entera*

whom (question) *quién/quiénes* (sg./pl.)

  whom (relative pronoun) *quien/quienes* (sg./pl.)

whose (relative pronoun) *cuyo/cuya/cuyos/cuyas* (m. sg./f. sg./m. pl./f. pl.)

  Whose … ? *¿De quién … ?*

why *por qué*

wide *ancho/ancha* (m./f.)

wife *esposa* (f.), *mujer* (f.)

win (to) *ganar*

  I hope they win! *¡Ojalá que ganen!*

wind *viento* (m.)

  It's windy. *Hace viento.*

window *ventana* (f.)

  display window *escaparate* (m.)

wine *vino* (m.)

  red wine *vino tinto*

  white wine *vino blanco*

wineglass *copa* (f.)

  glass of wine *copa de vino*

winter *invierno* (m.)

wish *deseo* (m.)

with *con*

  with you *contigo*

without *sin*

woman *mujer* (f.), *tía* (f.)

  businesswoman *mujer de negocios*

  policewoman *mujer policía*

wonder *maravilla* (f.)

wonderful *estupendo/estupenda* (m./f.)

wood *madera* (f.)

wooden *de madera*

wool *lana* (f.)

word *palabra* (f.)

work *trabajo* (m.)

work (to) *trabajar, funcionar*

  What do you do for a living? *¿En qué trabaja?*

working day *jornada* (f.)

world *mundo* (m.)

  world championship *campeonato* (m.) *mundial*

worldly *mundial* (m./f.)

worldwide *mundial* (m./f.)

worry (to) *preocuparse*

  Don't worry. *No se preocupe.*

  worry that ... (to) *preocuparse de que ...*

worse *peor* (m./f.)

worst (the) *el/la/los/las* (m. sg./f. sg./m. pl./f. pl.) *peor*

wrist *muñeca* (f.)

write (to) *escribir*

  write down (to) *anotar*

writer *escritor/escritora* (m./f.)

wrong *equivocado/equivocada* (m./f.)

wrong number *número* (m.) *equivocado*

Y

year *año* (m.)

  be ... years old (to) *tener ... años*

  fifties (the) *los años cicuenta*

  last year *año pasado*

  next year *año que viene*

  second year *segundo año*

  third year *tercer año*

  this year *este año*

yellow *amarillo/amarilla* (m./f.)

  yellow pages *páginas* (f. pl.) *amarillas*

yes *sí*

yesterday *ayer*

yet *todavía*

you (after a proposition) *ti* (infml. sg.)

  you (direct object pronoun) *lo/la/te/los/las/ os* (m. sg. fml./f. sg. fml./sg. infml./m. pl./f. pl./pl. infml)

  you (impersonal pronoun) *se*

  (to/for) you (indirect object pronoun) *le/les* (fml. sg./pl.), *se* (fml. sg./pl.) (used in place of le/les when preceding lo/la/los/las), *te/os* (infml. sg./pl.)

  you (subject pronoun) *usted/tú/ustedes/ vosotros/vosotras* (sg. fml./sg. infml./pl./m. pl. & mixed group infml. used in Spain/f. pl. infml. used in Spain)

young *joven* (m./f.)

  young boy *niño* (m.)

  young child *párvulo/párvula* (m./f.)

  young girl *niña* (f.)

  younger *menor* (m./f.)

  youngest (the) *el/la/los/las* (m. sg./f. sg./m. pl./f. pl.) *menor*

your (pl. fml. & infml.) *su/sus* (sg./pl.)

  your (pl. infml.) *vuestro/vuestra/vuestros/ vuestras* (m. sg./f. sg./m. pl./f. pl.) (used in Spain)

  your (sg. fml.) *su/sus* (sg./pl.)

  your (sg. infml.) *tu/tus* (sg./pl.)

yours (pl. fml. & infml.) *suyo/suya/suyos/suyas* (m. sg./f. sg./m. pl./f. pl.), *el de ustedes* (m. sg.), *la de ustedes* (f. sg.)

  yours (pl. infml.) *vuestro/vuestra/vuestros/ vuestras* (m. sg./f. sg./m. pl./f. pl.) (used in Spain)

  yours (sg. fml.) *suyo/suya/suyos/suyas* (m. sg./f. sg./m. pl./f. pl.), *el de usted* (m. sg.), *la de usted* (f. sg.)

yours (sg. infml.) *tuyo/tuya/tuyos/tuyas*
  (m. sg./f. sg./m. pl./f. pl.) (infml.)
yourself *se/te* (fml./infml.)
yourselves *se/os* (fml./infml.)
youth hostel *hostal* (m.)

Z

zero *cero*